THIS BOOK

Belongs to

Avery August Arnold

THE CHILDREN'S ILLUSTRATED BIBLE

THE CHILDREN'S ILLUSTRATED BIBLE

Stories retold by

SELINA HASTINGS

Illustrated by

ERIC THOMAS

and

AMY BURCH

DK

A Dorling Kindersley Book

Dorling Kindersley
LONDON, NEW YORK, DELHI, SYDNEY

Art Editor Shirley Gwillym

Project Editor Marie Greenwood

Senior Editor Emma Johnson

Designer Sarah Cowley

Additional design by
Heather Blackham, Muffy Dodson

Production Ruth Cobb, Marguerite Fenn

Managing Editor Susan Peach

Managing Art Editor Jacquie Gulliver

US Editor B. Alison Weir

Published in the United States by
Dorling Kindersley Publishing, Inc., 95 Madison Avenue
New York, New York 10016

This edition first published in 2000

10 9 8 7 6 5 4 3 2 1

Library of Congress Cataloging-in-Publication Data
Hastings, Selina.
The Children's illustrated Bible / illustrated by Eric Thomas: stories retold by Selina Hastings. — 1st American ed.
p. cm.
ISBN 0-7894-5331-2
1. Bible stories, English. [1. Bible stories.] I. Thomas, Eric, ill. II. Title.
BS551.2.H365 1994
220.9'505—dc20 93-30814
CIP
AC

For our complete catalog visit WWW.dk.com

Reproduced by Colourscan, Singapore
Printed and bound in China by L. Rex Printing Company

CONSULTANTS

Religious Consultants
Reverend John Glover
Rabbi Joseph Potasnik
Sister K.C. Young
Mary Evans
Jenny Nemko
Reverend Stephen Motyer
Bernadette Chapman
Father Philip Walshe

Educational Consultant
Geoffrey Marshall-Taylor

Historical Consultant, Old Testament
Jonathan Tubb,
Western Asiatic Department,
British Museum, London

Historical Consultant, New Testament
Carole Mendleson,
Western Asiatic Department,
British Museum, London

Editor's Note
The dates listed in this book are chronicled BC, meaning "before Christ," and AD, meaning "anno Domini," or "in the year of the Lord." However, much of the non-Christian world uses CE ("Common Era") and BCE ("Before the Common Era") to designate eras.

Introduction and section openers written by Geoffrey Marshall-Taylor

CONTENTS

Introduction to the Bible 8

THE OLD TESTAMENT

THE OLD TESTAMENT 14

The Creation 18

The Garden of Eden 20

Cain and Abel 22

Noah's Ark 24

The Flood 26

The Tower of Babel 28

THE PATRIARCHS 30

Abram's Journey 32

Abram, Sarai, and Hagar 34

Sodom and Gomorrah 37

Abraham's Two Sons 40

The Sacrifice of Isaac 42

Isaac and Rebekah 44

Esau and Jacob 46

Jacob's Ladder 49

Jacob and Rachel 50

Jacob's Wedding 52

Jacob's Return 54

Joseph's Dreams 56

Joseph the Slave 58

Pharaoh's Dreams 60

Joseph the Governor 62

Benjamin and the Silver Cup 64

LIFE IN EGYPT 66

Moses in the Bulrushes 68

Moses Is Called by God 70

Moses Warns the Pharaoh 72

The Plagues of Egypt 74

The Tenth Plague 76

The Crossing of the Red Sea 78

God Watches Over the Israelites 80

Moses Receives God's Laws 82

The Golden Calf 84

Balaam's Donkey 86

LIFE IN CANAAN 88

The Promised Land 90

Rahab and the Spies 93

The Battle of Jericho 94

The Call of Gideon 96

Jephthah's Daughter 98

Samson and the Lion 100

Samson and Delilah 102

Samson in the Temple 104
Ruth and Naomi 106
Samuel Is Called to Serve God 108
The Ark Is Captured 110
Saul, the First King of the Israelites 112
Saul's Downfall 114
God Chooses David 116
David and Goliath 118
Saul Turns Against David 120
David the Outlaw 122
David and Abigail 124
The Death of Saul 126
Long Live the King 128
David and Bathsheba 130
Absalom's Rebellion 132
King Solomon's Wisdom 134
Solomon's Temple 136
The Queen of Sheba 138
Elijah in the Wilderness 140
The Israelites Turn Against God 142
Naboth's Vineyard 144
Elijah's Final Journey 146
Elisha and the Woman of Shunem 147
Elisha and Naaman 150
CONQUERING NATIONS 152
The Prophet Isaiah 154
Hezekiah's Gold 155
Josiah and the Scroll of the Law 156
Jeremiah and the Potter's Wheel 158
The Israelites in Captivity 160
The Golden Statue 162
Belshazzar's Feast 165
Daniel in the Lions' Den 166
Esther Becomes Queen 168
Esther Saves Her People 170
The Rebuilding of Jerusalem 172
Jonah and the Great Fish 174
The Book of Psalms 176

THE NEW TESTAMENT

THE NEW TESTAMENT 180
A Son for Zechariah 184
An Angel Appears to Mary 186
The Birth of John 188
The Birth of Jesus 190
The Shepherds' Visit 192
The Presentation in the Temple 194
The Wise Men 196
The Flight into Egypt 198
Jesus Is Found in the Temple 200
John Baptizes Jesus 202
The Temptations in the Wilderness 204

JESUS OF GALILEE 206
DAILY LIFE IN JESUS' TIME 208
Jesus Calls His Disciples 210
The Marriage Feast of Cana 212
The Sermon on the Mount 214
Healing the Sick 216
The Centurion's Servant 218
Jesus Calms the Storm 220
The Gadarene Swine 221
Jairus' Daughter 222
The Sower 224
The Death of John the Baptist 226
The Feeding of the Five Thousand 228
Jesus Walks on the Water 230
The Good Samaritan 232
The Transfiguration 234
Mary, Martha, and Lazarus 236
Lost and Found 238
The Prodigal Son 240
The Unmerciful Servant 242
Lazarus and the Rich Man 244
The Pharisee and the Tax Collector 245
Jesus and the Children 246
The Rich Young Man 247
Zacchaeus the Tax Collector 248
Workers in the Vineyard 250
The Wedding Feast 251
The Wise and Foolish Maidens 252
The Parable of the Talents 254
Jesus Enters Jerusalem 256
Jesus and the Temple Traders 258
Judas Plots to Betray Jesus 260
Preparing for the Passover 262
The Last Supper 264
The Garden of Gethsemane 266
Peter's Denial 268
Jesus Before the Sanhedrin 270
Jesus Before Pilate 272
The Crucifixion 274
The Resurrection 276
On the Road to Emmaus 278
The Ascension 280
THE EARLY CHURCH 282
Tongues of Fire 284
Peter the Healer 286
The Death of Stephen 288
Saul's Journey to Damascus 290
Peter and Cornelius 292
Peter in Prison 294
PAUL'S JOURNEYS 296
The Adventures of Paul 298
Paul Is Arrested 302
Paul's Journey to Rome 304
Paul's Letters 306
The Book of Revelation 308

Who's Who in the Bible Stories 310
Index 314
Acknowledgments 320

Introduction to the Bible

MEDIEVAL BIBLE
A decorative page from an 8th-century Bible in the Royal Library in Stockholm.

THE BIBLE IS A collection of books written by different people during more than 1,000 years and dating from about 1450 BC. It is divided into two main parts, the Old Testament (or Hebrew Testament) and the New Testament.

The Old Testament books are the Scriptures, or sacred writings, of the Jewish people. They give an account of the people of ancient Israel over many centuries. By contrast, the New Testament, which consists of writings about Jesus and his first followers, covers a period of about 60 or 70 years. Both the Old and New Testaments make up the Christian Bible.

There are 66 books in the Bible. It is often said that it is more like a library because there are so many kinds of writing in it. For example, there are books containing laws, history, poetry, wise sayings or proverbs, diaries, and letters.

The Old Testament

The 39 books of the Old Testament have guided the Jewish people throughout their history. These are the Scriptures which Jesus read. For Jews, the most important part is the Torah – the first five books of the Bible. The word "Torah" means "teaching." The five books are Genesis, Exodus, Leviticus, Numbers, and Deuteronomy. Christians call this the "Pentateuch," a Greek word meaning "five books."

Each Sabbath Jewish congregations listen to a part of the Torah being read from scrolls in the synagogue. It takes a year of weekly readings to go from the beginning to the end. On the day when the last part of the Torah is reached and Genesis chapter one is due to be read again, there is a celebration called *Simchat Torah*, the "rejoicing of the law." A procession dances around the synagogue carrying the Torah scrolls high in thanksgiving.

In Christian services passages from the Old Testament are often read. The stories are considered important by Christians because of what can be learned from them about God, about others, and about themselves.

The Five Books of Moses

The Torah is special to Jews because its books contain God's words given through Moses to the Hebrew people, their ancestors. The Torah is sometimes referred to as "The Five Books of Moses" because of this. Its stories, songs, prayers, and laws teach about God and what he promises to his people and expects from them.

On Mount Sinai, Moses received God's laws.

For Christians, all the books of the Old Testament are equally important. They are divided into four sections: the law, history, poetry and wisdom writings, and the prophets.

At first the words of the earliest books of the Old Testament were passed on by one generation repeating them to the next. Eventually they were written down in the Hebrew language on parchment, which is made from animal skin. Each word was copied carefully by a scribe, as it is today.

A rabbi, or teacher, studies the words of the Torah.

A Jewish boy becomes Bar-Mitvah at the age of 13.

The Torah is studied by young Jews from an early age. When a Jewish boy reaches the age of 13 he becomes *Bar-Mitzvah*, which means "a son of the commandment." He is now a Jewish adult and, on the Sabbath after his birthday, he can read from the Torah in the synagogue. A Jewish girl becomes *Bat-Mitzvah* (daughter of the commandment) at the age of 12. In many synagogues she can also read from the Torah.

The Dead Sea Scrolls

In 1947 a shepherd boy came across some ancient scrolls in caves near the Dead Sea: they were fragments of all the books of the Old Testament, except for Esther, and had probably been written about the time of Jesus. It is thought that they came from the monastery at Qumran and were hidden in the caves by a group of Jews called the Essenes. The discovery showed how accurately scribes had copied these special words throughout the centuries.

Psalm 119 verse 105 explains why the Old Testament is so important to Jews and Christians. The writer says to God, "Thy word is a lamp unto my feet and a light unto my path."

DISCOVERY
The Dead Sea Scrolls, stored in pottery jars, were found in caves at Qumran (below). Some of the fragments date back to the 2nd century BC.

THE NEW TESTAMENT is made up of 27 books. The first four, the gospels of Matthew, Mark, Luke, and John describe the life, death, and resurrection of Jesus. The Acts of the Apostles tells of the growth of the Christian church and the journeys of St. Paul. The Epistles are letters from Christian leaders to Christians in the newly spreading churches. The book of Revelation contains letters to seven churches and writings about the future reign of Jesus in the world.

The Gospels

"Gospel" means "good news." The words of the gospels were first passed by word of mouth from person to person. Many people believe that Mark's gospel was the first to be written down and that Matthew and Luke referred to Mark's book in their own writings. John's gospel is quite different. It does not describe as many events in Jesus' life or include any of his parables. It concentrates on explaining who Jesus was and what he taught.

The gospels do not tell us everything about the life of Jesus. They concentrate on the three years before his death and on selected events and incidents during this time. They were written by his close followers to show to others why they believed that Jesus was the Messiah, the Son of God. Their purpose was to get across the message of Jesus' teaching to people living at the time, and to leave a written account for future generations.

THE LINDISFARNE GOSPELS
The Gospel writers were sometimes represented by living creatures: Matthew by an angel, Mark by a lion, Luke by an ox, and John by an eagle, shown here in these manuscript illustrations from the 7th-century Lindisfarne Gospels.

Early Editions of the Bible

Papyrus plant

The New Testament books were first written down on papyrus scrolls, an early form of paper made from reeds. Christians then began to copy them onto sheets of papyrus, which were bound and placed between two pieces of wood or tablets. This form of early book was called a codex.

The oldest part of the New Testament is from St. John's Gospel and dates from about AD 125. A complete New Testament in codex form was found at St. Catherine's monastery at the foot of Mount Sinai in 1844. The Codex Sinaiticus is in

St. Matthew

St. Mark

St. Luke

St. John

Codex Sinaiticus

ST. CATHERINE'S MONASTERY, MOUNT SINAI
The Codex Sinaiticus was found at St. Catherine's monastery, shown above in a painting by David Roberts.

Greek and dates from the 4th century AD. Manuscript fragments of the New Testament can be traced to the 2nd century.

As the Christian church spread, the New Testament was translated into Latin and other languages. It was not until 1382 that the first complete version of the Bible in English was published. It was translated by John Wycliffe and, at that time, the words were still copied by hand.

The first printed Bible was the Gutenberg, which appeared in 1456 with text in Latin. Printed translations in other languages soon followed, but it was not until 1535 that the first complete English Bible was published by Miles Coverdale. The first Authorized Version of the Bible appeared in 1611 in the form of the King James Bible. This was one of the great achievements of King James I of England's reign. There are now many versions of the Bible. It has been translated into over 1,900 languages. This means that most people in the world can hear it being read or can read it for themselves in words they can understand. This is important to Christians who believe that the Bible is one of the main ways in which people can find out about God's love for the world.

The New Testament tells of Jesus' teachings and how people of all ages were drawn to him.

THE OLD TESTAMENT

IN THE BEGINNING
GOD CREATED THE
HEAVEN
AND THE EARTH.

GENESIS 1:1

THE OLD TESTAMENT

MOST OF THE EVENTS OF THE Old Testament take place in a small area to the east of the Mediterranean Sea. From ancient times people have lived and traveled along a strip of land known as the "fertile crescent", which stretches from Egypt, through Canaan and Mesopotamia to Babylonia. There was enough water in this area to enable them to grow crops and graze animals. Many great civilizations have thrived here, and down the centuries there has been much fighting to control the land.

Canaan, the "promised land," where the Israelites flourished, is only about 150 miles (230 km) from north to south. It contains many different types of scenery, including plains and river valleys suitable for farming, lakes, hills, and rocky desert. The highest mountains are over 3,280 ft (1,000 m) high; the lowest point, at the Dead Sea, is 1,300 ft (400 m) below sea level.

The vegetation of Canaan in biblical times would have been different in many ways from that found today. When the Israelites entered Canaan, much of the hilly ground was covered by woods and forests. Since then many of these have disappeared, cut down and used for building and fuel. In recent years, however, trees have been planted in several areas and there are intensive irrigation projects under way to encourage the desert to "blossom as the rose" (Isaiah, chapter 35).

SPRING FIELDS
Wild flowers, like the ones in the photograph, grew in Canaan in biblical times. At that time, however, instead of the palm trees shown here, the landscape would have been covered with poplar, oak, and sycamore trees.

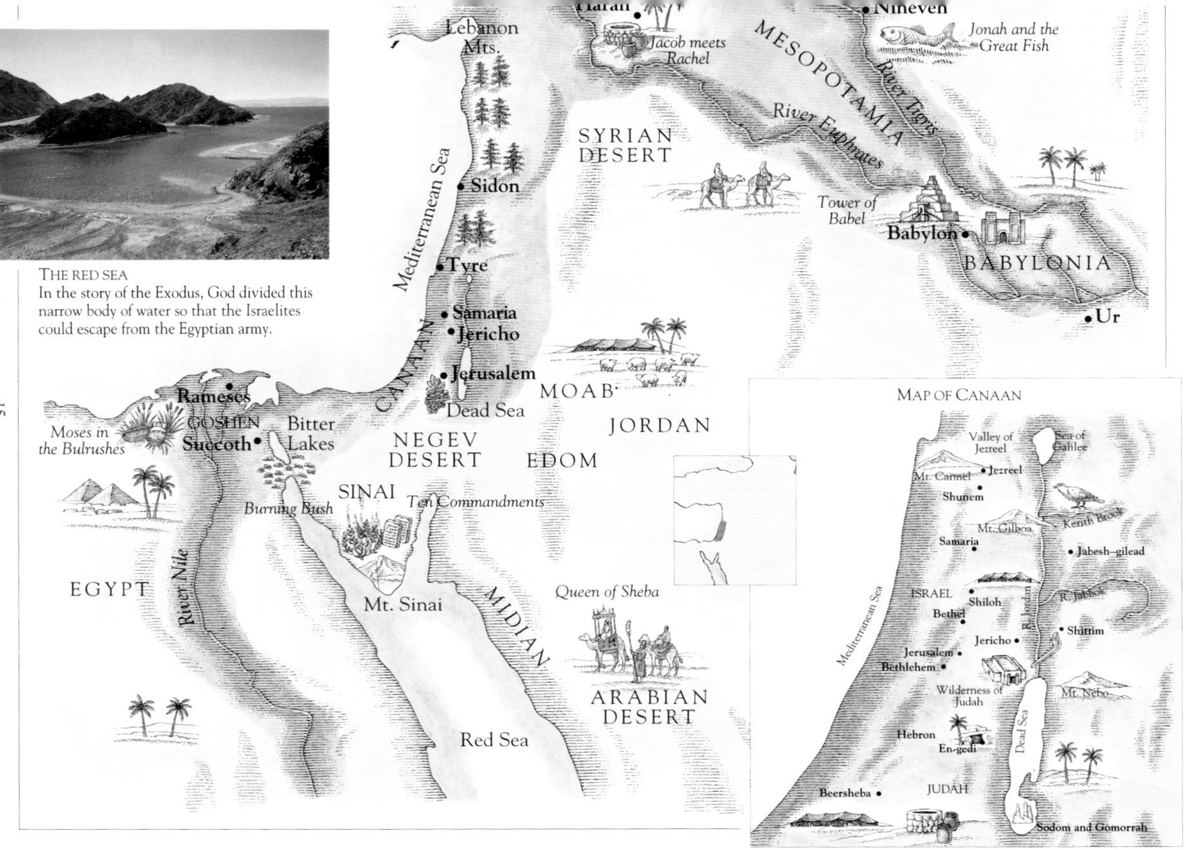

THE RED SEA
In the story of the Exodus, God divided this narrow body of water so that the Israelites could escape from the Egyptian army.

Abraham

IN ONE IMPORTANT way the people of Israel (the Hebrews) were different from others. Instead of many gods, they believed that there was only one God, a divine God. The Bible tells how God made this special promise, or covenant, with Abraham and his descendants, the people of Israel: "I will establish my covenant as an everlasting covenant between me and you, and your descendants after you, to be your God."

On Mount Sinai, God gave to Moses the main laws which the people were to follow: these "Ten Commandments," as they are called, are about ways of honoring God and treating others. There were also laws, or rules, covering many aspects of daily life from marriage to owning property. The Israelites believed that you could worship God not just in prayers and services, but by the way you lived your daily life.

The Ark of the Covenant

The Ten Commandments were written on two pieces of stone and were very precious to the Israelites. They kept them in a golden box called the "Ark of the Covenant." The Ark was also important to them, because it reminded them of God's covenant that he would be with them.

Because the people of Israel spent many years traveling before they found a place to settle, they made a portable tent, or "tabernacle," which they could set up anywhere. The Ark was kept in this tent, and in the area around it sacrifices and prayers were made each day to God. This was the most important place of worship for the Israelites.

The priests carry the box containing the Ten Commandments.

The tabernacle measured 45 feet (14 m) long, 13 feet (4 m) wide, and 16 feet (5 m) high. It was made of a wooden frame and covered with rich linen material in blue, purple, and scarlet. Over this were waterproof coverings. Inside, the tabernacle was divided into two rooms. The smaller of these was called the "most holy place" or the "Holy of Holies." Only the high priest was allowed into it and that was only once a year on the Day of Atonement. It was in this room that the Ark of the Covenant was kept.

THE TABERNACLE

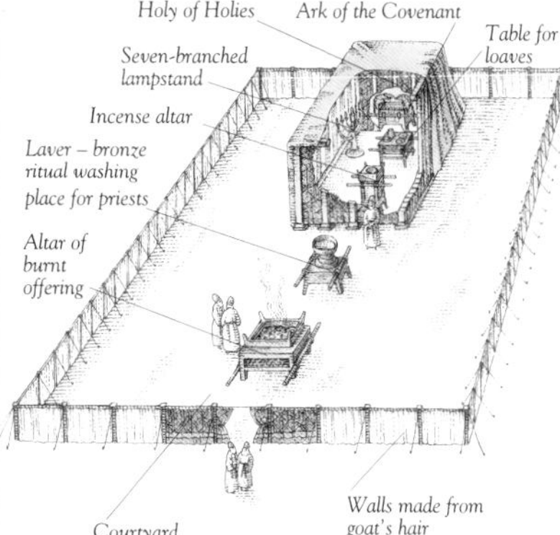

In the other, larger room was a bronze altar on which incense was burned each morning and evening. There was also a seven-branched gold lampstand, called a menorah, and a gold table on which, once a week, 12 loaves of bread were placed, one for each of the 12 tribes of Israel.

The tabernacle stood in a courtyard that was 54 yards (50 m) long and 27 yards (25 m) wide. Here, on a large altar, the priests burned animal sacrifices in their worship of God. Before the priests entered the tabernacle or offered a sacrifice, they washed their hands in a basin, called a laver.

Inside the tabernacle was the menorah, a seven-branched lampstand.

Many years later, when the people of Israel were no longer traveling all the time, King David decided to build a temple in Jerusalem where the Ark of the Covenant could be kept and God

KING SOLOMON'S TEMPLE

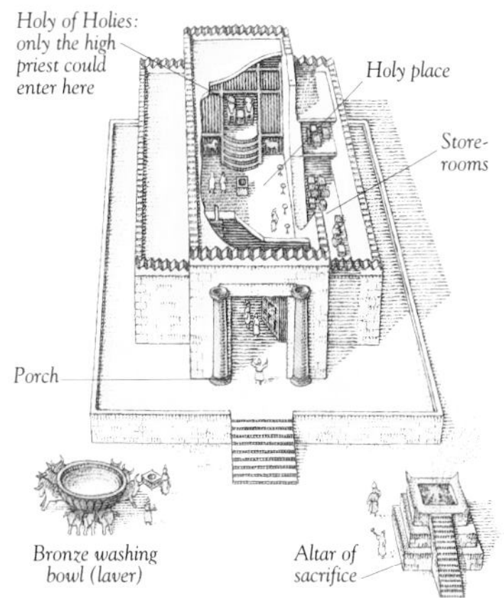

could be worshiped. It was David's son, Solomon, who ordered the temple to be built, along the lines of the tabernacle. When it was finished, King Solomon led a grand service to dedicate the temple to God.

A second temple replaced Solomon's in 515 BC, but the last Temple was built by King Herod the Great about 9 BC. This was much bigger and grander than the previous ones. It was destroyed by the Romans in AD 70.

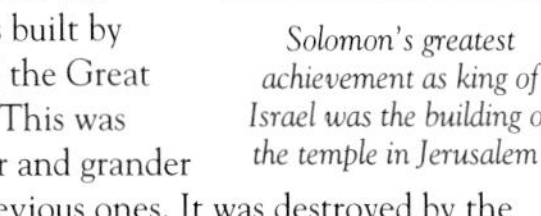

Solomon's greatest achievement as king of Israel was the building of the temple in Jerusalem.

Herod's Temple had several extra courtyards in addition to the one for priests: these were the Court of Women – the nearest that women could go to the "Holy of Holies" – and the Court of the Gentiles – the nearest people who were not Jews (Gentiles) could go. Although there were prayers and sacrifices every day, the temple was

HEROD'S TEMPLE

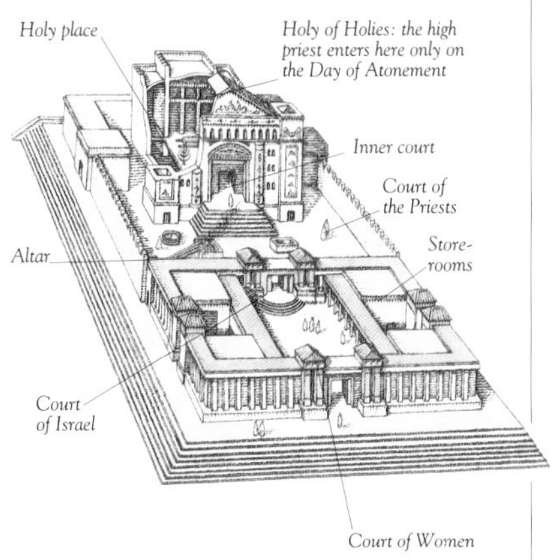

especially full at religious festivals. Often Psalms were sung by people as they went to the temple.

AT THE WESTERN WALL

This man is praying at the Western Wall. The *shophar*, or ram's horn, is blown at the start of a Jewish religious festival.

The Creation

IN THE BEGINNING God created heaven and earth. Water lay deep over the surface of the earth and the darkness was absolute. God said, "Let there be light." And suddenly there was light. And God saw that it was good.
God divided the light, which was day, from the darkness, which was night. And so ended the first day and night of creation.

Next God said, "Let there be sky over the waters," and called the sky heaven; and this was on the second day.

On the third day the land rose up through the waters, and God called the dry land earth, and the waters sea. At once grasses took root on the earth and every kind of plant; buds opened, seeds sprouted, and trees grew heavy with fruit. And God saw that it was good.

On the fourth day God said, "There must be lights in the sky to divide night from day

On the first day God creates light

On the second day God creates sky

On the third day God creates land, sea, and every kind of plant

and to mark the seasons." For this God created two lights: the greater, which he called the sun, to shine over the day, and the smaller, the moon, to shine at night. Around the moon God set the stars. On the fifth day God created all the creatures of the sea and sky. Birds flew through the air, while in the watery depths great fish swam silently..

On the sixth day God made all the animals, from the wild beasts of desert and jungle to cattle grazing in the fields. And God saw that it was good.

And God said: "I shall make people in my own image to rule over them." And so God created people, both male and female, in God's own likeness. And that was on the morning and the evening of the sixth day.

On the seventh day God rested, for the work was done, and all was well with the world.

On the fourth day God creates the sun, the moon, and the stars

On the fifth day God creates the creatures of the sea and sky

On the sixth day God creates animals and people

The Garden of Eden

SERPENT
Serpents, or snakes, such as the Egyptian cobra above, were thought by many people to represent evil or Satan. Satan opposes God and tries to upset God's plans.

CHERUBIM
Cherubim were often represented as winged sphinxes, or human-headed lions, as in this Assyrian ivory carving. In the book of Genesis, cherubim act as God's attendants. They guard the Tree of Life, which is the symbol of eternal life.

IN THE EAST, in Eden, God made a garden in which grew every tree and plant, and at the very center stood the Tree of Life and the Tree of Knowledge. God put the man into the Garden, telling him he might eat any fruit he wished, except from the Tree of Knowledge: for if he were to eat that, he would die.

God brought to the man, Adam, all the animals, so that he might name them. God then sent Adam into a deep sleep, and while he slept, took one of his ribs and out of it made a woman, so that Adam would have a wife. Both Adam and Eve, his wife, walked naked and happy in the Garden, and had no need of clothes.

Now the serpent, the most devious of all living creatures, questioned Eve, asking her if she could eat any fruit she pleased. "Yes," she said. "Any fruit except that from the Tree of Knowledge. If we eat that, we die."

"But you will not die," said the serpent. "Instead you will discover the difference between good and evil, and so will be equal with God."

The woman gazed at the Tree, and was tempted by the juicy fruit that would make her wise. She picked one and ate it; gave one to her husband, and he ate it. As they looked at each other, they

Adam and Eve are happy in the Garden of Eden

Eve picks fruit from the Tree of Knowledge and gives one to Adam

became aware of their nakedness. They quickly gathered some fig leaves, which they sewed together to cover themselves.

In the cool of the evening they heard the voice of the Lord as God walked in the Garden, and they hid so that God would not see them.

God called to Adam, "Adam, where are you?"

Adam said, "I heard your voice, and I was afraid so I hid."

"If you are afraid then I know you must have eaten from the Tree whose fruit I told you not to eat."

"It was the woman who gave me the fruit."

And Eve said, "It was the serpent who tempted and deceived me."

Then God cursed the serpent, and banished him from the Garden. He gave clothes to Adam and Eve, saying, "Now that you know both good and evil, you must leave Eden. You cannot stay for fear you might eat also from the Tree of Life, and if you did that you would live forever." And God drove them out of the Garden, and into the world. At the east of Eden he stationed cherubim and placed a flaming sword to guard the entrance to the Garden and to the Tree of Life.

God drives Adam and Eve out of the Garden into the world

Cain and Abel

wheat
lentils
almonds
pistachio nuts
olives
figs
grapes

CAIN'S OFFERING
God rejected Cain's offering for he did not give the best of his produce. Cain would have grown crops, such as the ones shown above.

Cain works in the fields

Abel is a shepherd

EVE GAVE BIRTH TO TWO SONS. Abel, the younger, was a shepherd, while his brother, Cain, worked in the fields. There came a time when they both made offerings to God: Cain from his crops, Abel from the finest and fattest of his flock. God was well pleased with Abel's offering, but not with Cain's. This made Cain very angry, and his face darkened with rage.

Abel offers the finest of his flock to God, while Cain offers fruit and grain

Cain kills Abel because God preferred his offering

"Why are you angry?" the Lord God asked him. "You will succeed if you work hard; and if you do not, the sin will be yours."

But Cain was not soothed by these words. He followed his brother into the fields, and there attacked and murdered him.

"Cain, where is your brother?" asked the Lord.

"I do not know," Cain replied. "Am I my brother's keeper?"

But God knew what had happened. "Cain, what have you done? I see your brother's blood staining the earth. Now you are cursed, cursed to wander the world, an outcast from man and God."

"This punishment is greater than I can bear!" cried Cain in agony. "You, my God, are going to turn your face away from me and condemn me to wander the world, to be killed by anyone who passes me on the road."

But the Lord reassured him. "The man who kills Cain will bring upon himself a terrible punishment." And God made a mark on Cain so that everyone would recognize him, and when they saw the mark would know they must leave him unharmed.

With a heavy heart Cain departed, and went to live in the land of Nod, which lies to the east of Eden.

ABEL THE SHEPHERD
Abel would have spent all day leading his flock of sheep to good pastures, and keeping them from harm. Sheep provided meat, milk, wool, and skins. The fattest, most perfect lambs were always offered to God.

God puts a mark on Cain and condemns him to wander the world

Noah's Ark

CYPRESS TREES
Cypress trees are found throughout the Bible lands. The wood is light, but strong and long-lasting. It was an ideal choice of timber for a boat as large as the ark.

AS THE YEARS PASSED, the descendants of Adam grew in number and spread to the four corners of the earth. But as they grew in number, so they grew in wickedness; and God, seeing violence and corruption everywhere, decided to destroy all the people and animals that had been created.

There was, however, one man whom the Lord loved, a good man who led an honest and hard-working life. His name was Noah, and God chose to save him, and to save also Noah's wife, and his three sons, Shem, Ham, and Japheth, and their wives.

"The world has grown wicked," God told Noah, "and I intend to destroy every living thing that I have made. But you, Noah, you and your family shall be saved.

Noah and his sons build the ark

Noah

"BUT WITH THEE WILL I ESTABLISH MY COVENANT; AND THOU SHALT COME INTO THE ARK, THOU, AND THY SONS, AND THY WIFE, AND THY SONS' WIVES WITH THEE."
GENESIS 6:18

"I shall cause a flood to rise over the land, and you must build an ark out of cypress wood that will float on the waters; it must be roofed with reeds and coated inside and out with tar. It must measure three-hundred cubits long, fifty cubits wide and thirty cubits high. It shall have three stories, with a door and a window in the side. In it you must make room for yourself and your family, and two – one male, one female – of every kind of creature, every kind of beast, reptile, and bird. And you must fill it with enough food for them and for yourselves. For it will rain for forty days and forty nights,

THERE WENT IN TWO AND TWO UNTO NOAH INTO THE ARK, THE MALE AND THE FEMALE, AS GOD HAD COMMANDED NOAH.
GENESIS: 7:9

The animals enter the ark, two by two

and life on earth will be extinct."

Noah did exactly as God had told him: he and his sons built the ark, making it watertight and stocking it with plenty of food of every variety for man and beast. When everything was ready, they led all the animals into the ark. Then they themselves went inside and God shut fast the door.

The skies darkened and it began to rain.

BOAT BUILDING
Noah and his sons would have built the ark by hand. The planks of wood were coated with tar to make the boat watertight. This traditional method of boat building is still practiced in parts of the Middle East today.

The Flood

THE DELUGE
This engraving by Gustave Doré captures the plight of people caught in the flood.

THE RAIN CONTINUED for forty days and nights. The flood waters rose, lifting the ark up with them until it was floating as high as the hills. Finally even the mountain ranges were submerged, and everything that was alive perished: there was no living thing left on Earth.

But God had not forgotten Noah, and all who were with him on the ark. After a time the rains stopped. The days went by, and then a great wind blew up; and after the wind a calm, and slowly the waters began to go down. Eventually the ark came to rest on a mountain peak in Ararat.

Every living thing perishes in the flood

AND THE WATERS PREVAILED, AND WERE INCREASED GREATLY UPON THE EARTH; AND THE ARK WENT UPON THE FACE OF THE WATERS.
GENESIS 7:18

Time passed, and Noah wanted to find out if the waters had subsided. Opening a window, he released a raven into the air to see if the bird would find anywhere to land. But the raven flew far and wide in every direction and saw nothing but water.

Next Noah released from the ark a dove; but she, too, flew in every direction without finding anywhere to land, for the waters still covered the earth. She returned to the ark, and Noah tenderly took her in. After seven days he again sent out the dove, and this time she came back in the evening with the leaf of an olive tree in her beak.

Noah knew by this that the waters were receding, and after waiting another seven days he sent out the dove once more. This time she did not return. Opening a window in the ark, Noah looked out and saw that the ground was dry.

God then spoke to Noah. "Now you must leave the ark, you, your wife, and your sons and their wives, and all the creatures you have with you. The world is for you and your children to govern, and the beasts on land and birds of the air and fish in the sea shall provide your food."

Then Noah built an altar in thanksgiving and made an offering on it to God. God was pleased with the sacrifice and blessed Noah and his family, telling them that they and their descendants would cover the earth.

As God spoke this blessing, a rainbow appeared in the sky. "This rainbow," God said, "is a sign that never again will the world be destroyed by flood; and in times to come when I cloud the sky with rain, afterward you will see a rainbow, and you will remember my promise, a promise made to you and to every living creature in the world."

ON DRY LAND
The mountainous area of Ararat in Turkey includes Mount Ararat where the ark is thought to have rested. Some people believe that Noah's ark still lies on this peak and expeditions have been sent to find its remains.

AND THE DOVE CAME IN TO NOAH IN THE EVENING; AND, LO, IN HER MOUTH WAS AN OLIVE LEAF.
GENESIS 8:11

The flood waters rise for forty days and nights

As Noah builds an altar in thanksgiving, a rainbow appears in the sky

The Tower of Babel

THE DESCENDANTS OF NOAH, having wandered for many years in the lands of the east, settled eventually on a wide plain in Shinar. Centuries had passed since the Flood, and now there were a great number of people, all speaking the same language. They decided between them to build a city out of brick, with a tower so tall its top would touch the clouds. This would give them a home, they thought, from which

BABYLON
Babel is traditionally thought to be the ancient walled city of Babylon, the capital of the empire of Babylonia. The earlier, biblical, name for Babylonia was Shinar.

The people of Babel build a tower out of bricks

no one could drive them out. More important, it would make them envied throughout the world.

And so they began to build, baking the bricks hard and using tar for mortar.

The Lord looked at the city that was taking shape, at the streets and the houses and the tower already rising up into the sky, and God said, "These people are growing vain. Soon there will be no limit to what they will want. I will confuse their speech, change the very words in their mouths, so that no one will understand what is said."

And so it was: soon everyone found that the words spoken by one person meant nothing to their neighbor.

This caused complete confusion. The building of the city, which was now called Babel because of the babble of voices within it, came to a stop. The people left the plain of Shinar and were scattered all over the world. And in every part of the world from that time on both men and women spoke in different languages.

ZIGGURAT
The tower of Babel may have been a ziggurat, or temple tower. Ziggurats have been found in Babylon and Ur. The pyramidlike buildings have outside staircases that lead to a temple at the top. Here, people believed they could be closer to the gods.

The tower reaches up into the sky

The building stops when the people's language is confused

MUD BRICKS
The tower of Babel would have been built out of mud bricks. This method of building is still used in parts of the Middle East today. Mud and straw are mixed together, shaped in wooden molds, then left to dry in the sun.

The Patriarchs

THE FIRST GREAT BIBLICAL leader of the people of Israel was Abraham. When he died, the leadership passed to his son, Isaac, and then in turn to Isaac's son, Jacob. These men are called the Patriarchs, which means male leaders or "fathers" of a family or tribe. The 12 sons of Jacob, including Joseph, were also considered Patriarchs, or founding fathers of Israel. They lived more than 1,500 years before Jesus.

During Abraham's life a special trust grew between his family and God. It began when the family left the great city of Ur and, together with their servants and animals, traveled first to Haran and then to the land of Canaan. When he left Haran, Abraham had no idea what sort of life awaited them. However, he believed that God wanted him to go to Canaan, so he set off on the long journey with his family. Because they trusted him, God made a covenant, or promise, with Abraham and his descendants: they would be his people and he would be their God.

God said to Abraham: "I will make nations of you and kings will come from you. I will give you the whole land of Canaan as an everlasting possession to you and your descendants. And I will be their God."

Although there were some towns in Canaan, the families of Abraham, Isaac, and Jacob moved from place to place, living in tents, finding areas where they could live without danger and where they had enough water and grazing for their sheep, goats, and other animals.

THE PATRIARCHS' FAMILY TREE

Abraham was the first of the Patriarchs. He was married to Sarah, but had a child (Ishmael) by Hagar, his wife's servant. Later, Sarah and Abraham had a son called Isaac.

Abraham's son, Isaac, married Rebekah. Her brother, Laban, was the father of Leah and Rachel who married Isaac's son Jacob.

Jacob was tricked into marrying Laban's eldest daughter Leah. Later he married her sister Rachel, whom he really loved.

Jacob had 12 sons and a daughter by his two wives and their servants, Zilpah and Bilhah. The 12 tribes of Israel were descended from his sons.

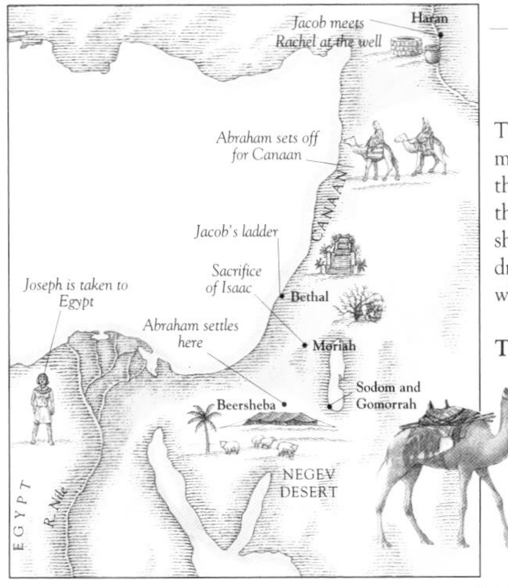

The map above shows the main events in the lives of the Patriarchs. Abraham and his people may have traveled across the desert to Canaan with camel caravans.

The God of Abraham, Isaac, and Jacob

Many important events happened to Abraham, Isaac, Jacob and other members of their family to test their faith in God and to give them greater understanding of God. For example, Abraham's obedience was shown when he was asked to sacrifice Isaac, his son. Later, when the time came for Isaac to be married, he learned to trust God through the way he met his wife, Rebekah. Years afterward, Jacob's faith in God became greater after he had a remarkable dream of a stairway stretching from Earth to Heaven.

These and other experiences helped the three men realize that God was involved in the things that happened to them in everyday life. Often they named places after something God had shown or taught them there. After Jacob had his dream, he decided to call the place "Bethal," which means "the house of God."

The Influence of the Patriarchs

Abraham, Isaac, and Jacob had great power, as did the heads of all families at that time. They were in charge of all family decisions, including the worship and sacrifices that were offered to God.

The Patriarch's word had to be obeyed and whenever he honored someone with a blessing, this could not be taken away. This is why Jacob, after he received a blessing from his father Isaac, became his heir, even though he had obtained the blessing by tricking his older brother, Esau.

The word "Israel" is first used in the Bible to refer to Jacob. One night Jacob wrestled with a stranger whom he thought was God. Afterward, God told Jacob that from then on he would be known as Israel, which means "the one who fights for God."

DESERT LIFE
Abraham and his people lived a nomadic life, moving from place to place. They probably lived on the outskirts of large towns, in tents similar to the Bedouin ones shown here.

Abram's Journey

ABRAM WAS BORN in Ur in Mesopotamia. Now elderly, he had settled with his wife Sarai in Haran. It was a sadness for both of them that they had had no children. One day God spoke to Abram. "You must leave this place, Abram, and take your wife and your relations and servants and everything you possess, and move to the land that I will show you. Once there you will have my blessing,
your name will be great,
and your people will become
a great nation."

ABRAM'S JOURNEY
The most likely route taken by Abram and Lot on their journey from Ur to Canaan. Lot finally settled in Sodom.

Lot's people

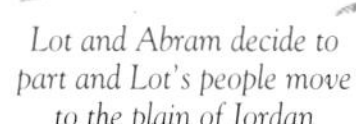

Lot and Abram decide to part and Lot's people move to the plain of Jordan

So Abram, with his wife Sarai and his nephew Lot, with his servants, his gold and silver, his tents, his donkeys and camels, sheep, and cattle, traveled south toward the land of Canaan.

But at the first place they settled there was not enough fertile land. Abram's shepherds began to fight Lot's shepherds for the best place to graze their flocks. Abram said to Lot, "Let us not quarrel. The whole country lies before us. If you go to the east, then I will go to the west, and there will be plenty for everyone."

TREASURES FROM UR
This gold helmet and dagger with its decorative sheath were discovered in Ur, a powerful city-state and the birthplace of Abram and Lot.

So Abram and his people settled in Canaan, while Lot looked to the east and saw the plain of Jordan. It was as lush and green as a well-watered garden. And there Lot agreed to go, he and his people settling in Sodom, one of the cities of the plain, whose inhabitants were known to be great sinners.

The Lord spoke again to Abram. "Look around you: all this land will belong to you and to your many descendants."

"But how can I have descendants?" said Abram, "I am an old man and I have no children."

"You will have a son," God told him. "And your son will have children, and his children's children will be as many in number as there are stars in the sky."

THE LORD MADE A COVENANT WITH ABRAM SAYING, "UNTO THY SEED HAVE I GIVEN THIS LAND, FROM THE RIVER OF EGYPT UNTO THE GREAT RIVER, THE RIVER EUPHRATES."
GENESIS 15:18

Abram's people settle in the land of Canaan

Sarai

Then God told Abram to make a sacrifice: to take a cow, a she-goat, and a ram; to kill the animals, cut them in half, and lay them side by side; to kill also a turtledove and a young pigeon.

This Abram did, dividing the animals in two, and leaving the birds whole. Later in the day he beat off the birds of prey, which greedily swooped down upon the carcasses. As the sun set he fell into a deep sleep, and while he slept he was seized with a terrible fear. But then he heard the voice of God speaking to him. He promised Abram that all would be well, and that he and his descendants would one day live in prosperity and die in peace in this land.

Night fell; and suddenly there came out of the darkness smoke and flames and a burning torch, which passed over Abram's sacrifice.

DESERT WANDERINGS
Abram and his family led a nomadic life. They traveled from place to place, looking for grazing land and water for their animals. They carried all their possessions on camels, and lived in tents. The Bedouin people live a similar life in the desert today.

Abram, Sarai, and Hagar

TENT DWELLERS
Desert dwellers today, such as these modern Bedouin, live much like Abram's family did. Because they constantly travel with their flocks to new grazing land, all of their possessions must be light, and easy to roll up. Waterproof tents woven out of coarse goat hair are homes well-suited to this way of living.

SARAI WAS GROWING OLD and still she had no children. She went to her husband, Abram, and told him that he should have a child by Hagar, her servant. "Look on Hagar," she said, "as though she were your wife."

This Abram did, but once Hagar realized she was going to have a baby, she began to be conceited and act rudely toward her mistress. "Hagar now looks down on me and insults me," Sarai complained to Abram.

"You must deal with her as you think right," Abram replied. Upon this Sarai began to treat her servant so harshly that Hagar ran away into the desert.

An angel found Hagar beside a spring in the wilderness, where she was weeping.

"What are you doing here?" he asked her.

"I am running away from my cruel mistress."

"You must return and behave well toward her. You are soon to give birth to

Hagar is expecting a child by Abram and begins to act rudely toward Sarai

Hagar runs into the wilderness and weeps, as Sarai has treated her harshly

a son whose name shall be Ishmael, and his descendants will be numbered in millions."

So Hagar returned and shortly afterward gave birth to a boy. Abram was then eighty-six years old. He looked at his son and gave him the name Ishmael, which means "God hears."

When Abram was ninety-nine, God appeared to him and said, "You shall be the father of many nations, and to mark this you must change your name to Abraham. I will keep my promise to you, and Canaan shall belong to you and your descendants forever; and I will be their God. Among your people every male must be circumcised now, and every male child of future generations. This will be a sign that you will keep your promise to me. From now on your wife must be called Sarah, and she will be the mother of your son."

Abraham laughed to himself at the idea that a man of one hundred and a woman of ninety should have a child. But God said, "Sarah will indeed have a son, and you shall call him Isaac, and he will be the father of princes. It will be with Isaac that my promise shall be continued, a covenant to be kept with all his descendants throughout all their generations.

"As for Ishmael, I will bless him and always look after him. He will lead a long and prosperous life, and will have many children. He will be a great power in the land, even though it is his brother, Isaac, whom I have chosen as the father of my people."

MOTHER AND CHILD
This Bedouin woman is holding her little child close to her. The Israelites considered children to be a gift from God. To be barren and unable to have a child, as Sarai was for many years, would have caused much heartache. Children spent most of their early years with their mothers.

Hagar returns home and gives birth to a boy, and Abram calls him Ishmael

Abraham and Sarah make the three strangers welcome

The three strangers tell Abraham and Sarah that they will have a son

DESERT MEAL
Sarah may have prepared a meal of bread, probably unleavened (made without yeast); milk, from a goat or sheep; curds, made from soured milk; and veal. Serving meat and milk together was not prohibited to Jews until after Moses, so this was a gracious meal then.

Time passed, and God appeared to Abraham near the trees of Mamre in the heat of the day.

Abraham was sitting at the entrance to his tent when he looked up and saw three strangers standing before him. At once, he came out to greet them. "My lords," Abraham said, bowing low. "If I have found favor with you, do not pass me by. Come, sit under this tree so you may wash your feet and rest, then we will bring you food, for we are your servants." Abraham then hurried back into the tent, giving orders to Sarah to bake bread, and for a tender young calf to be roasted. He stood by them under the tree while they ate.

"Where is your wife?" they asked.

"She is in the tent."

"Soon she will bear you a son."

Now Sarah was listening to this and she laughed at the idea that such an old woman should bear a child. But God heard her and rebuked her.

"Do you think there is anything too difficult for God to do?" he asked her.

Sodom and Gomorrah

GOD TOLD ABRAHAM that the cities of Sodom and Gomorrah would be destroyed, because their inhabitants were guilty of terrible crimes.

"If you find even ten righteous people," Abraham implored God, "will you have mercy and save these cities from destruction?"

"If I find ten good people," said the Lord, "I will not destroy them."

Two angels left for Sodom. They arrived there in the evening, where they were met at the city gates by Abraham's nephew, Lot. He welcomed them to his house, and spread before them a feast that he had prepared with his own hands.

No sooner had they finished eating than they heard the noise of a large crowd gathering. It was the men of Sodom: they were demanding that Lot hand over to them his two guests for their own pleasure.

Lot was full of anger and went out to speak to the crowd. "I would rather give you my daughters, to do with as you please," he said.

THE LORD SAID, "BECAUSE THE CRY OF SODOM AND GOMORRAH IS GREAT, AND BECAUSE THEIR SIN IS VERY GRIEVOUS, I WILL GO DOWN."
GENESIS 18:20-21

Lot goes out to speak to the crowd

A large crowd gathers threateningly outside Lot's home

"But these men you must not harm, for they are guests under my roof."

The crowd was in a frenzy and took no notice; the men only shouted louder and tried to force their way in. Suddenly Lot felt the angels' hands on his shoulders: they pulled him inside and shut the door. Then they struck the crowd with blindness, so that the men could no longer see where they were.

The two angels said to Lot, "Are there any other members of your family here? You must go to them and tell them to leave at once, or they will die when the city is destroyed." Lot hurried to his daughters' husbands and warned them of what was about to happen, but they would not listen and refused to move. Then the angels told Lot that he himself must leave. "Take your wife and both your daughters, and go quickly, for we must destroy this place and all its wickedness."

By now dawn was breaking, and the angels urged Lot to be gone.

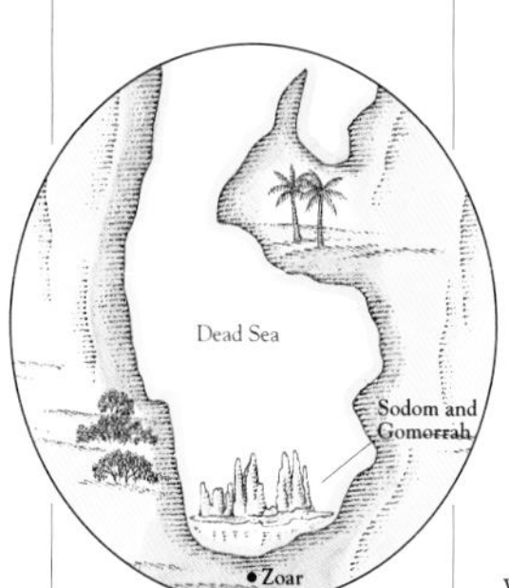

CITIES OF THE PLAIN
The cities of Sodom and Gomorrah probably lay in what is now the southern end of the Dead Sea. This area was once dry land that was very fertile. It is thought that an earthquake caused the Dead Sea to spread and cover the towns.

God rains down fire and brimstone on Sodom and Gomorrah

When they saw him hesitate, they took him by the hand and led him through the deserted streets and out beyond the city walls.

"Run as fast as you can, and make straight for the mountains. Do not look behind you, no matter what."

Lot's wife turns to look behind her and is transformed into a pillar of salt

Lot and his two daughters flee to the city of Zoar

"I cannot go so far," said Lot. "The mountains are too distant. Let me stay instead in the city of Zoar. Let me live there, and let it not be destroyed."

And to this the angels agreed.

By the time the sun had risen, Lot had reached Zoar. Then the Lord God rained down fire and burning stone on Sodom and Gomorrah, so that they and their people and the surrounding plain and everything that grew and moved upon it were utterly destroyed. Feeling the heat and hearing the noise, Lot's wife turned to look behind her. Instantly she was transformed into a pillar of salt.

The next morning Abraham rose early, and going to the place where he had talked with the Lord, he looked toward Sodom and Gomorrah. Instead of those two great cities of the plain he saw nothing but thick black smoke, like the smoke from a giant furnace.

PILLARS OF SALT
Because of the large amount of salt in the Dead Sea, nothing can live there – hence its name. There are clusters of salt in the water, serving as a reminder of the terrible fate of Lot's wife when she was turned into a pillar of salt.

Abraham's Two Sons

CIRCUMCISION
This painting by Fra Angelico shows Jesus being circumcised. In this ceremony the foreskin of a baby boy is removed. Many nations practiced circumcision, but for the Israelites it had a special meaning. It was a sign of the agreement, or covenant, between God and their people.

IT HAPPENED just as the Lord had said. When Abraham was a hundred years old, Sarah gave birth to a son whom they named Isaac from the word "laugh"; and when the baby was eight days old, he was circumcised. Both parents were overjoyed that at last they had a child, and Abraham gave a magnificent feast in celebration.

"Who would have thought that I at my age would have given birth," Sarah exclaimed. "God made me laugh with happiness so that all who heard should rejoice with me."

Sarah has a son by Abraham called Isaac

Abraham sends Hagar and Ishmael into the desert of Beersheba

WATER SKIN
The water carrier that Abraham gave to Hagar would have looked like this Bedouin water skin.

Soon, however, Sarah noticed that Hagar's son, Ishmael, was making fun of Isaac. "Ishmael must go!" she insisted. "You must turn him out, and his mother with him!

Abraham was saddened for he loved both his sons, but God reassured him. "Do as Sarah asks, for I will look after both Ishmael and Isaac. They will both live to be the founders of great nations."

Early the next morning Abraham gave Hagar some bread and a

leather skin filled with water and sent her into the desert of Beersheba with Ishmael.

The two of them wandered many miles through the hot, stony wilderness. Soon the bread was eaten, the skin dry, and there was no water to be found anywhere. Believing that death was near, Hagar laid her child under a bush, and then, weeping, went to sit by herself some way off so that she would not see him die.

Suddenly she heard the voice of an angel. "Do not be afraid," said the voice. "God will not let Ishmael die, for he has a glorious future before him. Go to him now, and take him by the hand."

As Hagar dried her eyes, she saw in front of her a spring. Eagerly she filled her skin, then went to Ishmael and gave him the water to drink.

Ishmael
The Arab people are traditionally believed to be the descendants of Ishmael.

An angel appears to Hagar

For some years Hagar and Ishmael made their home in the desert, where Ishmael grew up strong and brave, skillful with bow and arrow. In due course he married a young woman who came from the land of Egypt.

Hagar gives Ishmael water from the spring to drink

The Sacrifice of Isaac

NEGEV DESERT
Abraham and Isaac set off from their home in Beersheba. They journeyed through the Negev Desert, in southern Canaan, for three days until they reached Moriah.

GOD SPOKE TO ABRAHAM, in order to test his faith. "With your beloved son Isaac you must go to the land of Moriah, to a certain mountain which I will show you. There, instead of a goat or lamb, you must sacrifice your son on the fire."

The next morning, obedient to God's will, Abraham saddled a donkey, and set off for Moriah, taking Isaac and two servants with him. When they got to the mountains, Abraham stopped to cut some wood, giving it to his son to carry. He himself took a sharp knife and a flaming torch with which to light the fire. "You must stay here with the donkey," he told the two men. "We are going up the mountain to pray and make an offering to God."

"Father," said Isaac as they started on their way. "We have the wood for a fire, but where is the lamb to be sacrificed?"

"God will provide," answered Abraham.

When they reached the place chosen by God, Abraham built an altar on which he piled the wood; then, tying Isaac's arms tightly to his sides, he placed the boy on top of the pile. Abraham lifted the knife high above his head, preparing to plunge it into Isaac's breast. But at that moment he heard the voice of the angel of the Lord.

DOME OF THE ROCK
The mosque in Jerusalem is built on a rock, thought by many to be Mount Moriah, where Abraham was going to sacrifice Isaac. It is also the site of Solomon's Temple and Herod's Temple.

The two servants wait with the donkey

Abraham and Isaac go up the mountain to offer a sacrifice to God

"Abraham, Abraham, do not hurt your son. You have proved your perfect love of God by your willingness to sacrifice even your child."

The angel of the Lord tells Abraham not to hurt Isaac

A ram caught in a thicket is sacrificed instead of Isaac

RAMS IN THE THICKET
Abraham saw a ram, or male sheep, caught in a bush and sacrificed it instead of his son. The ram's horns may have become entangled as it tried to feed from the branches of the bush.

Looking around, Abraham saw a ram caught by the horns in the tangled branches of a bush. He untied Isaac, and seizing hold of the ram, put the animal on the altar in place of his son.

The angel spoke again. "Because you have done this for the love of God, you will be blessed, and your son, and your son's sons will be blessed; and they shall be as many in number as the stars in the sky."

Then Abraham and Isaac together came down from the mountain, and with the two servants returned to Beersheba.

"IN BLESSING I WILL BLESS THEE, AND IN MULTIPLYING I WILL MULTIPLY THY SEED AS THE STARS OF THE HEAVEN, AND AS THE SAND WHICH IS UPON THE SEASHORE."
GENESIS 22:17

Isaac and Rebekah

"Drink," says Rebekah, holding the jar out to the servant

servant

Rebekah

WATER CARRIER
Women like Rebekah often went to fetch water from a community well or cistern. These usually lay outside the city gates.

SARAH WAS DEAD, and Abraham knew he himself had not long to live. He sent for his most trusted servant. "My people are settled in Canaan, but I do not want my son to marry a Canaanite. You must go to the land of my birth, and from there bring back a wife for Isaac."

And so the servant set off for the city of Nahor in Mesopotamia, taking with him a train of ten camels laden with rich gifts. He arrived outside the city walls in the evening when the women were gathering to draw water at the well. As he watched them, he prayed to God for a sign: "Let her whom I ask for water be the wife for Isaac."

Almost before he had finished his prayer, a young girl carrying a water jar came to take her turn at the well. Her name was Rebekah, and she was very beautiful. The servant went up to her. "Will you let me drink from your jar?" he asked.

"Drink," she said, holding the jar out to him. "And now I will fetch water for your camels as well."

The servant was overjoyed at her kindness.

Covering her face with a veil, Rebekah walks toward Isaac

Isaac

From a saddlebag he took a heavy gold nosering and two bracelets of solid gold and gave them to her. "Where do you live?" he asked. "May I stay at your father's house?"

"You are welcome," replied Rebekah. Then she hurried home to tell her family. Her brother Laban welcomed the stranger, soon recognizing that it was God's will that Rebekah should return with him to Canaan.

Abraham's servant, having sent a prayer of thanks to God, made gifts to Rebekah of gold and silver jewelry and beautiful embroidered cloth. The next morning Rebekah said good-bye to her family, then set off with her nurse and servants for her new home.

Isaac was praying in the fields at twilight when he saw the camel caravan approaching through the dusk.

Covering her face with a veil, Rebekah dismounted. The servant described everything that had happened, and Isaac took Rebekah by the hand and led her to his tent.

Soon afterward they were married, and Isaac loved his wife and was comforted by her for the death of his mother, Sarah.

Camel
Abraham's large herd of camels was a sign of his family's wealth. The camel was used as a working animal. It was capable of carrying up to 400 lbs (180 kg) and could travel across the desert at about 8 to 10 miles (13 to 16 km) an hour.

Nosering
The nosering given to Rebekah may have looked like the one this Bedouin woman is wearing. Mesopotamian women often wore jewelry, including rings, necklaces, and bracelets.

Esau and Jacob

IBEX
Esau would have hunted game, such as the ibex, a type of wild goat, whose meat was highly prized. Ibex are still found in rocky areas of the Middle East today.

AFTER MANY YEARS of childlessness Rebekah gave birth to twin boys. The elder, who was covered from head to toe with thick red hair, they named Esau. The younger, born holding his twin's heel, they called Jacob. Esau, whom Isaac loved best, grew up a strong and adventurous hunter, while Jacob, his mother's favorite, preferred staying at home.

One day Jacob was cooking some lentil stew when his brother came in, faint with hunger. "Quick, I'm famished! Give me some of that!" Esau demanded.

"I will," Jacob replied, "if you give up your rights as firstborn to me."

Esau laughed. "What use to me are rights when what I want is a good meal!"

"Then give me your word." And Esau gave his word, and so exchanged his birthright for a plateful of stew and some bread.

Isaac, old and blind and near to death, asked Esau to shoot a deer and prepare the dish of venison he so loved. "I want to taste it one last time so that I may bless you before I die," he told him.

Esau, whom Isaac loves best, is a hunter

Jacob, Rebekah's favorite, prefers staying at home

Esau exchanges his birthright for a plateful of stew

Rebekah overheard these words and determined that Jacob, not Esau, should receive his father's blessing. "I will cook the dish," she said, "and you must take it to your father in Esau's place. Go now and fetch me two young goats."

"But he will know I am not Esau!" said Jacob. "Esau is covered in hair, and my skin is smooth. He will know that I am deceiving him, and will put a curse on me!"

"Do as I say, and all will be well." And Rebekah dressed Jacob in his brother's clothes and covered his hands and shoulders with goatskin. She gave him some bread and a bowl of stew made from goat's meat. Then she sent him to his father.

"Who are you?" Isaac asked, puzzled. "Come near me so that I may feel you. The voice is Jacob's voice, but the hands are the hands of Esau. Are you really my eldest son?"

"I am," Jacob lied.

So Isaac was deceived. Believing that it was Esau who was with him, he ate the food that had been brought to him. He blessed Jacob and promised that he should have everything due to the firstborn. "May you be happy and prosperous, and may good fortune come to all who wish you well."

Lentil stew
Esau sold his birthright to Jacob in exchange for a "mess of pottage," or red lentil stew, which he scooped up with thin, unleavened bread. This was a common meal in Old Testament times.

Rebekah discovers that Isaac is to give Esau his blessing

Rebekah helps Jacob to disguise himself as Esau

Isaac blesses Jacob instead of Esau, while Rebekah looks on

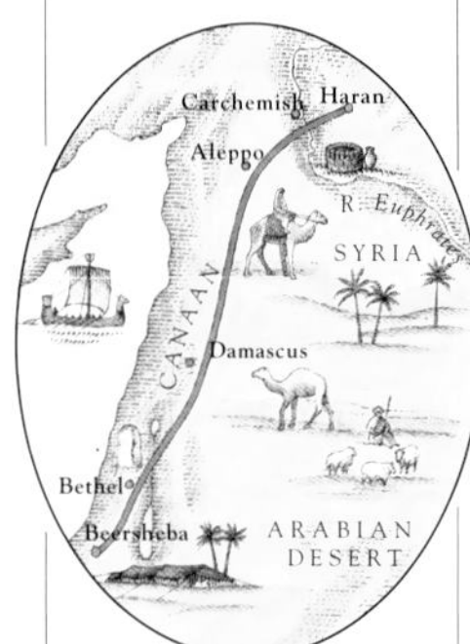

JACOB'S JOURNEY
Jacob set off from Beersheba in southern Canaan. He stopped at Bethel, where God appeared to him in a dream. From there he may have followed the route of the trade caravans and passed through major cities, such as Damascus, before reaching Haran.

Scarcely had Jacob left his father's tent than Esau arrived home from the hunt. Expertly he prepared the dish of venison and took it to Isaac. "Here is your favorite dish, father," he said.

"Who are you?" asked the old man.

"I am Esau, your eldest son."

"Then who is it who has just now been with me, and to whom I have given my blessing?" Isaac asked, his voice trembling.

When Esau heard his father's words, he cried out bitterly. He realized the trick that had been played, and he begged his father to bless him and give him his rights.

"I will bless you," said Isaac, "but I cannot give you what I have already promised to your brother." Isaac knew that the blessing was given before God, and it could not be altered.

Esau was filled with hatred for Jacob. He knew that Isaac would soon be dead, so he planned to kill Jacob as soon as the period of mourning for his father's death had passed. But Rebekah heard of his plot and was able to warn Jacob. "Your brother is planning to kill you," she told him. "Go at once to my brother Laban in Haran, and stay there until Esau's anger cools. I will let you know when it is safe to return." So Jacob left Beersheba and set out for Haran.

Esau cries out when he realizes that Isaac has blessed Jacob

Rebekah tells Jacob to leave for Haran, to escape his brother's anger

Jacob's Ladder

On his way to stay with Laban, Jacob stopped for the night. He picked up a large, smooth stone to use as a pillow and lay down to sleep.

He dreamed he saw a stairway reaching up to heaven, with angels moving up and down it. At the top of the stairway was God. "I am the God of Abraham and of your father Isaac," said the Lord to Jacob. "And I will give the land on which you lie to you and your descendants."

When Jacob awoke early the next morning, he was struck with wonder. "This is a holy place, for God was here and I did not know it." He took the stone which he had used as a pillow, and having stood it upright, poured oil over it. Then he named the place "Bethel," meaning the house of God.

He dreams of a stairway reaching like a ladder to heaven

Jacob falls asleep, using a stone as a pillow

And he dreamed, and behold a ladder set up on the earth, and the top of it reached to heaven: and behold the angels of God ascending and descending on it.
Genesis 28:12

Jacob and Rachel

Jacob

Rachel

Jacob watches as Rachel approaches the well

SHEPHERDESS
Rachel was a shepherdess. She would have tended her flock with care, protecting it from harm.

JACOB CONTINUED on his journey from Bethel. Eventually he came near Haran, in northern Mesopotamia. He saw a field in the middle of which was a well covered by a heavy stone. Around the well lay several flocks of sheep, being tended by shepherds. Every day when it was time for the sheep to drink, the shepherds would lift off the stone and draw water for the sheep from the well. They would then replace the stone over the mouth of the well.

Jacob greeted the shepherds. "Can you tell me the name of this place?" he asked.

"You are in Haran," they told him.

"Do you know Laban?"

"We know him well," they replied. "His daughter, Rachel, will be coming soon to draw water for their sheep."

Jacob sat down and waited, and then he saw Rachel approaching, driving before her a flock of sheep. Jacob thought she was very beautiful.

As she drew near, Jacob lifted the stone from the top of the well and helped her water her father's sheep. "I am Jacob, the son of Isaac. My mother is Rebekah, your father's sister," he told Rachel. Then he embraced and kissed her.

Rachel was delighted to see her cousin. She ran at once to tell her father the news.

Laban, too, was filled with joy, and hurried to meet his nephew.

JACOB'S KISS
On first meeting Rachel, Jacob kisses her. This painting by William Dyce captures the moment.

On hearing from Rachel that Jacob is here, Laban comes out to greet his nephew

Rachel and Leah wait to welcome Jacob

Throwing his arms around Jacob, he told him how glad he was that he had come. "You are welcome in my house," he said. "You, my sister's son, must come and stay with me."

They went back to his home where both Rachel and her elder sister, Leah, were waiting to welcome Jacob to their father's house.

So Jacob, having told his uncle all that had happened between himself and Esau, stayed with Laban for a month. During that time he worked hard, doing willingly whatever Laban asked him.

HEBREW BEAUTY
Rachel would have been young, with a natural beauty like this girl.

Jacob's Wedding

AND JACOB SERVED SEVEN YEARS FOR RACHEL; AND THEY SEEMED UNTO HIM BUT A FEW DAYS, FOR THE LOVE HE HAD TO HER.
GENESIS 29:20

WHEN JACOB HAD BEEN WORKING for his uncle for a month, Laban said to him, "It is not right that you should work for nothing. Tell me what I should give you in payment."

Now Jacob looked at Laban's two daughters, Rachel and Leah. Leah was plain, but Rachel was slender and beautiful, and it was she whom Jacob loved.

Laban

Laban gives a feast to celebrate the marriage of his daughter

"I will work for nothing," he said to Laban, "if at the end of seven years you will give me Rachel as my wife."

"I would rather she marry you than anyone," said Laban. "At the end of that time she shall be yours."

So for seven years Jacob worked as hard as he knew how. He loved Rachel so much and was so happy in her presence that the time passed quickly, each year seeming no more than a week in length.

At the end of seven years, Jacob went to Laban to claim his reward. "Now let me marry Rachel, as you promised."

Laban called together all his friends and family, and gave a great feast to celebrate the marriage of his daughter. But that night, when it was dark, he sent Leah to Jacob in Rachel's place. In the morning,

VEILED SECRET
On her wedding day, Leah would have worn a veil over her face, like the one this Bedouin woman is wearing. This explains how Jacob was tricked into believing that Leah was Rachel.

when Jacob saw the older, not the younger, sister lying by his side, he realized he had been tricked. "How could you do this?" he asked Laban angrily. "Did we not make a bargain? Have I not worked for you for seven years so that I might have Rachel as my wife?"

Laban shrugged. "In this country it is the custom for the elder daughter to marry first. Leah is the elder, so it is right that you should take her for your wife." He laid a hand soothingly on Jacob's arm. "However," he continued, "finish the wedding week's festivities. Then you may marry Rachel as well if you will work for me for another seven years."

To this Jacob agreed; a week later Rachel became his wife and for seven more years Jacob worked for Laban.

WEDDING FEAST
The Bible says that the wedding feast of Jacob and Leah lasted for one week. During this time family and friends would have gathered to sing, dance, and play music, as in this modern-day village wedding in Iran.

Jacob is angry with Laban for tricking him into marrying Leah

Laban

Jacob

Leah

Jacob marries Rachel a week after Leah

Of his two wives, Jacob loved Rachel best. But while Rachel remained childless, Leah bore her husband six sons and a daughter. Rachel grew envious of her sister, and in her unhappiness turned against Jacob. " Why do you not give me children?" she demanded.

"I am not God," Jacob coldly answered her.

But in time Rachel, too, conceived, giving birth to a boy, called Joseph. Once she had her baby, Rachel's sadness disappeared.

Leah

Rachel

While Leah has many children, Rachel remains childless

Jacob's Return

Jacob and his family journey home to Canaan

A stranger wrestles with Jacob

JABBOK RIVER
Jacob sent his family across the Jabbok River, so that he could spend some time alone. The fast-flowing Jabbok feeds into the River Jordan.

AFTER THE BIRTH OF JOSEPH, Jacob decided it was time to leave Laban, who was becoming jealous of his skills as a shepherd and his growing wealth. He sent a message to Esau to say he was on his way home and that he hoped Esau would look favorably on him. And then, taking with him his wives and children, all his servants, his herds and flocks, he started out for Canaan. Almost at once word came that Esau was coming to meet him with a force of four hundred men.

"I fear from this that he means to attack," said Jacob, and prayed to God to save him. He divided his own company into two parts, so that if Esau did attack at least half would escape. Then he chose a large number of cattle, camels, and donkeys to give to his brother.

That evening Jacob sent all the men, women, and children, together with his possessions, across the Jabbok River so that he might have some time alone.

Suddenly, and from nowhere, a stranger appeared and began to wrestle with him. All night they fought in silence.

ESAU MEETS JACOB
The dramatic reunion of the two brothers is realistically captured by Gustave Doré in this 19th-century engraving.

Jacob and Esau are reunited

At dawn the stranger said, "It is now morning, and I must leave. Tell me, what is your name?"

" My name is Jacob."

"You shall not be called Jacob any longer, but Israel, for you have struggled with God and with men, and you have prevailed." And with that the stranger was gone. As the sun rose and light returned to the fields, Jacob realized that he had come face to face with God.

He had hardly caught up with his people when they saw a cloud of dust on the road, signaling the approach of Esau and his four hundred men. Jacob hurried forward, then bowed down before his brother. Esau threw his arms around him and kissed him, and they both wept. "Welcome, brother," Esau said. "You and yours are welcome home."

JACOB BOWED HIMSELF TO THE GROUND SEVEN TIMES, UNTIL HE CAME NEAR TO HIS BROTHER. ESAU RAN TO MEET HIM, AND EMBRACED HIM, AND FELL ON HIS NECK, AND KISSED HIM: AND THEY WEPT.
GENESIS 33:3-4

Joseph's Dreams

saffron

cochineal

pomegranate

mollusk shell

kermes insect

NATURAL DYES
Joseph's coat could have been dyed with colors similar to those shown above. Orange came from the saffron flower, pink from the cochineal insect, blue from the rind of a pomegranate, purple from the mollusk shell, and red from the kermes insect.

JACOB LIVED IN CANAAN with his twelve sons. Of all his sons, he loved Joseph the most, as his mother was his beloved wife Rachel. He made Joseph a beautiful coat woven in all the brilliant colors of the rainbow. Jacob's other sons were jealous of Joseph because he was so favored, and when they saw him in his coat of many colors they hated him. One night Joseph had a dream, and when he had told his brothers his dream, they hated him even more.

"I dreamed," he said, "that we were in the fields at harvest, tying up sheaves of wheat. My sheaf of wheat stood upright, while your sheaves bowed down to it."

Soon afterward Joseph had another dream. "I dreamed," he said, "that the sun and moon in the sky and eleven stars were all bowing down to me."

When the brothers heard his words they were furious. A few days later they took their flocks to graze in fields some distance away. Jacob sent Joseph to see that all was well. The brothers had a clear view

Joseph tells his brothers his dreams

Jacob gives Joseph a beautiful coat

of the road and saw Joseph approaching in his multicolored coat. "Now is our chance – we could kill him and throw him into this pit. We can say that a wild animal attacked him."

But Reuben, who had a kind heart, spoke out. "Don't let us kill him: we don't want his blood on our hands. Much better just to throw him into the pit and leave him to his fate." And to this the brothers agreed – not knowing that secretly Reuben was planning to return later, rescue Joseph, and take him home.

When Joseph reached them, his brothers attacked him at once, ripping off his coat and throwing him into the pit. They left him there without food or water. Then they sat down to eat.

At twilight a group of Ishmaelites came by. They were on their way to Egypt with camels loaded with spices, balm, and myrrh. Judah suggested that they sell Joseph as a slave to the travelers. Then they would be rid of the brother they hated without having to kill him.

So Joseph was sold for twenty pieces of silver. And the Ishmaelites took him with them into Egypt.

Meanwhile the brothers killed a young kid and dipped Joseph's coat in its blood. Their father was filled with horror when they showed it to him. "This is Joseph's coat! My beloved son must have been killed by some wild beast!" Jacob tore his clothes in grief and wept, and no one was able to comfort him.

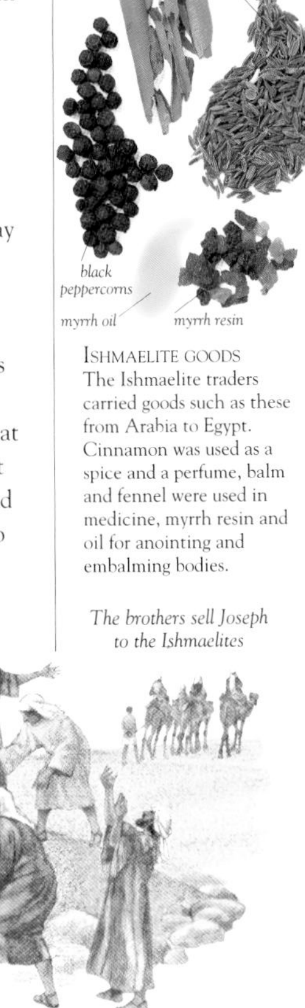

ISHMAELITE GOODS
The Ishmaelite traders carried goods such as these from Arabia to Egypt. Cinnamon was used as a spice and a perfume, balm and fennel were used in medicine, myrrh resin and oil for anointing and embalming bodies.

Joseph the Slave

AND SHE CAUGHT HIM BY HIS GARMENT, SAYING, "LIE WITH ME," AND HE LEFT HIS GARMENT IN HER HAND, AND FLED.
GENESIS 39:12

WHEN THE ISHMAELITES ARRIVED IN EGYPT THEY sold Joseph to one of Pharaoh's officers, Potiphar, captain of the guard. Joseph worked hard for Potiphar, who was so impressed by his skills that he made him head of his household.

Now Joseph was a handsome young man, and before long he

The Ishmaelites sell Joseph to Potiphar

Potiphar's wife tries to seduce Joseph

caught the eye of Potiphar's wife. She tried very hard to seduce him, but Joseph resisted her. "Your husband trusts me," he said. "You cannot ask me to betray him." Potiphar's wife did not care for her husband or for Joseph's objections. Day after day she lay in wait, teasing and tempting him. And still he refused her. Then one day in desperation she cornered Joseph and caught hold of him by the sleeve of his coat. But Joseph was too quick for her, and he made his escape, leaving her with nothing but an empty garment in her hands.

Then Potiphar's wife summoned all the servants. "Look what this Hebrew tried to do!" she said, holding up Joseph's coat. "He forced his way into my bedroom, and when I cried out, he fled, leaving his coat

WOMEN IN EGYPT
This Egyptian wall painting shows an official being offered food by his wife. Egyptian women, such as Potiphar's wife, could own and manage property.

behind." When her husband came home, he was told the same false story. Potiphar, enraged, immediately had Joseph thrown into prison. Fortunately, however, the jailer took a liking to the young man, and put him in charge of all the other prisoners.

It so happened that in the prison with Joseph were Pharaoh's cupbearer and the royal baker. One night each of them had a dream, which in the morning they asked Joseph to explain. "In my dream," said the cupbearer, "I saw a vine with three branches, bearing ripe grapes. I squeezed the juice from these grapes into a cup, which I gave Pharaoh to drink."

"Your dream," said Joseph, "means that in three days Pharaoh will pardon you."

Potiphar and his wife have Joseph arrested

Potiphar has Joseph thrown into prison

Joseph meets the baker and the cupbearer in prison

"I," said the baker, "dreamed that I had three baskets of bread for Pharaoh stacked on my head, and a flock of birds flew down and ate every crumb."

Joseph looked grave. "I am sorry to say that your dream means that in three days Pharaoh will have you hanged."

And it happened just as Joseph said: within three days the cupbearer was restored to his job, while the baker was hanged.

WALL PAINTING
The houses of officials, such as Potiphar, would have been decorated with brightly colored wall paintings like this detail of a hunting scene. Raw materials, such as carbon for black and copper for green, were used as paints.

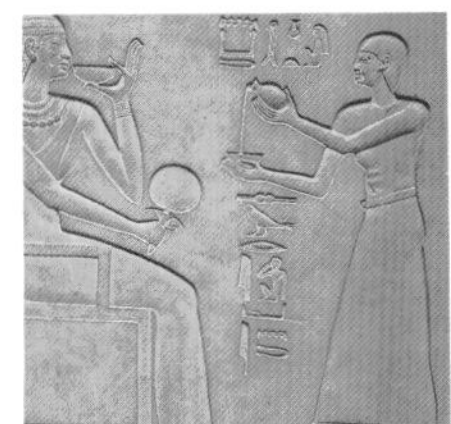

CUPBEARER
This limestone relief shows a cupbearer serving an Egyptian princess. The Pharaoh's cupbearer was a high-ranking official who held an important position of trust. His main duty was to taste food and drink before serving, to check for poison.

Pharaoh's Dreams

PHARAOH'S THRONE
The Pharaoh would have had a special throne for religious ceremonies. It is thought that this gold-plated throne, found in Tutankhamen's tomb in Egypt, was used for such occasions.

TWO YEARS HAD PASSED and still Joseph was in jail. Then one night Pharaoh had a strange dream: he was standing by the River Nile and while he watched, seven cows, fat and healthy, came out of the water to feed. A while later seven thin cows came out of the river, so lean and bony they could barely stand. The thin cows ate up the fat cows. Pharaoh woke with a start. Then he fell asleep and dreamed again. This time he saw seven ears of wheat growing plump and golden on a single stalk. Then he saw seven shriveled ears of wheat, which ate up the seven large ears.

In the morning Pharaoh demanded that someone be found to explain his dreams. All the wise men and magicians were brought before Pharaoh, but no one could tell him the meaning of his dreams.

Joseph is brought before Pharaoh and tells him the meaning of his dreams

Joseph

Pharaoh promotes Joseph to the highest office

It was then that the cupbearer remembered Joseph and told Pharaoh how he had correctly interpreted both his and the baker's dreams. Joseph was immediately released from prison and brought before Pharaoh. After thinking for a moment Joseph said, "God has revealed to me what your dreams mean: Egypt is about to enjoy seven years of great plenty, to be followed by seven years of terrible famine. In the time of plenty you must save grain from the harvest and store it, so that there will be enough to eat during the famine."

Pharaoh was so impressed by Joseph that he decided to promote him to the highest office. Pulling the ring from his own finger, he gave it to Joseph, then he hung a heavy gold chain about his neck and dressed him in fine linen robes. He presented him with a magnificent chariot. "You shall be ruler of the whole of Egypt," he declared, "second in power only to myself."

Under Joseph's supervision, grain was gathered and stored during the seven years of good harvest. Then, when the lean years arrived, there was more than enough for all. There was so much that people came from distant lands to buy grain, for the famine was everywhere.

AND JOSEPH GATHERED WHEAT AS THE SAND OF THE SEA, VERY MUCH, UNTIL HE LEFT NUMBERING; FOR IT WAS WITHOUT NUMBER.
GENESIS 41:49

CHARIOT
Egyptian chariots were driven by royalty and high officials, as well as by warriors and hunters. When Pharaoh gave a chariot to Joseph, it was a sign of his new status.

Under Joseph's supervision, grain is gathered and stored

Joseph the Governor

FAMINE
This statue of a starving man with a begging bowl was found in Egypt and dates from the Middle Kingdom around 2000 BC. It reflects the suffering of ordinary people during times of famine, an ever-present threat in the ancient world. The famine in Egypt would have been caused by a drop in the water level of the River Nile. The river usually provided the Egyptians with plenty of water for their crops.

Simeon is taken prisoner

The brothers kneel down in front of Joseph

THE FAMINE HAD SPREAD to Canaan. Joseph's father, Jacob, saw that his people were hungry, so he sent ten of his sons to Egypt to buy wheat. He kept Benjamin, his beloved youngest son, at home with him.

The brothers set off on their long journey from Canaan to Egypt. They found their way to the governor, who was their brother Joseph. Once in his presence they knelt humbly before him, their faces pressed to the ground. Joseph knew at once who they were, but they did not recognize him in his fine clothes.

He spoke accusingly. "You are spies, coming here to spy on Egypt."

"No," they protested. "We are from Canaan, come here to buy grain. We were twelve, but the youngest is at home with our father and one of us is dead."

"Why should I believe you?" Joseph demanded. "You must prove you are not spies. You shall return to Canaan to fetch the youngest. Then I will know if you are telling the truth."

AND JOSEPH COMMUNED WITH THEM, AND TOOK FROM THEM SIMEON, AND BOUND HIM BEFORE THEIR EYES.
GENESIS 42:24

Joseph has his brothers' sacks filled with wheat, and their silver is secretly replaced

On the journey home one of the brothers opens his sack and finds the silver

But first Joseph had the brothers thrown into prison for three days. On the third day they were brought again before him. "Take this wheat back to your land," he said. "But bring your youngest brother here or I shall have you all put to death. And to make sure you obey me, I shall keep one of you here as hostage."

The brothers trembled. They felt guilty and believed that this was a punishment for the way they had treated Joseph.

As they whispered among themselves, Joseph listened, silently weeping at the sight of their frightened faces. He had spoken through an interpreter, and knew they did not realize he could understand everything they said.

Suddenly he gave the order for one of the brothers, Simeon, to be bound in front of them and put in jail. Then he had the sacks of the others filled with wheat, and the silver they had brought to pay for it secretly replaced. Lastly he gave them food before sending them on their way.

Overnight on the journey home one of the brothers opened his sack to get wheat for his donkey, and saw the returned silver. "What does this mean?" they asked each other nervously.

Once back in Canaan they told Jacob everything.

"My children are being taken away from me. First Joseph, then Simeon," said Jacob. "And now you want to take Benjamin. But you shall not take my youngest child from me – if harm came to him I would go to my grave in sorrow."

RECORDING A HARVEST
In Egypt grain was stored in large granaries. Clerks kept a record of stocks, as shown in this Egyptian wall painting. Joseph was a good organizer, and was able to provide his brothers with a supply of wheat from his stores.

PIECES OF SILVER
In the days before coins, silver was often used as money. Joseph's brothers would have paid for their grain with pieces of silver weighed out on scales.

Benjamin and the Silver Cup

WINE FUNNEL
The brothers "drank and were merry" at Joseph's feast. Wine making was commonly practiced in Egypt. Funnels were used to strain the sediment from the wine.

EGYPTIAN FEAST
The Egyptians ate well, and Joseph would have offered his brothers a variety of foods at the feast. This could have included savory dishes of duck, cucumbers, leeks, onions, garlic, and olives, followed by sweet dishes of pomegranates, dates, figs, walnuts, almonds, and wild honey.

Joseph meets his brothers at the feast and weeps at seeing Benjamin

SOON ALL THE GRAIN WAS GONE, and Jacob told his sons that they must go again into Egypt and buy food. "We cannot go without Benjamin," said Judah. Jacob was unhappy, but Judah promised to look after his brother and bring him safely home.

"You must take a present for this all-powerful governor," said Jacob. "Take the best our land has to offer – honey, spices, balm, myrrh – and plenty of silver to pay for the wheat."

Again the brothers went to Joseph, who invited them to eat at his house. There they were welcomed by his steward and joyfully reunited with their brother Simeon. When Joseph entered, they bowed low and laid their presents before him. At the sight of Benjamin, Joseph was so moved that he left the room and wept. On returning, he offered them the best he had in food and wine, and to Benjamin he gave five times more to eat and drink. After dinner Joseph ordered his men to fill the brothers' sacks with grain, and to put back the money they had brought with them. In Benjamin's sack he hid a silver cup of his own.

The brothers left as soon as it was light, but they had not gone far when Joseph's steward caught up with them. He searched their sacks in turn. When the cup was found in Benjamin's sack, the steward had them all arrested and taken back to the city.

SILVER CUPS
These silver cups date from the Middle Kingdom (2133-1786 BC), the time when the events in the Joseph stories probably took place. The theft of a silver cup was a serious crime because silver was a luxury, which was imported into Egypt from Syria. Also, the cup belonged to Joseph, the governor, second in importance only to the Pharaoh.

The silver cup is found in Benjamin's sack

Once more at Joseph's house the brothers threw themselves on the ground, begging for mercy. "You may all go," said Joseph, "except the man in whose sack the goblet was found. He shall stay and be my servant."

"Do not keep Benjamin," Judah implored him. "If he does not return, my father will die of grief, for he loves him dearly, and he has already lost one son. I beg you to keep me instead."

Then Joseph felt his heart would break, and he could bear it no longer. "I am Joseph, your brother, whom you sold as a slave. But now I am Pharaoh's chief adviser and governor of all Egypt. You must come and settle here, for there are five more years of famine to suffer. Bring all you have, your flocks and your herds, and I will look after you. Tell my father what you have seen." And he threw his arms around Benjamin and wept, and then he kissed all his brothers.

The brothers returned to Canaan, and told Jacob that Joseph was alive. Jacob was full of joy at the news. He agreed at once to go with them to Egypt, and there they made their home.

THEY SPEEDILY TOOK DOWN EVERY MAN HIS SACK TO THE GROUND, AND OPENED EVERY MAN HIS SACK. AND HE SEARCHED, AND BEGAN AT THE ELDEST, AND LEFT AT THE YOUNGEST: AND THE CUP WAS FOUND IN BENJAMIN'S SACK.
GENESIS 44:11-12

Life in Egypt

WHEN JOSEPH'S FAMILY and friends went to live in Egypt, to escape from famine in their own country, they were given land in Goshen, in the north of the country. This area was part of the Nile Delta, where the River Nile breaks up into many smaller rivers before flowing into the Mediterranean Sea. Because there was plenty of water there, the Israelites were able to grow a great many crops.

An Egyptian schoolboy once described in a letter the comfortable way of life:

FROM CANAAN TO EGYPT
The wall paintings above are from an Egyptian tomb at Beni-Hasan. They show a group of people, probably Canaanites, coming into Egypt with their belongings.

"The countryside provides a wealth of good things. Their pools are full of fish, their lagoons are thick with birds, their meadows are covered with green grass. Their storehouses are full of barley and wheat that tower up to the sky. There are onions and chives to season the food, also pomegranates, apples, olives, and figs from the orchards. People are glad to live there."

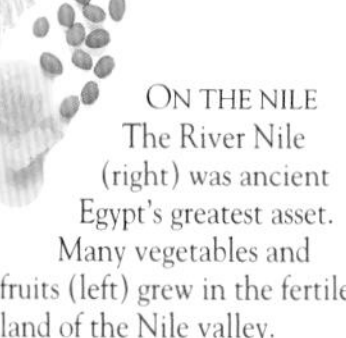

ON THE NILE
The River Nile (right) was ancient Egypt's greatest asset. Many vegetables and fruits (left) grew in the fertile land of the Nile valley.

Rulers and Slaves

The rulers of Egypt, the pharaohs, were at the center of Egyptian society. They lived in great luxury and built rich palaces, temples, and tombs. They were buried inside huge stone pyramids, with their treasures, often made of gold and silver.

Many Israelites became wealthy and some, like Joseph, who had been sold into slavery, rose to have great influence in Egypt. Then, 300 years after Joseph's time, their fortunes changed. In about 1500 BC the Egyptian rulers turned against people who had come from other countries: this included the Israelites. They became slaves and had to work for others rather than for themselves.

The Egyptian court was one of the richest of the ancient world.

The Israelites were harshly treated by the Egyptians.

Slaves carried out most of the building work, making bricks from a mixture of mud and straw. Royal buildings were usually made of stone. Israelite slaves may have built the cities of Pithom and Rameses, and the great city of Thebes in the south. The impressive buildings at Thebes and in other parts of Egypt show the skill of builders and craftsmen.

Moses in Egypt

One of the greatest leaders of the Israelites was Moses, who was found as a baby by the pharaoh's daughter. He grew up in the grand palaces of the Egyptian court and as a boy would have learned to read and write in hieroglyphics and take part in popular sports, such as archery and gymnastics.

Moses left Egypt after he had killed an Egyptian. He never forgot that he was an Israelite, and later he returned to free his people and lead them out of Egypt at God's command.

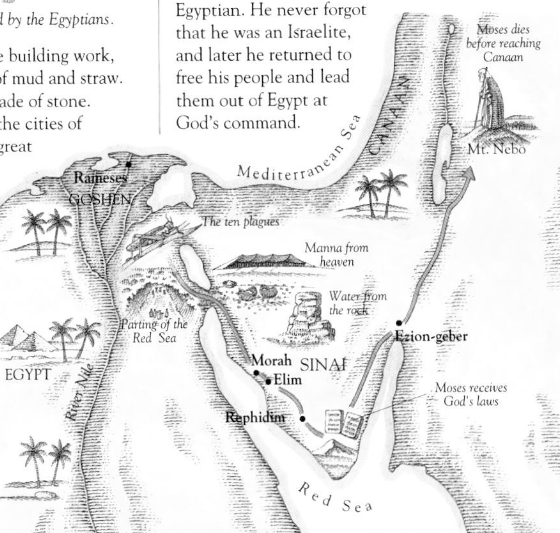

MAP OF THE EXODUS
The route of the Exodus, or exit, from Egypt is not certain. It is likely, however, that the Israelites, led by Moses, avoided the most direct route along the Mediterranean coast so that they did not confront the Philistines in that area.

Moses in the Bulrushes

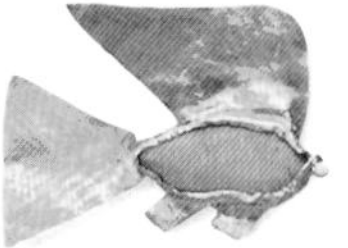

GOLDEN FISHES
These lucky charms may have been worn to protect against accidents on the River Nile. Made of gold, children probably wore them in their hair.

IN EGYPT A NEW PHARAOH came to the throne. Since Joseph's time, the children of Israel had grown powerful and numerous, and the new king was frightened that they would overrun his country. "We must take precautions against them," he said to his counselors. "If war breaks out, they may side with our enemies and defeat us." First, he gave orders that the Israelites should be treated as slaves, and made to work in gangs, building roads and cities. Then he made a ruling that any male child born to an Israelite woman should immediately be put to death.

Pharaoh rules that any male child born to an Israelite should be put to death

Now there was a young married woman of the tribe of Levi who had recently given birth to a boy. Both parents were delighted, and they made up their minds that their son should escape Pharaoh's cruel command.

For the first three months of the baby's life, his mother managed to hide him in the house. But soon he grew too big to hide, and she knew that she could no longer keep him. With a heavy heart, she made a covered cradle out of dried reeds, which she made watertight by covering it with tar and clay. In this she tenderly placed her baby, and left him hidden among the bulrushes on the banks of the Nile.

BASKET
This Egyptian basket and lid dates from 1400 BC. Baskets were used as containers for clothes and food in many households. Moses' mother would have found it easy to make one out of papyrus reeds.

All this was watched by the baby's sister, who remained near at hand so that she could see what would happen.

It was not long before Pharaoh's daughter, accompanied by her maids, came down to the river to bathe. Catching sight of the little cradle, she sent one of the girls to bring it to her. As the princess gently removed the cover, the baby began to cry, and her heart was touched. "This must be a Hebrew child," she said.

At that moment, the baby's sister came forward and, curtsying low to the princess, asked if she could be of help. "Shall I find a nurse from among the Hebrew women to look after the baby?" she said. The princess was delighted with the suggestion, and the girl ran quickly home to fetch her mother. The princess was happy to employ the woman. "If you will look after the boy," she said, "I will pay you well."

So the baby's real mother was able to bring him up. In time Pharaoh's daughter, who had grown to love the child, adopted him as her son. "I will call him Moses, which means 'to draw out,' " she said, "because I drew him out of the water."

KEEPING COOL

Fans made from ostrich feathers were used by servants, known as fan-bearers, in the Egyptian royal court. This ivory-handled fan dates from the time of Moses (c1300 BC). Ostriches were a common sight throughout the desert lands of Sinai and Israel in biblical times.

An Israelite woman hides her baby among the bulrushes on the banks of the Nile

The baby's sister watches as the princess and her servant girl find her brother

WHEN SHE HAD OPENED IT, SHE SAW THE CHILD: AND, BEHOLD, THE BABE WEPT. AND SHE HAD COMPASSION ON HIM, AND SAID, "THIS IS ONE OF THE HEBREWS' CHILDREN".
EXODUS 2:6

Moses Is Called by God

Moses kills an Egyptian for beating an Israelite

ALTHOUGH BROUGHT UP AS AN EGYPTIAN, Moses never forgot that he was one of the children of Israel. One day he saw an Egyptian savagely beating an Israelite slave. Looking around to see that no one was watching, he killed the attacker and buried his body in the sand. However, word of what he had done eventually came to Pharaoh's ears, and Moses knew that his life was in danger. He left Egypt and went to the land of Midian.

Presently, he sat down to rest near a well. The seven daughters of Jethro, a priest in Midian, came to the well to draw water. But the local shepherds drove them away. Moses rebuked the men, then helped the young women to fill their jars. When they told their father what had happened, Jethro was so grateful that he gave Moses his daughter Zipporah in marriage.

One day while tending Jethro's sheep, Moses led them far into the desert, to the holy mountain of Sinai. The flock was quietly grazing when suddenly the Lord appeared, from the middle of a bush that had

MOSES FLED FROM THE FACE OF PHARAOH, AND DWELT IN THE LAND OF MIDIAN: AND HE SAT DOWN BY A WELL.
EXODUS 2:15

Jethro's daughters come to the well

Moses drives the shepherds away

MOSES' FLIGHT
Moses fled across the harsh and waterless Sinai Desert before reaching Midian. While tending sheep on Mount Sinai, God appeared to him out of a burning bush. There, Moses was later to receive God's laws.

burst into flames. But as Moses looked at the flames licking and crackling among the leaves, he saw that the blazing bush was not being destroyed by the fire.

Then Moses heard the voice of God calling him. "Moses, do not come any nearer, for you are standing on holy ground." At this Moses put his hands over his eyes, for he was afraid to look at God.

"I have seen how my people are suffering in Egypt, where they are treated as slaves," said the Lord. "I will free them from that cruel country and give them a land of their own, a land flowing with milk and honey. You, Moses, must go and bring my people out of Egypt."

"But how am I to do this?" asked Moses.

"I will be with you," said the Lord. "You must tell the Israelites that I am the God of their ancestors, the God of Abraham and Isaac, and they will follow you. Tell them that God, whose name is 'THAT I AM' has sent you.

A bush bursts into flames in front of Moses and God speaks to him

"You must go to Pharaoh and ask him in my name to release the Israelites. He will be angry and refuse your request. But I will curse Egypt and cause such horrors to fall upon the land that Pharaoh will no longer defy me, and he will let you go."

"But what if they do not believe that I am sent by God?"

"Moses, what are you holding in your hand?"

"A staff," said Moses.

"Throw it to the ground." And Moses threw down his staff, which instantly became a serpent writhing in the dust.

"Now lift it up by the tail."

As Moses picked up the snake, it turned back into a wooden staff.

"Now look at your hand," God commanded him. And Moses saw with horror that his hand was covered with running sores.

"Look again." And Moses looked, and his hand was smooth.

"But Lord, I am slow of speech," said Moses.

"Then your brother Aaron shall speak for you. Now go, do as I have told you, and I will be with you," said God.

YAHWEH

The four-letter Hebrew word YHWH was the name which God used to reveal himself to Moses. It is usually written as "Yahweh" and comes from the Hebrew verb "to be." It means "the one who is always there."

Moses Warns the Pharaoh

Moses and Aaron stand before Pharaoh and ask him to let their people go, but Pharaoh refuses

AFTER GOD HAD SPOKEN TO HIM, Moses returned home. God had told Moses that the men who wanted to kill him were now dead, and it would be safe for him to go back to Egypt. Moses told his father-in-law of his plan, and asked for his blessing. "Go in peace," said Jethro fondly.

So Moses left Midian, taking with him the staff of God. And accompanied by his wife, his sons, and his brother, Aaron, he came once more to Egypt. He and Aaron went at once to see Pharaoh. "I have come at the command of the God of Israel to ask you to let his people go," said Moses.

Pharaoh smiled coldly. "Why do you stir up trouble among my slaves? I will teach you what it means to defy me!" And he gave orders that the Israelites, who had been put to make bricks out of mud and straw, should no longer have straw provided: they must find it for themselves in the fields.

The Israelites, already worked to exhaustion by their masters, were in despair. "How can we make bricks if we must also gather the straw?" they cried. But their cries were ignored, and those who failed to make as many bricks as before were savagely beaten.

"Look at your people, Lord," said Moses. "They are being treated even more harshly, and there is no hope of release."

SLAVERY

The Egyptians generally treated their slaves well, but as the Israelites grew in number the Egyptians felt threatened and dealt with them harshly. They forced them to build their homes and temples and tend their crops and animals in the hot sun. If they did not work long or hard enough, a supervisor punished them.

The Israelites are beaten by their Egyptian masters

The staffs of Aaron and the royal magicians turn into serpents

"Speak again to Pharaoh," said God. "And demand that he let my people go."

So the brothers stood a second time before Pharaoh and his court, only to receive the same answer. But Moses, remembering what God had told him, signaled to Aaron to throw down the staff. Aaron did so, and as the staff touched the ground it turned into a serpent. At this Pharaoh gave the order to his royal magicians, and they all threw down their staffs, which all turned into serpents. These were swallowed up by Aaron's serpent.

But Pharaoh remained unmoved.

"Go to the banks of the Nile," said the Lord to Moses. "And when Pharaoh comes down to the river, ask him again to let my people go. And if he will not, strike the surface of the water with your staff."

And so Moses and Aaron went down to the river, and waited for Pharaoh to come.

PHARAOH
The powerful rulers of Egypt were called pharaohs. This statue is of Rameses II, who ruled Egypt during the 13th century BC. It is thought that he was the pharaoh to whom Moses spoke. Rameses II was responsible for building more monuments and statues than any other pharaoh. Because of these fine achievements, he is often referred to as Rameses the Great.

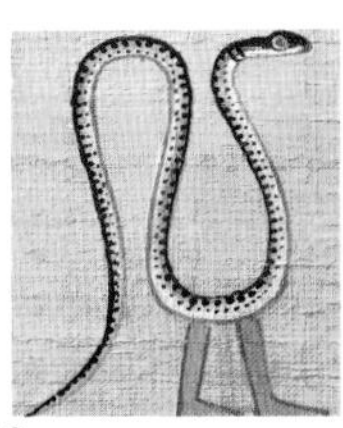

SERPENT
One of the gods worshiped by the Egyptians was the serpent god, Sito, shown above. When Aaron's serpent ate the Egyptian serpents, it showed God's power over the Egyptian gods.

The Plagues of Egypt

The waters of the Nile turn to blood and all the fish die

ONCE MORE, Moses and Aaron pleaded with Pharaoh to let the people go. When Pharaoh refused to listen, they struck the waters of the River Nile. At once the water turned to blood, and all the fish died, and the dead fish rotted in the sun and stank. For seven days the whole of Egypt ran with blood, and there was no water to drink. But Pharaoh refused to free the Israelites. So Moses and Aaron, following God's command, stretched their sacred staff over the Nile. At once, throughout all Egypt, frogs in their hundreds and thousands came hopping out of rivers, streams, and ponds, hopping into people's houses, into their cupboards and ovens, even into their beds.

Frogs hop into people's houses

Horrified, Pharaoh sent for Moses. "Ask your god to take away this plague," he implored. "And I will let your people go at once!"

Overnight the frogs died. They lay several deep in the villages and fields, until they were gathered up into evil-smelling heaps.

Lice crawl over every man and woman

And when Pharaoh saw that the plague was over, he went back on his word.

Then Aaron struck the sand beneath his feet, and the millions of grains of sand turned into millions of lice that crawled and seethed over every man, woman, and beast that lived in the land.

But Pharaoh's heart was like stone.

Next came a cloud of flies: fat, black flies that crawled into people's mouths and under their eyelids.

Again Pharaoh begged Moses, in return for the Israelites' freedom, to rid him of the plague. And when the flies were gone, again he broke his word.

A cloud of flies attack the people

All the oxen are struck by disease

This time the Lord sent to Egypt disease that killed every horse and camel, all the oxen, the goats, and the sheep, every one.

But still Pharaoh would not let the children of Israel leave.

People are covered in boils

God said to Moses and Aaron, "Take a handful of ashes from the fire and throw it up into the air." And as they did this, the ashes spread a hideous sickness that broke out in boils, covering the skin of both men and animals.

But Pharaoh was not moved.

Heavy hail flattens whole fields

Then God told Moses to stretch his hand toward the heavens, and instantly there was a crash of thunder, red-hot lightning zigzagged along the ground, and a heavy hail fell from the sky, flattening whole fields and smashing open the trunks of trees.

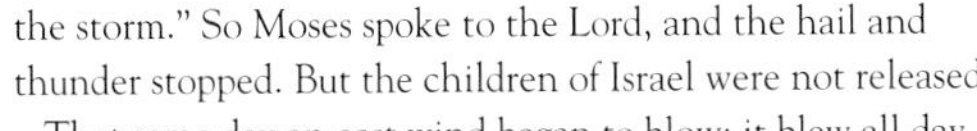

Pharaoh summoned Moses. "Now I will do as you ask if you will stop the storm." So Moses spoke to the Lord, and the hail and thunder stopped. But the children of Israel were not released.

Locusts cover the sky and fields

That same day an east wind began to blow; it blew all day and all night, and with the wind came the locusts. They came in such numbers that the sky was black, and they covered the land so that the land was black, and they ate every remaining blade of grass, every leaf, every fruit left hanging from the tree.

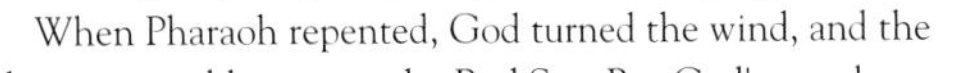

When Pharaoh repented, God turned the wind, and the locusts were blown into the Red Sea. But God's people were kept captive still.

Darkness falls for three days

So God told Moses to stretch out his hand, and darkness fell upon Egypt, and there was no light for three days.

Pharaoh sent for Moses. "Now you may go, you and all your people, but you must leave your flocks behind."

"That I may not do," said Moses.

"Then I shall keep your people as slaves, and I forbid you ever to come into my presence again. If you disobey me in this, you will die."

The Tenth Plague

The Israelites daub the doorposts of their houses with blood

In every Egyptian family, the eldest child draws its last breath and dies

PASSOVER FEAST
Today, Jewish people celebrate Passover each spring. The various foods symbolize the Exodus: unleavened bread, a nut and apple paste called *charoseth*, horseradish and lettuce (the bitter herbs), a roasted lamb bone, eggs, and salt water.

THE LORD SPOKE TO MOSES. "I shall bring one last plague to Egypt, a plague so terrible that Pharaoh will have no choice but to let my people go. At midnight tonight every first-born child throughout the country will die. Not one shall escape: all will die, from the firstborn of Pharaoh himself, to the firstborn of the poorest slave, to the firstborn of the cattle in the fields. Only the children of Israel will remain untouched.

"This day shall forever afterward be known as Passover, for tonight I will pass over the whole of Egypt, and my people will be freed. From now on, the day must be kept holy and counted as the first day of the year. Every household must kill a lamb, which shall then be roasted and eaten with bitter herbs and bread that is unleavened. Your doorposts must be daubed with the blood of the slain animal, so that when I pass in the night I shall know to leave untouched the houses marked with blood."

Moses called together all his wise men and counselors and told them what God had said, and how they were to keep this day, the first Passover, holy forever after.

Midnight fell, and suddenly a terrible wailing and screaming was heard, as the Lord passed over the land. Except for the Israelites, not one family was left unharmed. Death was everywhere. Everywhere,

AND PHARAOH CALLED FOR MOSES AND AARON BY NIGHT, AND SAID, "RISE UP AND GET YOU FORTH FROM AMONG MY PEOPLE, BOTH YE AND THE CHILDREN OF ISRAEL; AND GO, SERVE THE LORD, AS YE HAVE SAID."
EXODUS 12:31

Taking all their possessions with them, the Israelites leave Egypt

from Pharaoh's palace to the darkest prison, from the rich merchant's house to the open pasture, the firstborn, both man and beast, drew their last breaths and died.

Pharaoh, rising from his bed in grief, sent for Moses and Aaron. "Take your people and go! Go from my country, and take all your flocks and herds!" By now, the Egyptians were so frightened they begged the Israelites to leave as quickly as possible, and heaped their former slaves with silver, gold, and jewels.

And so it was that after four-hundred-and-thirty years in the land of their captivity, the children of Israel, six-hundred thousand of them, all on foot, men, women, and children, with their flocks and herds and all their possessions, at last left Egypt.

SADDLEBAG
On leaving Egypt, the Israelites may have carried their possessions in saddlebags, similar to this Bedouin one made of goat's hair and wool.

The Crossing of the Red Sea

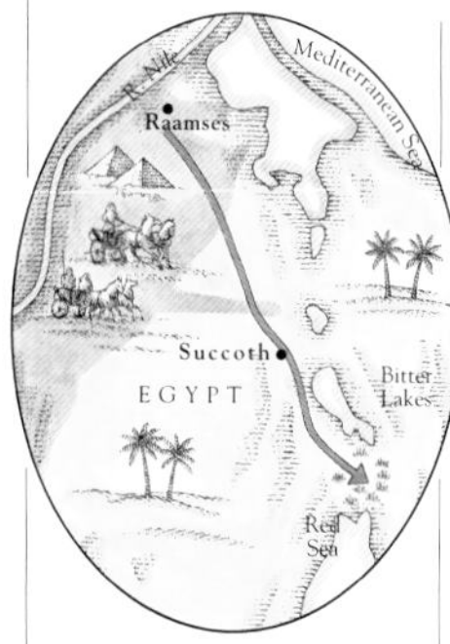

CROSSING THE SEA
The Hebrew words originally translated as "Red Sea" in fact mean "sea of reeds." It is possible that the Israelites crossed over a marshy swamp to the north of the Red Sea.

GOD LED HIS PEOPLE OUT OF EGYPT and through the wilderness at the edge of the Red Sea. God led them by day as a column of cloud and by night as a column of fire, so they should know which way to go.

But Pharaoh again hardened his heart, angry that he had let his slaves leave. He gave orders to the officers of his army to make ready, and he himself led a force of six hundred chariots, as well as horsemen and foot soldiers, against the Israelites.

The Israelites were camped on the shore when they saw the Egyptian army approaching. They turned in terror to Moses. "Why did you take us from our comfortable captivity only to let us die here in the wilderness?"

"Do not be afraid," Moses reassured them. "The Lord will protect you from harm."

As he spoke, the column of cloud moved over the Egyptians, so that they were in darkness. Then, following the word of the Lord, Moses stretched his hand over the sea. Immediately a strong wind sprang up, and the waters parted, and a passage of dry land appeared along the seabed. Moses led his people along this path, the waters like a high wall on either side of them.

THE RED SEA
The Israelites could have camped at a spot like this by the Red Sea. The sea usually looks blue, but when the algae that grow in the water die, the sea becomes a reddish-brown.

As soon as Pharaoh saw what was happening, he and his army came galloping in pursuit. But as his horsemen and his hundreds of chariots thundered over the dry sand, the Lord commanded Moses again to stretch out his hand. The waters of the Red Sea closed over the Egyptians, and every man was drowned.

But the children of Israel reached the far side of the sea in safety, and when they saw how God had protected them, they gave grateful thanks to God and to the prophet Moses. They sang a song of praise, recalling the happy escape of the children of Israel from their long years of slavery, and their crossing of the Red Sea.

Then Miriam, Aaron's sister, took up her tambourine, and calling the women to follow her, led them in a dance along the water's edge.

The Crossing of the Red Sea

> AND THE CHILDREN OF ISRAEL WENT INTO THE MIDST OF THE SEA UPON THE DRY GROUND.
> **EXODUS 14:22**

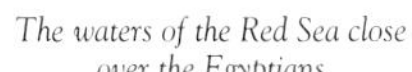

The waters of the Red Sea close over the Egyptians

Miriam takes a tambourine and dances with the other women

Moses and his people cross on dry land and reach the far side in safety

God Watches Over the Israelites

QUAILS
Migrating quails fly across the Sinai Desert twice a year. Tired from the long flight, they fly low and are easily caught.

MANNA
Some scholars think that the manna may have come from the hammada shrub, above, which grows in southern Sinai. When insects feed on its branches, it produces a sweet, white liquid. Today, Bedouin people use it as a sweetener.

Flocks of quails appear in the desert

The Israelites catch the quails and roast them

THE ISRAELITES WANDERED in the Sinai Desert for many weeks, hungry and exhausted. They began to whisper against Moses and Aaron. "At least in Egypt we had plenty to eat, but here we may die of starvation."

The Lord heard what they were saying, and told Moses to summon his people. "They shall be well provided with food," God promised.

In the morning the ground is covered with manna from heaven

The people are told to gather as much as they can eat in a day

That same evening flocks of quails suddenly appeared, which were caught and roasted.

The next morning the ground was covered with small round shapes, white and tasting of honey. The Israelites were puzzled. "What is this?" they asked each other. "It must be manna, for it falls from Heaven."

"This is bread sent by God," said Moses. "Let the people gather as much as they can eat in a day, and no more." But some were greedy and took more than their share. Secretly they hoarded the manna in their tents, and overnight it turned black, and became full of worms and stank.

On the sixth day, Moses told them they could collect enough food to last for two days. "Tomorrow is a holy day of rest, as decreed by God. Today you must gather up what you need, and eat as much as you want and keep the rest for the Sabbath. It will stay fresh and good overnight, for tomorrow you will find no manna on the ground."

Most people did as Moses said, but a few disobeyed and went out on the Sabbath looking for food.

"When will the people learn to obey my rules?" the Lord asked Moses.

The days passed and the Israelites, as they made their slow way through the burning desert, complained of a lack of water. "Why did you bring us out of Egypt just to die of thirst?" they asked angrily.

But God told Moses to go to a certain rock and strike it with his staff. As he did so, water cold and pure gushed out of the rock, so that all could drink their fill.

As Moses strikes the rock with his staff, water gushes out

"BEHOLD, I WILL STAND BEFORE THEE THERE UPON THE ROCK IN HOREB; AND THOU SHALT SMITE THE ROCK, AND THERE SHALL COME WATER OUT OF IT, THAT THE PEOPLE MAY DRINK." AND MOSES DID SO IN THE SIGHT OF THE ELDERS OF ISRAEL.
EXODUS 17:6

Moses Receives God's Laws

AND MOSES DREW NEAR UNTO THE THICK DARKNESS WHERE GOD WAS.
EXODUS 20:21

AFTER THREE MONTHS the children of Israel arrived at the foot of the holy mountain of Sinai, where they made their camp. Moses went up the mountain to pray to God, who told him that in three days God would speak to the people.

On the morning of the third day the sky turned black, and thunder and lightning crashed and rumbled through the darkness. The mountain itself belched smoke and fire like a great furnace, and the ground shook. Then the voice of God was heard like a mighty trumpet, calling Moses to him.

God calls Moses to him and gives him the ten commandments carved on two stone tablets

"I am the Lord your God, who brought you out of Egypt and these are my commandments, to be obeyed by all my people.

You shall worship no other God but me.

You shall not make any statue or picture to worship.

You shall not speak the name of the Lord except with reverence.

You shall keep the sabbath, the seventh day, as a holy day of rest, for in six days I made the world, but on the seventh day I rested.

You shall show respect to your father and mother.

You shall not commit murder.

You shall not be unfaithful to your husband or wife.

You shall not steal.

You shall not speak falsely against others.

You shall not envy another person's possessions."

When the people heard the thunder and saw the flames and the smoke, they were terrified and would not come near. But Moses reassured them. "Do not be afraid," he said. "God has come to us so that we may learn his commandments and keep ourselves free of sin."

But still the people shrank back, and again Moses went up the mountain alone, to the dark cloud on the summit where God was.

Mount Sinai
Moses received God's laws on Mount Sinai, or Mount Horeb, as it is sometimes called in the Bible. Mount Sinai is believed to be the mountain Jebel Musa or "Mountain of Moses," part of a group of peaks in the south of the Sinai Peninsula. It is 7,500 feet (2,300 m) high and is made of red granite.

The Israelites camp at the foot of the holy mountain of Sinai

The Golden Calf

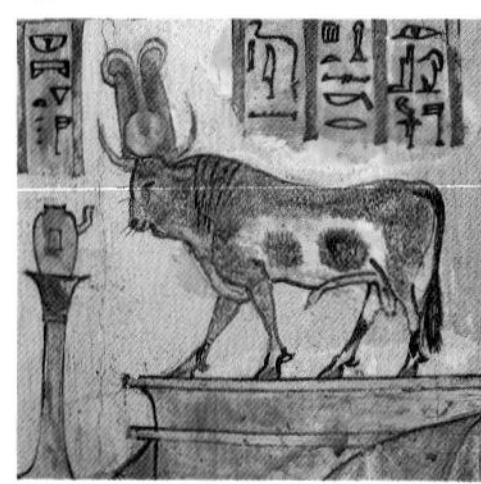

EGYPTIAN BULL GOD
Aaron's golden calf could have been based on Apis, an Egyptian bull god depicted in this painting from Thebes in Egypt. Pagan gods were often represented as bulls in ancient times. Bulls were known for their strength and fearlessness and were used as symbols of fertility and power.

WHEN THE PEOPLE SAW THAT MOSES had not returned from the mountain, they gathered around Aaron saying, "You must make us a god, for we do not know what has happened to this Moses who brought us out of Egypt."

"Then bring me gold," said Aaron, "and I will give you what you want."

So both men and women brought Aaron their gold jewelry, which he melted down and formed into the shape of a monstrous golden calf. He built an altar to the calf, and the people prayed to it and offered sacrifices, and danced and feasted in front of it.

Looking down from his mountaintop, God said to Moses, "How quickly are my commandments forgotten! Now shall the full force of my anger be felt!"

But Moses begged the Lord to forgive them. "Did you bring them out of Egypt, your chosen people, only to destroy them in your fury?"

Calmed by these words, God sent Moses down the mountain carrying two stone tablets on which were engraved his ten commandments.

As he came near the Israelites' camp, Moses heard loud laughter and music; he saw the statue of the calf, and the smoking sacrificial fires, and drunken figures wildly dancing. Full of anger, he flung the stone tablets to the ground where they broke into pieces. He knocked over the golden idol and threw it on the flames. Then he turned to Aaron. "How could you have let this happen?" he demanded.

Summoning the people together at the entrance of the camp, Moses solemnly addressed them. "Let those who are on the side of the Lord come and stand by me." Only the men of the tribe of Levi went to him, the rest remaining where they were. "Now," he said to the Levites, "go through the camp and with your swords put to death every man you see. For this is the will of God."

Over three thousand men were killed that night, and the next day Moses went again to the Lord to beg forgiveness for his repentant people. "I will send an angel to lead them to the promised land," said God. "But they have made a false idol and must suffer for it."

AND IT CAME TO PASS, AS SOON AS HE CAME NIGH UNTO THE CAMP, THAT HE SAW THE CALF, AND THE DANCING: AND MOSES' ANGER WAXED HOT, AND HE CAST THE TABLES OUT OF HIS HANDS, AND BRAKE THEM BENEATH THE MOUNT.
EXODUS 32:19

The people dance and feast in front of it

Aaron builds a golden calf

Moses flings the stone tablets to the ground in anger

Balaam's Donkey

THE LAND OF MOAB
Balak felt threatened by the Israelites when they camped in the plains of Moab, to the east of the Dead Sea.

BALAK, KING OF THE MOABITES, looked with fear on the tribes of Israel who were surrounding his land. He sent messengers to the fortune-teller, Balaam, asking him to curse this people so that he might defeat them in battle.

But God had spoken to Balaam. "You must not curse the people of Israel," he said, "for they are my chosen people."

When Balak's messengers arrived, Balaam told them he would not do as they wished.

"If Balak were to give me his own house, every room heaped with gold and silver, still I could not go against the word of God," said Balaam.

But that night God spoke again to Balaam. "Go with these men, and do just as I tell you."

The next day Balaam saddled his donkey and set off with Balak's messengers. Suddenly the angel of the Lord appeared, blocking the way, drawn sword in his hand. The donkey saw the angel, and shied away, turning off the road and into a field. But Balaam saw nothing and he beat his mount angrily. Next the angel barred a path that led through a vineyard between high walls. Again

On seeing the angel, Balaam's donkey lies on the ground

Balaam journeys with Balak's messengers to visit Balak in Moab

THE LORD OPENED THE EYES OF BALAAM, AND HE SAW THE ANGEL OF THE LORD STANDING IN THE WAY, AND HIS SWORD DRAWN IN HIS HAND: AND HE BOWED DOWN HIS HEAD, AND FELL FLAT ON HIS FACE.
NUMBERS 22:31

the donkey saw him, and squeezed up against the wall, crushing Balaam's foot; and again she was beaten. The angel appeared a third time, standing in the middle of a narrow path where there was no room to turn either to the left or the right. When the donkey saw the angel she lay down on the ground. Balaam was angrier than ever and beat her twice as hard.

Then God gave the animal the power of speech. "Why do you hit me?" she asked. "Because you disobeyed me!" her master furiously replied. "If I had a sword, I would kill you!" Then the Lord opened Balaam's eyes and he saw the angel. Appalled and astonished, he fell flat on his face, begging for forgiveness.

Balak greeted Balaam and took him into the mountains.

BEAST OF BURDEN
The donkey, or ass as it is often called in the Bible, was one of the earliest "beasts of burden." A donkey could carry heavy loads, or burdens, as well as pull the plow.

clay bones

model of sheep's liver

TOOLS OF THE TRADE
Balaam was a diviner, or fortune-teller. In ancient times diviners used objects, such as a clay model of a sheep's liver and animal bones, shown above, to make predictions. The bones were thrown down and the pattern they made was studied.

Balaam then went still higher up the mountain where God spoke to him, telling him to bless the Israelites.

Balaam looked down across the wide wilderness and saw the tribes of Israel in their tents and he blessed them. This made Balak very angry. "I called on you to curse my enemies: instead you bless them! I promised you great riches if you would obey me, but now you must go away empty-handed!"

So Balaam returned to his home in Pethor by the River Euphrates.

Life in Canaan

THE BIBLE TELLS US THAT when the Hebrew people escaped from Egypt, they settled in Canaan, the "promised land." Eventually the land they conquered was divided among the 12 tribes, who were the descendants of Jacob, later called Israel. For this reason they were also known as the Israelites. In the valley of the River Jordan, in the east of the country and on the coastal plain in the west, there were many kinds of crops and fruits. Compared to the barren land through which the Israelites had traveled for 40 years, Canaan was a land "flowing with milk and honey."

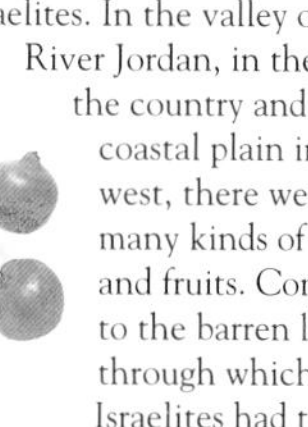

The Israelites found Canaan a rich and fertile land with many fruits and plentiful crops.

The Israelites were experienced in tending their flocks and living simply off the land, but in Canaan, they found workers skilled in many other crafts and trades. In addition to the farmers, there were stonemasons, potters, builders, metal workers, jewelers, carpenters, and musicians.

The Canaanites were skilled craftsmen.

Canaanite Gods

The Canaanites worshiped many gods and goddesses, including one called Baal. At Ugarit, which is now Ras Sharma in Syria, a statue of Baal was found showing him as a warrior god.

The religion of the Israelites was very different: they worshiped only one God and did not have any statues or carved images. These religious differences led to clashes between the Israelites and the followers of Baal.

THE PROMISED LAND
Date palms grow in the lush landscape of the Jordan Valley.

The Twelve Tribes of Israel

According to the Bible the 12 tribes of Israel were descended from the 12 sons of Jacob. No tribe was named after Joseph, Jacob's best-known son, but two tribes, Manasseh and Ephraim, took their names from Joseph's sons. Each of the 12 tribes had its own identity and each was given territory when Canaan was conquered. The Levites, who were named after Levi, had no territory, because they were responsible for organizing and carrying out the worship of God in the tabernacle, the sacred meeting tent.

Judges and Kings

To begin with, the Israelites did not have a king. They were linked by the law of God given to them by Moses and by their understanding and worship of God. Moses appointed judges to make sure that the people lived according to God's laws. Later these judges became leaders of the people. The Bible tells us that when they were being attacked by their chief enemy, the Philistines, the Israelites decided that they wanted a central government, to be ruled by a king. As a result, Saul became the first king of Israel. He was succeeded by his son-in-law David and David's son Solomon.

Saul

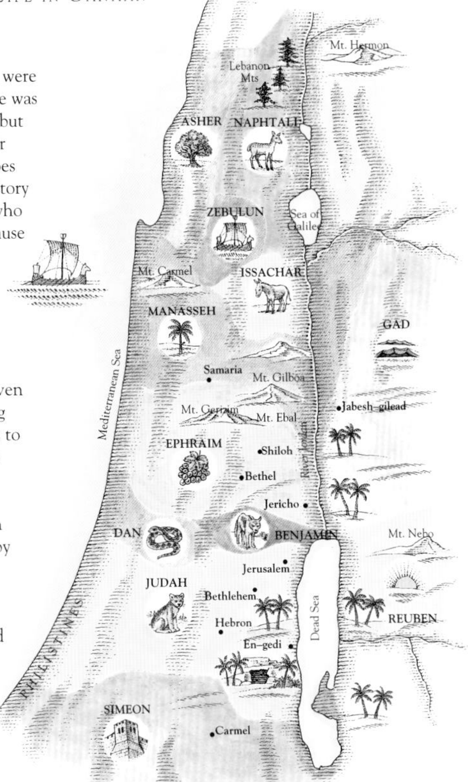

The map above shows the kingdoms of the 12 tribes of Israel, each with its own emblem, or symbol.

THE KINGS OF ISRAEL AND JUDAH

Saul — *David* — *Solomon* — *Rehoboam* / *Jeroboam*

King Saul was succeeded by David and then Solomon. On Solomon's death the kingdom was split between Rehoboam and Jeroboam.

Later the kingdom was divided into two: Israel, in the north, ruled by a series of kings beginning with Jeroboam, and Judah in the south, ruled by Solomon's descendants, beginning with his son Rehoboam. Israel was destroyed by the Assyrians after 200 years, but Judah (from which the word Jew comes) lasted for another 135 years before Jerusalem was destroyed by the Babylonians and the people taken to live in exile in Babylon.

The Promised Land

CLUSTER OF GRAPES
The large, juicy grapes brought back from Canaan were important to the Israelites. Grapes could be eaten fresh, dried as raisins, boiled to make grape syrup, or pressed to make wine.

FROM HIS CAMP IN THE PARAN DESERT, Moses sent twelve men to spy out Canaan, the land which God had promised to the people of Israel. The men carefully explored the country, and after forty days returned, bringing with them handfuls of grapes, figs, and pomegranates.

"It is a rich country flowing with milk and honey," they told Moses and Aaron. "But the people are strong and they live in great walled cities. We would never be able to overcome them."

In spite of this report, Caleb, from the tribe of Judah, was eager to invade at once and take possession of the country. But the others,

The men return from Canaan, bringing with them grapes, figs, and pomegranates

AND THEY TOLD HIM, "WE CAME UNTO THE LAND WHITHER THOU SENTEST US, AND SURELY IT FLOWETH WITH MILK AND HONEY."
NUMBERS 13:27

Moses calls Joshua and says that he must lead the people into Canaan

AND MOSES CALLED UNTO JOSHUA AND SAID UNTO HIM IN THE SIGHT OF ALL ISRAEL, "BE STRONG AND OF A GOOD COURAGE: FOR THOU MUST GO WITH THIS PEOPLE UNTO THE LAND WHICH THE LORD HATH SWORN UNTO THEIR FATHERS TO GIVE THEM."

DEUTERONOMY 31:7

who had been with him on the expedition, were afraid. "We would be defeated," they said. And to make their argument convincing, they pretended they had seen a race of giants in Canaan, beside whom the Israelites would look like grasshoppers.

For forty years the children of Israel continued to wander in the wilderness. In time Aaron died, and Moses knew that he, too, would soon die. He called Joshua, son of Nun, and said, "Iam old and will never reach Canaan. You must lead our people there. Be strong and of good heart. Do not be afraid, for God will be with you."

Then Moses inscribed the law of God on two tablets of stone, for he knew that without his guidance the Israelites would soon take to evil ways. The priests kept the tablets in a golden chest called the Ark of the Covenant, which had been made as a holy resting place for the ten commandments.

Having blessed his people, Moses went to the summit of Mount Pisgah where God showed him the whole of the promised land, stretching from Gilead, Dan, Judah, and the distant sea in the west to the southern valley of Jericho, city of palm trees.

There Moses died and was buried, and the people wept for thirty days. Since his death there has never been a prophet like him in Israel. He was a man who had the courage to defy Pharaoh and lead his people out of Egypt; a man who stood face to face with God.

CANAAN
In the northern part of Canaan is the valley of Jezreel (pictured here). Although known as a land "flowing with milk and honey", Canaan is a land of variety. The area descends from fertile hills and fields to a barren desert watered by springs.

Moses is shown the promised land before he dies

Rahab and the Spies

While the two spies hide on her roof, Rahab swears to the officers that there is no one inside

JOSHUA LED HIS PEOPLE to the River Jordan, which was all that divided them from the promised land. He sent two men as spies across the river and into the city of Jericho. There, they were hidden in the house of a woman called Rahab.

The king of Jericho had heard reports that spies were in the city, and he gave orders for every street and every house to be searched. When his officers came to Rahab's door, she, having hidden the two Israelites under some flax on her roof, swore that there was no one inside. The danger over, she said to the men, "Because I have saved your lives, you must swear by the Lord that no harm will come to any member of my family."

"We swear," they said. And it was agreed that Rahab should tie a scarlet thread to her window so that the invaders would know not to attack her house. Then, Rahab let the spies down by a rope, and they escaped into the night.

Rahab lets the spies down by a rope

FLAX
Flax plants were grown for making linen. The plants were picked and the stems placed in water to separate the fibers. They were left to dry on flat roofs, like Rahab's. A comb was used to separate the threads. These were then woven together to make linen.

The Battle of Jericho

The priests carry the Ark of the Covenant across the River Jordan, which had stopped flowing

AFTER THE TWO MESSENGERS had returned from Jericho, they reported to Joshua, and he assembled all his people on the banks of the Jordan. "Listen carefully to what I have to say. As soon as the priests carrying the Ark of the Covenant put their feet in the water, the river will stop flowing. The waters coming from the source will cease, and a path of dry land will appear. On this you will all be able to cross safely to the other side." And it happened exactly as Joshua had described. The people left their tents and came down to the riverbank; the priests lifted up the Ark and approached the water. At once the waters stopped and divided, and the priests walked to the middle of the riverbed. There they stood, holding the Ark up high, while all of Joshua's people passed safely to the far side. The priests

The Israelite army circles the city

The seven priests blow their trumpets made from rams' horns

"WHEN THEY MAKE A LONG BLAST WITH THE RAM'S HORN, AND WHEN YE HEAR THE SOUND OF THE TRUMPET, ALL THE PEOPLE SHALL SHOUT WITH A GREAT SHOUT; AND THE WALL OF THE CITY SHALL FALL DOWN FLAT."
JOSHUA 6:5

then followed, and no sooner had they stepped onto dry land, than the waters closed over behind them.

Joshua then gathered his army together. Over forty-thousand men stood ready to fight on the plains of Jericho. All of them were willing to die for Joshua, for he was as inspiring a leader as Moses: his people both trusted him and feared his anger, for they knew that, like Moses, he was loved by God.

Jericho was in a state of siege, the gates bolted shut against the Israelite army. The Lord said to Joshua, "Each day for six days you and all your men shall walk once around the city walls. The Ark shall be carried behind you, led by seven priests holding trumpets made out of rams' horns. On the seventh day, you shall circle the city seven times, the priests shall blow their trumpets, and the people shout to the skies. Then will the walls of Jericho fall to the ground. All who live in the city will be killed except for Rahab and her family and household. They shall be spared, because it was she who hid our messengers."

And so it happened. Joshua warned his men not to make a sound for six days; but on the seventh day, as they walked for the seventh time around the city, Joshua said to his people, "Shout! For the Lord has given this city to you."

And so the Israelites raised a great shout, the priests blew their trumpets, and the walls of Jericho fell to the ground. Every man, woman, and child in the city was killed: only Rahab and those living in her house survived.

SHOFAR
Joshua's men would have steamed a ram's horn to make it soft, and then bent the wide end to form a trumpet, or *shofar*. The deep, mournful sounds of this horn are still heard in Jewish synagogues on certain holy days, such as the Day of Atonement, when the people think about the wrongs they have done.

The walls of Jericho fall to the ground

The Call of Gideon

AND THE ANGEL OF THE LORD APPEARED UNTO GIDEON, AND SAID UNTO HIM, "THE LORD IS WITH THEE, THOU MIGHTY MAN OF VALOR."
JUDGES 6:12

THE ISRAELITES HAD A NEW AND POWERFUL ENEMY, the people of Midian. As soon as the grain was ready for harvest, the Midianites would attack, burning the wheat and slaughtering the animals. The Israelites had begun to worship other gods, but in their despair they appealed to God for help.

The Lord sent an angel to Gideon. "It is you who must save your people from this scourge," said the angel. Gideon, hot and tired from threshing the small amount of wheat he had managed to hide, looked at the angel in astonishment. "But I am only a poor farmer," he said.

"The Lord will be with you," the angel assured him.

That night, in obedience to God's word, Gideon smashed the altar that had been built to the god Baal. In its place he put up an altar to the Lord. The next morning the Israelites gathered around the fallen altar. "Who has done this terrible thing?" they demanded.

Soon it became known that Gideon was the man. "He must die!" shouted the crowd. But Gideon's father said, "If Baal is a god, then let

Gideon smashes the altar of Baal

Gideon takes his men down to the spring to drink, and chooses those who are to fight with him

him take his own revenge!" And to this the people agreed.

Gideon then gathered his forces and pitched camp by the spring of Harod. "If there are any among you who are afraid, let them go now," he commanded. At these words, over half his army of twenty-two thousand men turned for home. Then God told him to take the remaining ten thousand men down to the spring, and watch how they drank. God said to Gideon: "Those who cup the water in their hands, keep with you; but those who put their faces into the water, send away."

At last, with a company of only three hundred, Gideon looked down on the Midianite army camped in the valley below. When darkness fell, he gave each of his men a trumpet made of ram's horn and a flaming torch covered by an earthenware jar. Silently the army of Israelites surrounded the enemy camp, and at a signal from Gideon, blew their trumpets, smashed the jars to reveal the light from the torches, and shouted as loud as they could. Confused and terrified, the Midianites began fighting each other as they fled into the night.

So Gideon won his victory without striking a single blow.

SPRING OF HAROD
At God's command, Gideon watched to see how his soldiers drank from the waters of this spring. Those who cupped the water in their hands, rather than put their faces in the water, were chosen to fight. One interpretation is that God chose those who were the most alert and ready for battle.

Gideon's army attacks the Midianites at night

Jephthah's Daughter

AMMONITE HEAD
This limestone statue shows the head of an Ammonite king. The Ammonites lived in eastern Canaan from about 1200 BC to 600 BC. Because they were descended from Lot, the Israelites left them in peace at first, but the Ammonites later became their sworn enemies.

TIMBREL
A timbrel is a kind of tambourine made from skins stretched over a wooden hoop. Israelite women played timbrels in feasts and processions while chanting God's praises, or to celebrate the return of war heroes.

JEPHTHAH WAS THE SON OF GILEAD, but as he did not share the same mother as his brothers, they resented him and eventually turned him out of the house, telling him he was not a worthy member of the family. Knowing he would not be allowed to stay near them, Jephthah went to live in the land of Tob.

Time passed, and the Ammonites declared war on the children of Israel. Having heard of his courage and skill as a soldier, the Israelites went to Jephthah and asked him to return; they begged him to be their general and lead them in battle against the enemy.

"But I was turned away from my home," said Jephthah. "Why do you

Jephthah promises God he will sacrifice whatever he sees first if he is given victory over the Ammonites

come to me? I am no longer one of you."

Eventually, however, they persuaded him and he agreed to go back as commander of the army.

First, he sent a messenger to the Ammonite king demanding that he withdraw his troops from Canaan. But the king refused. So then Jephthah prayed to the Lord. "O God, if you will give me victory over the Ammonites, I will sacrifice to you whatever I first see on reaching home."

With Jephthah as their leader, the Israelites easily defeated the enemy. Many Ammonites were killed, and the rest ran for their lives.

Jephthah arrived home, where his only child, his daughter, came running out of the house to greet him. She was brightly dressed, and

Jephthah's daughter weeps with her friends for the life she is about to leave

Jephthah tears his clothes in grief when his daughter runs out to meet him

danced around him, laughing and shaking her timbrel. But her father tore his clothes in grief and covered his face in his hands and sobbed. "I have made a promise to God. I cannot go back on my word, but if I keep it, you, my daughter, will die!"

"You must keep your promise," she said. "The Lord has given you victory over the enemy, and it is right that you fulfill your side of the bargain. But let me have a few weeks to prepare for what is to come." So for two months she wandered the mountains with her friends, and wept for the life that she was about to leave. Then she returned to her father, and he sacrificed her, according to the vow he had made.

AND JEPHTHAH CAME TO MIZPEH UNTO HIS HOUSE, AND, BEHOLD, HIS DAUGHTER CAME OUT TO MEET HIM WTIH TIMBRELS AND WITH DANCES: AND SHE WAS HIS ONLY CHILD.

JUDGES 11:34

Samson and the Lion

LION
Lions were the most dangerous animals living in Canaan. They roamed wild in forests and thickets, and were a threat to other animals and people. Samson was so strong, he killed a lion with his bare hands.

FOR FORTY YEARS the children of Israel had suffered at the hands of the Philistines, a fierce enemy from the lands near the sea. Then an angel appeared to an Israelite couple who had long been childless. "You will have a son who will win a great victory over the Philistines," the angel told them. "But you must be careful never to cut his hair." The angel then warned the woman. "While you are carrying the child, you must not touch wine or any strong drink, for your son will be a Nazirite, and his life will be dedicated to God."

Samson kills a lion, tearing it apart with his hands

Samson eats honey, found in the lion's carcass

The child was called Samson, and he grew tall and strong. One day Samson said to his father, "Father, I have seen a beautiful Philistine woman at Timnah, and I want her for my wife." His parents were unhappy that he had chosen a Philistine. "There are many Hebrew women who would make you a good wife: will you not look among them first?" But when they saw that Samson was determined, they did not stand in his way.

Samson and his parents went to Timnah, and as they walked through the vineyards a young lion leapt out at them. As easily as if he were swatting a fly, Samson killed it, tearing it apart with his hands. Then he went to the woman's house and they talked together, and she delighted Samson. It was not long before he asked her to marry him. A little later, he saw in the lion's carcass a honeycomb covered in bees; this he scooped out and ate as he walked, with no thought of being stung. He gave some to his parents, but did not say how he had come by it.

To celebrate his wedding he invited thirty of his wife's friends to a feast, which was to last seven days, for this was the custom of the country. On the first day, he put a riddle to his guests, promising rich rewards to anyone who could answer it. "Out of the eater comes meat; out of the strong comes sweet: what does this mean?" No one could guess. For three days they puzzled over it until finally one of the Philistines went to Samson's wife. "You must make your husband tell you the answer, or we will burn your house to the ground!"

Very frightened, Samson's wife went to him weeping. "How can you say you love me if you will not tell me the solution to your riddle? It is not much to ask!"

"I shall tell nobody," said Samson. "Not even you." But his wife coaxed and cried, until on the seventh day he told her. At once she ran to her friends with the news. And when that evening Samson again put the riddle, one of them stood up. "I can answer that!" he shouted. "There is nothing sweeter than honey. There is nothing stronger than a lion." Samson, realizing he had been tricked, was very angry. In his rage he killed thirty Philistines. Then he returned to his father's house and never saw his wife again.

BRAIDED HAIR
Samson was a Nazirite, a person dedicated to God. Nazirites had to promise never to cut their hair. Samson wore his uncut hair braided, like the prince in the stone sculpture above.

Samson and Delilah

Delilah ties Samson fast with seven bowstrings

She binds Samson with rope

She weaves Samson's long hair into the fabric of her loom

DELILAH SAID TO SAMSON, "TELL ME, I PRAY THEE, WHEREIN THY GREAT STRENGTH LIETH."
JUDGES 16:6

TIME PASSED, AND SAMSON fell in love with a woman called Delilah. The Philistine lords went to Delilah and told her she must uncover the secret of Samson's great strength. "Find out how we may take him prisoner, and each one of us will give you eleven-hundred pieces of silver."

When Delilah was alone with Samson, she questioned him prettily.

"Tell me, what is the secret of your strength? And how could you be made captive?"

"If I were bound with seven new bowstrings, then I should be helpless as a child," Samson replied.

As if in play, Delilah then tied him fast with seven bowstrings given her by the Philistines, who were lying in wait in the next room. "The Philistines are upon us!" she cried. But Samson snapped the strings as easily as if they had been frail threads.

"Why did you not tell me the truth?" Delilah asked crossly.

"The truth?" said Samson. "The truth is that I can be held only by ropes that have never been used."

As before, Delilah bound him fast, and as before the Philistines burst in upon them, only to see Samson break the ropes as easily as if they had been spun of spider webs.

The third time Delilah put her question, Samson told her that if she wove his long hair into the fabric on her loom, then he would be

WEAVING
In weaving, threads are intertwined to make cloth. This nomadic woman is weaving on a horizontal loom, similar to the one Delilah would have used.

weak. But again, when the Philistines tried to lay hands on him, he broke away effortlessly.

"How can you say you love me," sobbed Delilah, "when you tell me nothing but lies!" And she needled and nagged him until at last Samson, sick to death of her pestering, told his secret. "If my hair is cut, then my strength is gone."

PHILISTINE HEADDRESS
The Philistines lived along the Mediterranean coast in southwest Canaan from 1200 BC to 600 BC. They had a well-organized army. The soldiers wore distinctive feathered headdresses, as shown in the stone carving above, which made them appear very tall. They fought with iron swords and spears.

Delilah watches as the Philistines arrest Samson

Samson is led away in shackles

He fell asleep, exhausted, on her lap; and while he slept Delilah signaled to one of the Philistines, who crept in and cut off the strong man's hair. "Samson, the Philistines are upon us!" she cried. And Samson, not knowing that his strength had left him, jumped to his feet; but at once was overpowered.

His captors blinded him, and took him to Gaza where he was thrown into prison. There brass shackles were locked around his ankles, and he was put to work grinding wheat. But slowly his hair began to grow.

SAMSON TOLD DELILAH ALL HIS HEART, AND SAID UNTO HER, "THERE HATH NOT COME A RAZOR UPON MINE HEAD; FOR I HAVE BEEN A NAZIRITE UNTO GOD FROM MY MOTHER'S WOMB: IF I BE SHAVEN, THEN MY STRENGTH WILL GO FROM ME, AND I SHALL BECOME WEAK, AND BE LIKE ANY OTHER MAN."
JUDGES 16:17

Samson in the Temple

Samson pushes against the pillars of the temple

HE PHILISTINES WERE IN THE TEMPLE celebrating and offering sacrifices to their god, Dagon. "Thanks be to Dagon, for he has delivered the enemy into our hands!" they chanted. As the singing and dancing became louder and wilder, there were shouts for Samson.

"Bring him out! Let us see the Israelite champion! Where is his strength now!"

The blind prisoner was led into the temple and put to stand between the pillars of the doorway, so that everyone could see him. The crowd grew from hundreds to thousands, all of them laughing and jeering at Samson's helplessness.

"O Lord God, give me my strength once more!" Samson silently entreated.

Bracing his hands against the pillar on either side of him, Samson pushed with all his might. There was a noise as though the earth were cracking open, and suddenly the temple, roof and walls, crashed to the ground, killing everyone inside it, including Samson.

So, in dying, Samson won a final victory over the Philistines.

AND SAMSON CALLED UNTO THE LORD, AND SAID, "O LORD GOD, REMEMBER ME, I PRAY THEE, AND STRENGTHEN ME, I PRAY THEE, ONLY THIS ONCE, O GOD, THAT I MAY BE AT ONCE AVENGED OF THE PHILISTINES FOR MY TWO EYES."
JUDGES 16:28

The temple comes crashing down on the Philistines

Ruth and Naomi

Orpah returns to Moab, while Ruth and Naomi journey together to Bethlehem

Boaz watches Ruth working in his field

BETHLEHEM
Ruth and Naomi would have traveled from Moab for about 50 miles (80 km) before reaching Bethlehem. The town is set high up on a hill and is surrounded by fertile fields. Bethlehem is the birthplace of David and Jesus.

FOR MANY YEARS the widow Naomi had made her home in Moab. Her husband had died there, and so had her two sons. Their wives, Orpah and Ruth, lived with her. During a time of famine, Naomi decided to return to her own country, to Bethlehem. "We will come with you," said her daughters-in-law.

"No," said Naomi. "Your place is not with me, an old woman. You must stay in Moab where you belong."

Orpah was content with this, but Ruth loved Naomi and would not be parted from her. "Where you go, there shall I follow," she said. "Your home shall be mine; your people, my people; your God, my God." And so Ruth and Naomi journeyed together to Bethlehem.

They arrived at harvest time, and Ruth went into the fields to gather the leftover barley. Boaz, a cousin of Naomi's, who owned the fields, noticed the young woman and asked who she was. He was

Ruth gathers the barley that is left over

HARVESTING
The picture above shows women cutting and gathering grain during harvest time. Poor people, like Ruth, would come later to collect any leftover grain. This is known as gleaning.

While Boaz sleeps, Ruth lies down at his feet

touched to hear about her kindness to Naomi, and went over to her. "Come and eat with us. You are safe here with my people."

That evening Naomi told Ruth to return to Boaz. "Wait until he has fallen asleep, then go quietly and lie down beside him."

As soon as she saw that Boaz slept, Ruth lay down at his feet. In the middle of the night, he woke with a start and saw the form of a woman in the darkness. "Who are you?"

"I am Ruth, and I have come to ask for your protection."

"There is someone closer to you in the family than I: but if he does not wish to look after you and Naomi, then I shall take care of you."

And so it turned out. Ruth and Boaz were married, and Ruth gave birth to a son, who brought great happiness to Naomi in her old age.

WHEN BOAZ HAD EATEN AND DRUNK, AND HIS HEART WAS MERRY, HE WENT TO LIE DOWN AT THE END OF THE HEAP OF WHEAT: AND SHE CAME SOFTLY, AND UNCOVERED HIS FEET, AND LAID HER DOWN.
RUTH 3:7

Samuel Is Called to Serve God

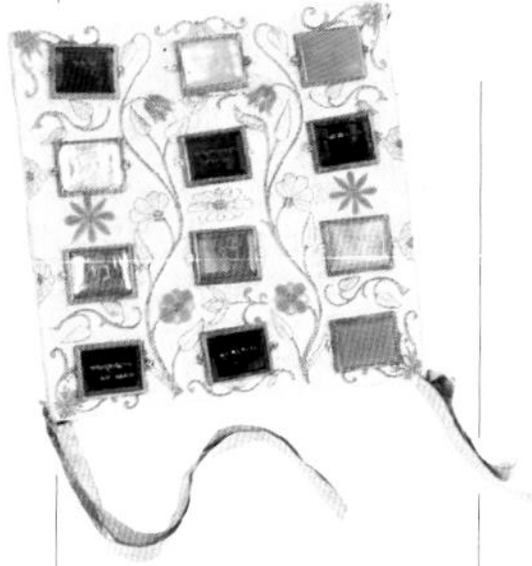

BREASTPIECE
Eli was a high priest and would have worn a linen breastpiece like the one above. It is inset with 12 gemstones, representing the 12 tribes of Israel. The breastpiece was tied to an *ephod*, a two-piece apron, which the high priest wore over his blue robe.

HANNAH WAS ONE of the two wives of Elkanah. Penninah had children, but even though Elkanah loved her, Hannah had none. Every year they went to pray at Shiloh, where the Ark of the Covenant was kept, and every year Penninah would mock Hannah because she had no children. One night Hannah went to the temple and prayed to God. "Lord, please send me a son, and I promise to devote his life to your service." Eli, the high priest, watched her praying, then he blessed her as she left. "May God grant your wish," he said. In due course Hannah gave birth to a son, whom she called Samuel.

Eli watches as Hannah prays to God for a son

Hannah gives her son, Samuel, to Eli to look after

TEACHING THE LAW
As a high priest, Eli would have taught Samuel to obey God's laws. In the same way, a rabbi – a teacher of Jewish laws – instructs the young today.

Hannah nursed the child, then, not forgetting her promise to God, she took Samuel to the temple and gave him to Eli to look after. Every year, when she came with her husband to pray at Shiloh, Hannah brought with her a little coat for Samuel. Eli cared for him lovingly and brought him up to obey God's word. The child grew as straight and true as Eli's own two sons were dishonest and sly.

One night Samuel was awakened by a voice calling his name. "Here I am," he said, and jumping from his bed ran to see what Eli wanted.

"I did not call you," said the old man. "Go back to bed."

But in a short while the boy heard the voice again – "Samuel, Samuel!" – and again he went in to Eli, but the priest assured him that he had not spoken. The third time Samuel heard the voice, Eli told him that it must be the voice of God.

So Samuel lay down in the dark and waited. "Samuel, Samuel."

"Lord," the child replied. "I am your servant, and ready to listen."

"The sons of Eli are evil men. You must tell their father that they cannot serve as priests or be pardoned for their wickedness."

The next morning Samuel told Eli what God had said. "So be it," said Eli. "It is the word of the Lord."

The Lord came, and stood, and called as at other times, "Samuel, Samuel." Then Samuel answered, "Speak; for thy servant heareth."
I Samuel 3:10

While Eli sleeps, Samuel is awakened by a voice calling him

The Ark Is Captured

AND WHEN THE ARK OF THE COVENANT OF THE LORD CAME INTO THE CAMP, ALL ISRAEL SHOUTED WITH A GREAT SHOUT, SO THAT THE EARTH RANG AGAIN.
I SAMUEL 4:5

THE ISRAELITES, badly defeated in battle by the Philistines, decided to fetch the Ark of the Covenant from Shiloh. When the Ark was near they believed that God was with them, and would save them from their enemies. The Ark was carried into the camp and a great shout went up, a shout that struck fear into the hearts of the Philistines.

"The Israelite God is a terrible god," they said to one another.

The Philistines find the statue of Dagon lying broken next to the Ark

"We must fight with all our strength not to be overcome." And again the Philistines fought and defeated the people of Israel, and then they seized the Ark.

A man from the tribe of Benjamin fled from the battle and went to Shiloh where he found Eli, the old priest.

"What has happened, my son?" asked Eli.

"The Philistines have defeated us, we have suffered heavy losses, and the Philistines have taken the Ark."

When Eli heard that the Ark of the Covenant – which he had watched over for so many years – had been captured, his heart stopped and he fell to the ground dead.

The Philistines took the Ark to Ashdod, and put it in the temple of Dagon beside a statue of their god. The next morning, the statue of

DAGON
The chief god of the Philistines was Dagon, god of grain and fertility. He is sometimes represented as part fish, part man, as shown here.

Dagon was found lying on the ground in front of the Ark. Puzzled, the priests set the golden image upright, but the following day Dagon was found again on the ground, with his head and both hands broken off. Soon afterward the Philistines were struck by a plague of boils, and their land was overrun with rats.

"We must send the Ark back with a peace offering," they decided. They laid the Ark on a cart, and beside it they placed a casket of gold. They wanted to see how powerful the God of the Israelites was, so they put untrained cows between the shafts and, without a driver, the cows pulled the cart straight down the road.

Some Israelites were harvesting wheat in the fields when they looked up and saw the cart approaching.

Overjoyed, they ran to it and gently lifted the sacred chest to the ground. A burnt sacrifice was made, and they thanked God that the Ark was safely in their hands once more.

OX AND CART

The Israelites used trained oxen to pull simple wooden carts, like the one in the picture above. Valued for their strength, oxen were also used for plowing and threshing.

Some Israelites are cutting wheat in the fields when they see the cart, carrying the Ark, approaching

Saul, the First King of the Israelites

HORN AND OIL
Samuel anointed Saul king with oil contained in an animal's horn. It was a sign that Saul was chosen by God and belonged to the Lord in a special way. Samuel would have used olive oil, perfumed with spices and myrrh. The Israelites had many other uses for oil. They used it in cooking, to soothe cuts and bruises, for preparing a body for burial, and as fuel for lamps.

SAMUEL GREW OLD, and the people asked him to appoint a king to rule over them. Samuel asked God what he should do.

"There is a man called Saul, of the tribe of Benjamin, and he is the one you must choose. He will make himself known to you."

Shortly afterward, a tall young man came up to Samuel on a hill outside the city. "I have lost three of my donkeys," he said. "I know you are a prophet: can you tell me where they are?"

"Your donkeys are safe," Samuel replied. "Now come with me, for you are to be the first king of Israel." Saul was astonished. "But I am unimportant!" he exclaimed. "I am of the tribe of Benjamin, the smallest of all the tribes of Israel, and my family is the least important family in the tribe." Samuel reassured him, and led the astonished Saul back to his house, where he gave him food and then anointed him with oil, pouring it over his head.

"With this oil," he said, "I declare you king. Now you must return home. On your way you will see two men who will tell you your donkeys are found. Next you will meet three men, the first leading three young goats, the second carrying three loaves of bread, the third a bottle of wine; they will give you two of their loaves. Lastly, you will come across a group of prophets making music and singing praises to God, and you will join with them."

Everything happened exactly as predicted, after which Samuel called the children of Israel together. "I am here to show you your king," he told them. "Where is Saul, of the tribe of Benjamin?" But Saul, overwhelmed, was hiding among some baggage. He was soon found, however, and brought before Samuel, where he stood head and shoulders taller than any man there.

SAMUEL SAID TO ALL THE PEOPLE, "SEE YE SAUL WHOM THE LORD HATH CHOSEN, THAT THERE IS NONE LIKE HIM AMONG ALL THE PEOPLE?" AND ALL THE PEOPLE SHOUTED, AND SAID, "LONG LIVE THE KING!"
I SAMUEL 10:24

Samuel calls the Israelites together and declares Saul king

"Here is your ruler!" said Samuel. "The man God has chosen to be your king."

And the people shouted, "Long live the king!"

Afterward Samuel wrote down the rules of kingship, dedicating his account to God. Then he told all the people – men, women, and children – to return to their homes.

Saul hides among baggage before he is found and brought before Samuel to become the first king of the Israelites

Saul's Downfall

The Israelite army defeats the Ammonites and frees the city of Jabesh

Saul summons his entire army to attack the Ammonites

THE CITY OF JABESH was under siege by the Ammonites, who agreed to make peace on one condition: that the right eye of every citizen should be put out. The people were appalled. They wept and wailed, but not one of them could think of a way to avoid this cruel punishment.

Toward evening Saul came in from the fields, driving a herd of oxen before him. He was astonished to find the entire population in a state of terror. "What is the matter?" he asked. "What has happened?"

When he heard what the enemy was threatening to do, Saul was full of anger. Immediately he summoned his army together. He sent messengers to the people of Jabesh, promising that the very next day, by the time the sun was at its highest, they would be safe. The Israelites attacked the Ammonites early the next morning. By midday they had either slain

Samuel reproaches Saul for lighting the sacrificial fire himself

SAMUEL SAID TO SAUL, "THOU HAST DONE FOOLISHLY: THOU HAST NOT KEPT THE COMMANDMENT OF THE LORD THY GOD, WHICH HE COMMANDED THEE: FOR NOW WOULD THE LORD HAVE ESTABLISHED THY KINGDOM UPON ISRAEL FOR EVER."
I SAMUEL 13:13

or put to flight every one of them. Saul and his people were overjoyed, and celebrated their victory with sacrifices to the Lord.

Two years after Saul had become king, the Philistines gathered on the Israelites' border in enormous numbers, preparing for invasion. Samuel told Saul to wait for seven days, at the end of which he would come and make the burnt offering before the battle. But at the end of seven days, there was no sign of Samuel, and Saul grew impatient. He decided to wait no longer, but to light the fire himself.

Suddenly he found Samuel by his side. "Why have you disobeyed me?" Samuel asked.

"Because you did not come, and my men were scattered. The Philistines may attack at any moment. I was afraid that if I did not make a burnt offering to the Lord, we would be defeated."

"You have done wrong to disregard God's commandment," Samuel reproached him. "If you had obeyed God's word, you would have been the founder of a great kingdom. But because you went against his word, your sons will now never succeed you: another family, not yours, will rule Israel."

CANAANITE ALTAR
The Israelites were not the only people to sacrifice animals on altars – it was a common practice in the ancient Middle East. The Canaanites made sacrifices to their gods on rectangular – or oval – shaped altars. These were made of uncut field stones, like the one above. Canaanite altars were usually built on "high places" – hilltop sites dedicated to the worship of the gods.

God Chooses David

"THE LORD SEETH NOT AS MAN SEETH; FOR MAN LOOKETH ON THE OUTWARD APPEARANCE, BUT THE LORD LOOKETH ON THE HEART."
I SAMUEL 16:7

OD SPOKE TO SAMUEL, telling him to go to Bethlehem where he would find a man called Jesse. "I have chosen one of the sons of Jesse to be the next king," he said.

In Bethlehem, the news of Samuel's arrival made the people tremble, for he was now a great and powerful man. But Samuel

Jesse

Jesse's youngest son, David, watches over the sheep

Samuel

Samuel blesses seven of Jesse's sons, but knows that none of them has been chosen by God

reassured them. "I come in peace, to bless you and pray with you."

One by one, seven of Jesse's sons came to the prophet to be blessed. When Samuel saw the men standing before him, tall and handsome, he thought to himself, "Surely, one of these must be the chosen one." But as each of the brothers came before him in turn, he heard the Lord's voice, "This is not the man. God does not judge in the way people do. Do not look at the face but into the heart."

Finally, Samuel turned to Jesse and said, "God has chosen none of these men. Are all your children here?"

"All but the youngest, David, and he is out in the fields looking after the sheep."

"Fetch him," said Samuel.

The boy, fresh-faced and strongly built, came running in. "This is he," said God. Then Samuel took the holy oil and anointed David in front of his whole family. And from that day on the spirit of the Lord was with him.

SHEPHERD BOY
David was the youngest, and therefore the least important, of Jesse's sons. He looked after his father's sheep in the hills around Bethlehem. Out in all kinds of weather, his life would have been a lonely one as he led his sheep to good pasture, and protected them from harm. One story in the Bible tells how David risked his life by killing a bear and a lion that threatened the sheep.

Samuel anoints David the next king of the Israelites

David and Goliath

Saul's army gathers to do battle against the Philistines

David hurls a stone from his sling

SLINGSHOT
As a shepherd, David would have carried a sling for hurling stones at animals that threatened his sheep. The shepherd placed a stone in his pad, held the two ends of the sling, then swung it around at high speed. When he let go of one end, the stone would fly toward its target. Also used by soldiers, the sling was a deadly weapon.

HE PHILISTINES WERE READY for battle. On two hilltops, with only a narrow valley between, the armies were assembled, the Philistines on one, Saul and the Israelites on the other.

All of a sudden a giant man came striding down toward the valley from the Philistine camp. Goliath of Gath towered above everyone; on his head was a massive bronze helmet; he wore a breastplate of bronze, and his legs and arms were sheathed in bronze. In one hand he carried a bronze dagger, in the other an iron-headed spear as big as a tree.

"I challenge you, Saul!" bellowed Goliath. "I challenge you to send one of your men to fight me! Let the two of us decide the outcome of the war!"

At these words, Saul trembled, and the Israelites were filled with fear.

Three of Jesse's sons were among Saul's soldiers, and their brother David had left his sheep to bring them food. As he reached the camp, he heard Goliath's boastful challenge, and saw that no one dared answer it.

"I will fight the giant," he said to Saul.

"But you are only a boy. Goliath is a famous man of war."

Eventually, however, Saul was persuaded. Refusing both weapons and armor, David went to a nearby stream and picked out five smooth pebbles, which he put in his shepherd's pouch. Then, with his sling in

DAVID PUT HIS HAND IN HIS BAG, AND TOOK THENCE A STONE, AND SLANG IT, AND SMOTE THE PHILISTINE IN HIS FOREHEAD.
I SAMUEL 17:49

one hand, his staff in the other, he walked toward Goliath.

"Get out of my way, boy!" the champion shouted, his voice heavy with contempt. "I do not fight with children!"

"You come to me with a dagger and a spear, but I come to you with God on my side," said David. He put down his staff, and placed a pebble in his sling. Whirling it around once, he let it fly. The stone struck Goliath in the middle of his forehead, and the giant crashed to the ground, dead.

When the Philistines saw their great champion dead, they turned and ran, leaving the Israelites to celebrate their victory.

PHILISTINE HEAD
The Philistines were one of the "Sea Peoples" who originally came from the islands in the Aegean Sea. They buried their dead in clay coffins, or sarcophagi. Strange-looking human features were engraved on the head ends of the coffins.

Saul Turns Against David

HARP
David's harp may have looked like this Jewish harp, called a *nebel*. It is made out of animal skin stretched over a rounded box. Or, David may have played a *kinnor*, a small, stringed instrument with a wooden frame.

SO DELIGHTED WAS SAUL with David's magnificent victory, that he gave him a high command in the army, and the young man came to live in Saul's own house. There David was made welcome by Saul's son, Jonathan, whom he quickly came to love as a brother. Jonathan spoke so highly of David to his father that Saul, too, soon came to look on him as a member of his own family. After a while, Saul gave his daughter, Michal, to David as a wife. Michal, a scholar, had long been in love with David, and so the match was a happy one.

To the people of Israel David was a hero. As he walked through the streets he was cheered and applauded, songs were sung and stories recounted about his defeat of Goliath. Women with tambourines danced joyfully in front of him, chanting, "Saul has slain thousands, but David has slain tens of thousands!"

Saul tries to kill David

David dodges Saul's spear

Saul listened to their words, and he began to grow jealous. "If the people think so much more of him than of me," he said to himself, "he will soon be in possession of my kingdom." From that moment he began to brood, and to watch David closely.

One day David was playing his harp while Saul listened. In Saul's hand was the spear which always hung from his belt. Suddenly overcome by a passionate surge of hatred, Saul threw the spear at the young man's head. David dodged the blade, but realizing his life was now in danger, left Saul as soon as he could and went into hiding. He went first to Michal, but she quickly convinced him it was not safe to stay. She lowered him on a rope from the window, and from there he disappeared into the darkness and made his escape.

That night soldiers sent by Saul appeared at David's house demanding to see him. "He is ill in bed," said his wife. Pushing her to one side, the men burst into David's room where they saw what appeared to be a man asleep. But it was only a statue covered in goat's hair which Michal had placed under the covers to deceive them.

So David made his escape. But Saul thought only of his hatred, and how to bring about the young man's death.

Michal places a goat's hair rug under the covers, so the soldiers think it is David

Michal helps David to escape through a window

SO MICHAL LET DAVID DOWN THROUGH A WINDOW: AND HE WENT, AND FLED, AND ESCAPED.

I SAMUEL 19:12

David the Outlaw

David goes into hiding

Jonathan fires an arrow to signal that David's life is in danger

WARNING SHOTS
The Israelites used bows made of wood and bone, and arrows tipped with metal, for fighting and hunting. A quiver held up to 30 arrows.

JONATHAN went in secret to see David in his hiding place. "What have I done to make Saul hate me? Does he really want to kill me?" David asked his friend in anguish.

"Do not worry, I will find out my father's real feelings," said Jonathan. "Meanwhile you must stay hidden until I give you a signal: then you will know if you are safe, or only a step away from death."

Returning home, Jonathan found his father at dinner and sat down opposite him. "Where is David?" the king demanded.

David holds up a piece of material cut from Saul's robe, to show how close he came to killing him

Saul is overcome with guilt

"He has gone to visit his family in Bethlehem. Believe me, Father, he has done you no harm," said Jonathan.

His face crimson with rage, Saul staggered to his feet, grabbed a spear, and flung it drunkenly at his son. "How dare you take sides against me. Bring David to me now, for he must die!" he shouted.

The next morning, as arranged, Jonathan went into the meadow where David was hiding. He fired an arrow to fall far beyond where his friend lay concealed. This signaled that David's life was in danger. The two men embraced sadly. Then they parted, Jonathan to go back to the city, David to go into the wilderness, where he was joined by a band of loyal followers.

Saul set out with his men to look for David in the desert land around En Gedi. The day was hot, and he retired into a cave – the same cave in which David and his men were hiding. Quietly David crept up behind Saul and cut off a piece of his coat. Once Saul had left the cave, David called out, "My lord king, it is I, David. See how close I came to killing you, and yet I spared your life! I would not harm someone who has been anointed by God."

At these words, Saul was overcome with guilt. "David, I have treated you badly, but you are a much greater man than I. May God be with you, and long may you reign as the future king of Israel!"

HIDEOUT

In the rugged hills and valleys around En Gedi, by the Dead Sea, there were plenty of natural caves where David and his followers could hide. In a cave, such as the one above, David would have had the advantage of seeing Saul and his army approaching from a distance.

David and Abigail

AFTER WEEKS OF WANDERING in the desert, David and his followers came within a short distance of Carmel. This was the home of Nabal, a man famous for his enormous wealth. Having always treated Nabal well, David did not hesitate to send several of his men to ask for food. Nabal, however, received them rudely. "Who is this David?" he demanded. "Why should I give you anything?" And with that he turned the men away.

But Abigail, his wife, a kind and beautiful young woman, hearing what had happened, was distressed by her husband's meanness.

FIG CAKES
Abigail brought David cakes made of figs. This sweet, seedy fruit formed part of the Israelite diet. The figs could be eaten fresh, or dried and pressed into cakes. Figs were one of Canaan's most important crops.

Abigail loads her donkeys with provisions and takes them to David

She kneels before him and begs for his mercy

Secretly, she loaded five donkeys with provisions – wine, meat, bread, raisins, and fig cakes. Riding through a mountain ravine, Abigail met David and his loyal followers. Kneeling before David, she begged for his mercy. "My husband is much to blame for refusing you food," she said. "But I implore you not to take revenge!"

David, moved by her words, promised that he would leave Nabal unharmed.

When Abigail returned to Carmel, she found her husband holding a feast, surrounded by his friends and very drunk. So drunk was he that not until next morning was she able to tell him of her visit to David. As she spoke, Nabal's blood ran like ice in his veins. His heart failed him and became like stone, and within ten days he was dead.

Later, David asked Abigail to be his wife.

AND IT WAS SO, AS ABIGAIL RODE ON THE ASS, THAT SHE CAME DOWN BY THE COVERT ON THE HILL, AND BEHOLD, DAVID AND HIS MEN CAME DOWN AGAINST HER; AND SHE MET THEM.
I SAMUEL 25:20

David's loyal followers watch close by

WADI
Abigail met David in a mountain ravine near Carmel. A ravine, or wadi, is formed by a stream that floods during the rainy season, but remains dry for the rest of the year. When dry, wadis were used as roadways. Wadis are common in the desert regions of the Middle East.

The Death of Saul

The witch of Endor summons the spirit of Samuel from the dead

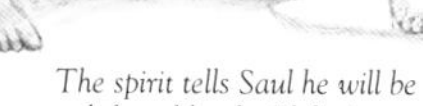

The spirit tells Saul he will be defeated by the Philistines

Saul realizes that the voice of the spirit is indeed Samuel's

SHEOL
The Israelites saw the world as a flat disk surrounded by seas and resting on pillars. Deep in the depths of the earth was Sheol, the resting place of the dead. Saul would have believed that Samuel's spirit was called up from Sheol.

SAMUEL WAS DEAD, and the whole country mourned for him, for he had been much loved. The Philistines were ready yet again for war, and yet again the Israelites were preparing to defend themselves. When Saul realized the power and size of the enemy, his heart was filled with a deadly fear. He prayed to God, but only silence answered his prayers.

Then in his misery he remembered hearing talk of a witch at Endor. Carefully disguising himself and attended by two of his men, he went by night to see her. "Ask the spirits what is to happen to me," he begged. Knowing that witchcraft was against the law, the woman was nervous, and at first refused. But Saul reassured her.

"Whom do you wish me to call up?" she asked him.

"Samuel."

No sooner had he spoken than the witch cried out in alarm.

"What do you see?" asked Saul.

"I see an old man covered in a cloak," she said. At once Saul knew that it was indeed Samuel whom she had called up from the dead.

"God has left you," said the voice of Samuel. "Tomorrow the Philistines will be victorious in battle, and you and your sons shall be slain."

The next day the Philistine army in their thousands fell upon the Israelites, who were swiftly and bloodily defeated. Hundreds were slaughtered, hundreds more ran for their lives. Jonathan and his brothers were killed. Saul, already mortally wounded, turned to his armor bearer. "Kill me!" he commanded.

But the man was afraid: he could not bring himself to kill his king. "My lord, I cannot!" he said.

So Saul plunged his sword into his breast. When the armor bearer saw the king fall, he, too, turned his blade upon himself so that he might die with him.

MOUNT GILBOA
Mount Gilboa, shown above, was the setting for the horrific battle between the Israelites and the Philistines. The mountain is in northern Canaan and overlooks the valley of Jezreel.

Saul, mortally wounded, commands his armor bearer to kill him

Long Live the King

IN THE TOWN OF HEBRON all the tribes of Israel gathered to proclaim David the new king of the Israelites. David took his people to Jerusalem, a city belonging to the Jebusites – for Jerusalem was to be his capital. But the Jebusites refused to open their gates, leaving the newcomers camped outside the walls.

However, some of David's men climbed up a waterpipe, which took them deep inside the city, and from there they were able to unlock the gates. Once inside, the Israelites defeated the Jebusites and captured the city.

The Ark of the Covenant was brought to Jerusalem, escorted by a crowd of thousands, singing and playing on pipes and tambourines.

JERUSALEM
Above is Jerusalem, also known as the "City of David," which became the Israelites' political and religious center. On the left is the Dome of the Rock, a Muslim mosque. It now stands on the site of Solomon's temple, which David made plans for and Solomon built.

DANCING FOR JOY
The picture above shows folk dancing in modern-day Syria. When the Israelites danced, it was a way of expressing their delight in God. On entering Jerusalem, the Israelites danced to thank God for their victory and to praise him.

The people escort the Ark into Jerusalem

As they entered the gates, trumpets sounded, and David took off his royal robes and danced for joy before the Ark of the Covenant.

When the Ark arrived at the ceremonial tent, or tabernacle, which had been built to house it, David offered burnt sacrifices to the Lord. Then he blessed his people, and gave everyone cakes and wine.

Michal, David's wife, watched him from a window as he mingled freely with the crowd. "How shameful to see the king of Israel dancing with the common people!" she said scornfully.

But David replied, "Nothing I do for the honor of God is shameful: the shame lies with those who despise me for it!" Then David resolved to build a temple in honor of the Lord.

Michal looked through a window, and saw king David leaping and dancing before the Lord; and she despised him in her heart.
II Samuel 6:16

Michal watches David with scorn

David dances before the Ark

David and Bathsheba

King David

Bathsheba

David watches from the roof of his palace as Bathsheba bathes

BATHING
This clay figure of a woman bathing dates from around 1000 BC. After washing, Bathsheba would have rubbed scented oil into her skin.

KING DAVID'S ARMIES were away fighting in the field, but the king himself stayed in Jerusalem. One evening as he was sitting on the flat roof of his palace, he saw a lovely woman bathing and combing her hair. He sent a messenger to find out who she was. The answer came back that her name was Bathsheba, wife of Uriah the Hittite.

David was so struck by her beauty and grace that he gave orders for Bathsheba to be brought before him. He talked to her, courted her, and made love to her. In time she told him she was carrying his child.

Immediately David recalled her husband, Uriah, who was one of his best generals. He asked for a report on the war, and then told him to return to his own house. The next day, however, David was informed that Uriah had spent the night sleeping at the door of the palace.

"Why did you not go home and see your wife?" David asked him.

"How can I eat and drink with my wife, and sleep safe under my own roof when I know that your whole army is encamped in the

Bathsheba's husband, Uriah, is killed in battle

open, ready to fight for the nation?" asked Uriah.

David sent Uriah back to the field with a letter to Joab, the commander of the army: "You must place Uriah in the front line, and keep him where the fighting is fiercest." Joab did as he was ordered, and during the next battle Uriah was killed.

Bathsheba grieved for her husband, but once the period of mourning was over, she agreed to marry David. After a while, she gave birth to a son.

God was displeased, and sent Nathan the prophet to show David the cruelty of his treatment of Uriah, who had been such a brave and loyal servant.

Nathan began by telling David a story. "There were two men," he said. "One was rich, with many flocks and herds, the other poor, his only possession a little ewe lamb that he loved as a daughter and fed from his own plate. A traveler arrived at the rich man's house asking to be fed. The rich man, not wishing to lose one of his own sheep, instead killed the poor man's little lamb, roasted it, and fed it to his guest."

David was shocked by Nathan's story. "The rich man should be punished!" he shouted angrily.

"But you are like the rich man," said Nathan. "And it is you who must be punished. You have sinned against God, and for this your son will die!"

PET LAMB
Generally, the Israelites did not keep animals as pets, but a lamb that had lost its mother would have needed special care. A shepherd, or shepherdess, may have taken an orphaned lamb into the family home to look after it, much as the poor man cared for his ewe lamb.

THE POOR MAN HAD NOTHING, SAVE ONE LITTLE EWE LAMB, WHICH HE HAD BOUGHT AND NOURISHED UP; AND IT GREW UP TOGETHER WITH HIM, AND WITH HIS CHILDREN.
II SAMUEL 12:3

The poor man feeds his ewe lamb with his own food

Absalom's Rebellion

Absalom and his men rebel against David, but are defeated in battle

Absalom

Absalom waits at the city gate and talks to anyone who comes to see the king

Absalom makes himself popular with the people

AS NATHAN had predicted Bathsheba's son died, but later she gave birth to another boy, who was called Solomon. God loved Solomon, but King David had many other children by many different wives, and most of them squabbled with each other. One, called Absalom, quarreled with and killed his half brother. He was then forced to flee and go into hiding. Eventually, however, David relented and allowed Absalom to return to Jerusalem.

Absalom was a young man of exceptional beauty, particularly proud of his long, thick hair. He was also ambitious, secretly determined that he should be the next king of Israel. He bought a chariot and horses and every morning he would stand at the city gate and talk to anyone who came to see the king.

Having made himself popular with the people, Absalom went to Hebron. There he raised a powerful army, with which he challenged his father to battle for the kingship.

But David rode out of Jerusalem at the head of many thousand men. As he gave his instructions to his captains, he said, "Be gentle with Absalom, for my sake."

After a long battle, the rebels were put to flight. Absalom himself escaped on the back of a mule, which, frightened by the noise of fighting, bolted into the shelter of a forest. As it galloped through the

HAIR
In Canaan, both men and women often wore their hair long and groomed. This carving shows an Assyrian official with long hair that has been carefully curled. Absalom cut his hair with a razor once a year.

trees, Absalom's long hair was caught in the branches of an oak, and he was left dangling helplessly.

There he was found by one of David's men, who went to tell Joab, the commander of the king's army. "You have seen Absalom!" Joab exclaimed. "Why did you not kill him on the spot? I personally would have given you a handsome reward!"

"I would not have accepted it," said the soldier. "I will not lift a finger against him, for King David asked us to deal gently with his son."

Enraged, Joab grabbed three heavy spears.

Absalom's long hair is caught in the branches of an oak tree

Joab and his armor bearers ride to where Absalom hangs

Together with his armor bearers he rode to where Absalom was hanging, a prisoner in the branches of the tree, and drove the spears into his chest. Then he gave orders for Absalom's body to be flung into a pit in the depths of the forest and covered with stones.

When David heard the news of Absalom's death, he was overcome with grief. "My son, oh my son!" he wept. "If only I had died instead of you!"

OAK TREE
The kermes oak, above, was one of several species of oak tree that grew in Canaan in ancient times. Oak trees are still found in the Middle East today.

King Solomon's Wisdom

AND THE KING SAID, "BRING ME A SWORD." AND THEY BROUGHT A SWORD BEFORE THE KING. AND THE KING SAID, "DIVIDE THE LIVING CHILD IN TWO, AND GIVE HALF TO THE ONE, AND HALF TO THE OTHER."
I KINGS 3:24-25

Solomon orders that the baby be cut in two

One woman agrees with the order

The other woman pleads for her baby's life

WHEN DAVID WAS DYING, he summoned his son, Solomon. "Soon I shall no longer be here to advise you," he said. "Always be strong and true, and always obey the word of God. If you do that, the Lord will be with you."

After David died, Solomon in his turn became king of Israel, and married the daughter of Pharaoh, king of Egypt, with whom he had made a treaty.

One night God appeared to him in a dream. "Ask for what you most want, and I will give it to you."

"You have made me king of a great people," Solomon replied. "But I have no more idea of how to govern than a child. Lord, give me wisdom."

Pleased with this answer, God said, "Because you asked nothing for yourself, neither for long life, nor wealth, nor victory over your enemies, I will grant your wish. If you do right and obey my laws, I will give you a wise and understanding heart, and you shall become known as a good king."

Soon afterward two women came before Solomon. They shared a house, and each had recently given birth to a child, but one child had died, and now both mothers were claiming the living baby as theirs.

"It is her baby who died," the first woman insisted. "Do you think I do not know my own child!"

"No, no!" cried the other. "It is her baby who is dead: in the night while I slept, she stole mine from my side!"

"Bring me my sword," said Solomon. The sword was brought. "Cut the child in two, and give half to each of the women standing here."

"Yes, O wise King, let neither of us have him," said one. "Cut him in two!"

But the other woman burst into tears and wrung her hands. "Do not kill my baby!" she cried. "I would rather give him away than have him hurt!" By this Solomon knew that she was the true mother, and he gave the child to her.

When the people heard of the judgment of Solomon they looked at their king with new respect, for they knew such wisdom could come to him only from God.

KING SOLOMON
Solomon was renowned for his wisdom, and this is shown in the story of the two women: he knew that the real mother would not agree to her baby being killed. The king wrote many wise sayings: most of the Book of Proverbs is thought to have been written by him. Under Solomon's rule the Israelites entered a golden age of peace and prosperity. This was crowned by the building of the temple, named after him, in Jerusalem.

The baby is given to the true mother

Solomon's Temple

CEDARS OF LEBANON
Large, evergreen cedar trees covered the hills of Lebanon in Solomon's time. Cedarwood was valued for its beauty, fragrance, and strength.

NOW THAT THERE WAS peace at last, Solomon's greatest wish was to carry out the plan of his father, David, to build a temple for the worship of God. He sent word to Hiram, king of Tyre, asking him for wood from the great cedars of Lebanon. The huge trees were felled, then roped to rafts and floated down the coast. At the same time thousands of laborers quarried and cut the stones for the foundations and outer walls of the temple.

It took four years to lay the foundations, and three to build the temple upon them. Inside the temple, the walls were of cedarwood, carved with flowers and trees and painted with gold. The altar, too, was covered in gold.

When it was finished, Solomon, accompanied by the priests and tribal leaders, brought the Ark of the Covenant to the temple, where it was placed carefully in the inner sanctuary.

Suddenly the temple was filled with a cloud, so the priests could not carry out their duties. It was the glory of God filling the house of the Lord.

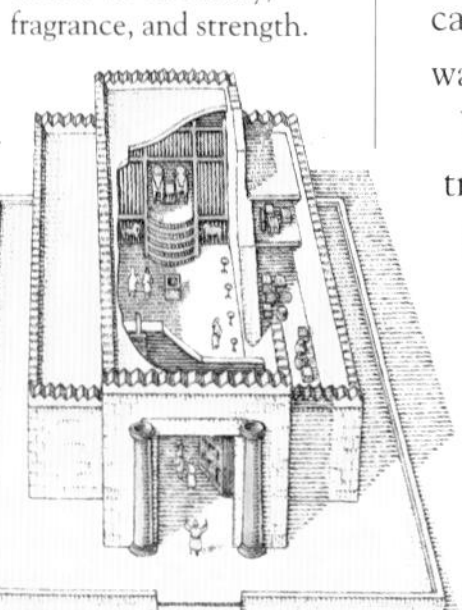

SOLOMON'S TEMPLE
Solomon's temple replaced the tabernacle, or sacred tent, in providing a permanent home for the Ark of the Covenant. The Ark, flanked by two golden cherubim, was placed in the innermost room, the Holy of Holies. The temple was at the center of the Israelites' faith because it was the place where God was (see page 17).

Laborers cut the stones for the temple

It takes seven years to build Solomon's temple

Winged cherubim are carved for the inside of the temple

CARVED IVORY
Cherubim, winged creatures, were carved on the inside of the temple. They may have looked like this sphinx from Nimrud in Assyria.

The Queen of Sheba

THE QUEEN OF SHEBA had heard about the wisdom of Solomon, and she wished to see for herself if all she had heard was true. So she traveled a long way from the distant land of Sheba with a great camel caravan, loaded with spices and gold and precious stones, until she came to Jerusalem.

The king received her courteously, and she asked him many

THE QUEEN'S JOURNEY Sheba was probably in southwest Arabia. The queen of Sheba traveled about 1,000 miles (1,600 km) to visit Solomon. On the way, she would have taken the King's Highway, a major international trade route that was controlled by Israel during the reigns of David and Solomon.

The queen of Sheba travels to Jerusalem

She is accompanied by a great camel caravan, loaded with spices and gold and precious stones

difficult questions. But none was too difficult for Solomon: he answered them all.

Then she looked around her, at his servants and his ministers, at his magnificent golden palace and happy, prosperous people, and she knew that here was a man both wise and good. "I would not believe it, until I had seen with my own eyes," she said. "Israel is fortunate in its king."

She gave Solomon many magnificent gifts, while he in his turn presented her with everything her heart desired. His wealth and generosity were without limit, and the queen returned to her own country laden with the riches of Israel.

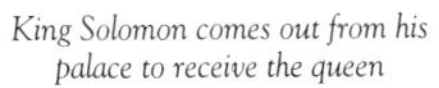

King Solomon comes out from his palace to receive the queen

PRECIOUS GIFTS
Sheba became a wealthy land by trading spices, gold, and jewels. When the queen of Sheba visited King Solomon and brought expensive gifts with her, she may have wished to make a trade agreement with the king.

AFRICAN QUEEN
Legend has it that the queen of Sheba ruled over Ethiopia and Egypt.

Elijah in the Wilderness

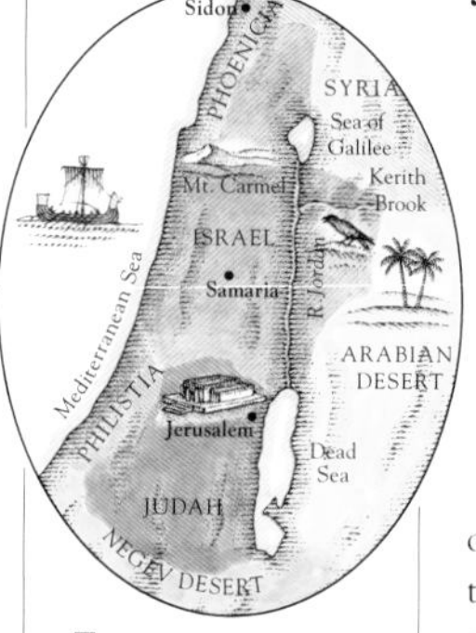

TWO KINGDOMS
Solomon, who belonged to the tribe of Judah, had not always treated the northern tribes well. When Rehoboam became king these tribes rebelled. The kingdom was then split into two: Israel, with Samaria as its capital, in the north; Judah, with Jerusalem as its capital, in the south.

AFTER THE DEATH of Solomon, his son Rehoboam became king. There was unrest among the tribes in the north, but Rehoboam did not listen to the people's troubles. The tribes rebelled and the kingdom was split in two, into Israel and Judah. Then, the people of Israel turned against God. The times were so wicked that the prophet Elijah foretold there would be a drought lasting many years.

The Lord spoke to Elijah. "Go to the stream that runs in the valley of Kerith, and live there in secret. You can drink from the brook, and the ravens will bring you food." And indeed every morning and evening ravens appeared with bread and meat in their beaks; but soon the stream dried up from the lack of rain.

In obedience to God, Elijah then went to the city of Sidon, where he met a woman gathering sticks

Elijah drinks from the brook and is fed by ravens

Elijah brings the woman's son back to life

outside the city walls. "Please, give me something to eat," Elijah asked her.

"I have nothing but a jar of flour and a little oil," she said. "And with that I must feed myself and my son, or we will starve."

"Go to your house, and there you will find enough flour and enough oil to last until the rains come." And it happened just as the prophet said. There was food every day for the woman, her son, and for Elijah.

But then the woman's son fell ill and died. "Do you call yourself a man of God!" she cried to Elijah. "You, who have let God take my son from me!" Elijah gently lifted up the boy, laid him on his own bed, and three times he bent over him.

"O Lord," he prayed. "Let this child's life return." And in a short while the boy took a deep breath, opened his eyes, and sat up. Elijah lifted the child and brought him to his mother, who was overjoyed. "Now I know you are truly a man of God," she said.

RAVENS
According to Old Testament law, a raven was unclean and could not be sacrificed or eaten. In spite of this, God sent ravens to bring food to Elijah in the desert, showing that the most humble can serve God.

The Israelites Turn Against God

BAAL
This bronze idol from about 1400-1300 BC probably represents Baal, the chief Canaanite god. The Israelites may have begun to worship Baal because he was supposed to control rainfall, which the Israelites depended on for survival.

THE DROUGHT HAD LASTED FOR THREE YEARS when Elijah the prophet went to Samaria to see Ahab, king of Israel, who had become a follower of the god Baal. He told Ahab to summon the children of Israel and all the priests, and bring them together on Mount Carmel. There Elijah said to them, "You cannot worship both Baal and God!" But the people remained silent. He told them to build an altar to Baal while he built an altar to God. They laid wood and a sacrificial calf on each of the altars. "Let the true God set alight the altar fire!" cried Elijah.

The priests of Baal lifted up their arms and called on their god to send them fire. "O, Baal, hear us!" they shouted. But the hours passed and nothing happened, and the fire remained unlit.

"Perhaps he sleeps!" mocked Elijah. He gave orders for barrels of

Elijah builds an altar to God, and it roars into flames

The priests build an altar to Baal, but it remains unlit

water to be emptied over his altar, so that the wood was soaked and impossible to burn. He spoke quietly to God. "Lord God of Israel, I ask you to send fire so that the hearts of your people may return to you."

"THERE ARISETH A LITTLE CLOUD OUT OF THE SEA, LIKE A MAN'S HAND."
I KINGS 18:44

Elijah

servant

A little cloud appears, no bigger than a man's hand

Elijah tells his servant to let Ahab know that the rains have come

Instantly the pile of sodden logs roared into flames, and within seconds the calf, the wood, and the stones on which they lay were burnt to blackened ashes. At this, the people fell on their faces and honored God.

Then Elijah went to the summit of Carmel and told his servant to look out to sea. "There is nothing," said the young man, "only a clear sky and a calm sea." Elijah told him to look again. "Still I see nothing." Seven times he looked, and after the seventh time he turned to the prophet saying, "Still I see nothing – nothing but a little cloud, no bigger than a man's hand."

"Go quickly to Ahab, and tell him that the rains have come!" Almost before Elijah had spoken, the sky grew black, and the rain came lashing down, and a great wind arose that drove the water inward over the whole country. Ahab rode off to the town of Jezreel, but Elijah, tucking his cloak into his belt, ran ahead of Ahab.

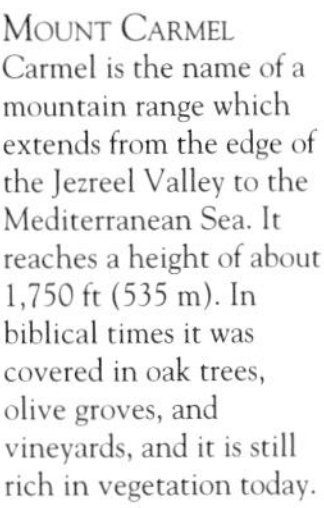

MOUNT CARMEL
Carmel is the name of a mountain range which extends from the edge of the Jezreel Valley to the Mediterranean Sea. It reaches a height of about 1,750 ft (535 m). In biblical times it was covered in oak trees, olive groves, and vineyards, and it is still rich in vegetation today.

Naboth's Vineyard

NEXT TO THE PALACE of King Ahab in Samaria was a vineyard. The king wanted to buy the vineyard, and offered the owner, Naboth, a good price for it.

But Naboth refused. "The Lord will not let me part with my inheritance," he told the king.

Ahab, who was used to being obeyed, was enraged. He flung himself down on his bed, turned his face to the wall, and refused both food and drink. His wife, Jezebel, was worried. "Please tell me what is troubling you," she begged him. But when she heard what the matter was, she laughed. "Now you may eat and drink with a light heart! I will see that you get your vineyard – in fact it is as good as yours already."

Jezebel wrote to all the officials and noblemen of the city, signing the letters with Ahab's name, and sealing them with the royal seal. In them she gave instructions that a day of fasting should be held. Naboth was to be set up in a position of great importance. Two men were to sit opposite him and accuse him of speaking against God, a crime that carried a sentence of death.

VINEYARD
This Assyrian carving shows a king and queen in a vineyard. The vines are trained and lifted off the ground by supports.

Everything happened as Jezebel had planned. Naboth was accused, seized, taken outside the city walls, and stoned to death. "Now the vineyard is yours," said Jezebel in triumph to her husband.

Ahab lost no time in going to the vineyard, anxious to inspect his new property. But he found he was not alone. God had spoken to the prophet, Elijah, and sent him to rebuke the king. "This vineyard has been bought with the death of an innocent man!" thundered Elijah. "And just as the dogs lick his blood from the roadside, so will they lick yours. For your death, and that of Jezebel, will be as cruel and violent as Naboth's!"

Ahab was appalled when he heard the prophet's words and was overcome with shame. He tore his clothes, dressed himself in sackcloth to show his remorse, refused to eat, and fell into deep despair.

When God saw that Ahab was truly sorry for what he had done, the Lord spoke again to Elijah. "Because this man has seen the error of his ways, I will be merciful to him. He may live out his days in peace, but because of the serious wrong done, there will come a time when disaster will fall upon his descendants."

Naboth is seized by soldiers and taken outside to be stoned, as Jezebel looks on

King Ahab takes possession of Naboth's vineyard

Elijah rebukes him for killing Naboth

Ahab is overcome with shame and dresses in sackcloth

Elijah's Final Journey

Elijah beats the surface of the River Jordan with his cloak and the waters divide

ONE DAY ELIJAH WAS TRAVELING WITH ELISHA, whom he had chosen to be his successor. Elijah, knowing that he was soon to die, asked Elisha to go with him no farther. Elisha loved the older man, and wanted to stay with him. "I shall not leave you," he said. So the two men continued on their way.

At Bethel, Elijah again turned to Elisha. "You must stay here, while I go on alone." But still Elisha would not leave him.

Finally, they came to the River Jordan. Elijah took off his cloak and beat the surface of the water with it. The waters divided, and the prophets crossed the river, walking on a pathway of dry land.

Suddenly a chariot of fire appeared out of the sky, drawn by horses flaming scarlet and gold. Before Elisha knew what was happening, Elijah was whirled up into the chariot, which, with the sound of a shrieking, rushing wind, disappeared from sight. Elisha, staring up into the clouds, cried out in wonder. But Elijah was never seen again.

Slowly Elisha took up Elijah's cloak and hit the surface of the river, calling on God to help him. The waters parted and he walked to the other side on dry land. The spirit of Elijah was now with him.

Elijah is whirled up into the skies in a chariot of fire

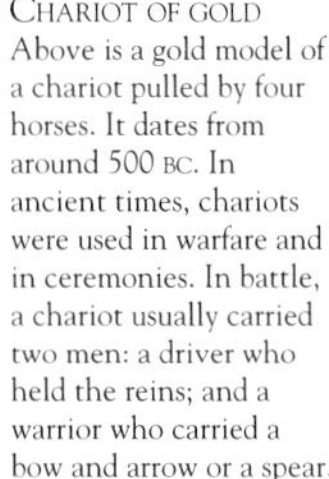

CHARIOT OF GOLD
Above is a gold model of a chariot pulled by four horses. It dates from around 500 BC. In ancient times, chariots were used in warfare and in ceremonies. In battle, a chariot usually carried two men: a driver who held the reins; and a warrior who carried a bow and arrow or a spear.

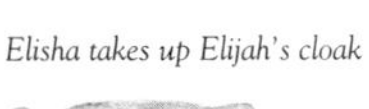

Elisha takes up Elijah's cloak

Elisha and the Woman of Shunem

ON HIS TRAVELS ELISHA often visited the city of Shunem. In the city lived a rich woman who invited him to eat with her and her husband every time he passed by. The woman said that Elisha could stay whenever he wished, and made ready a little room for him on the roof, with a bed, a table, a stool, and a lamp.

One evening as Elisha lay on his bed, he called his servant, Gehazi. "How can I repay the kindness of this woman?" he asked.

"I know that what she wants most is a child," Gehazi replied. "But her husband is too old to father children."

"Ask her to come here," said Elisha. The woman came, and stood in the doorway to hear what Elisha had to say.

"Soon," he told her, "you will have a son."

"No, that cannot be," she protested. But just as the prophet said, within a year she gave birth to a boy.

ELISHA
The painting above is of the prophet Elisha. When Elisha took up Elijah's cloak, it symbolized that he was chosen by God to succeed Elijah as the prophet of Israel. In the Bible, Elisha is described as being bald-headed, and once he was mocked by some children for his baldness. Two bears then appeared and attacked the children.

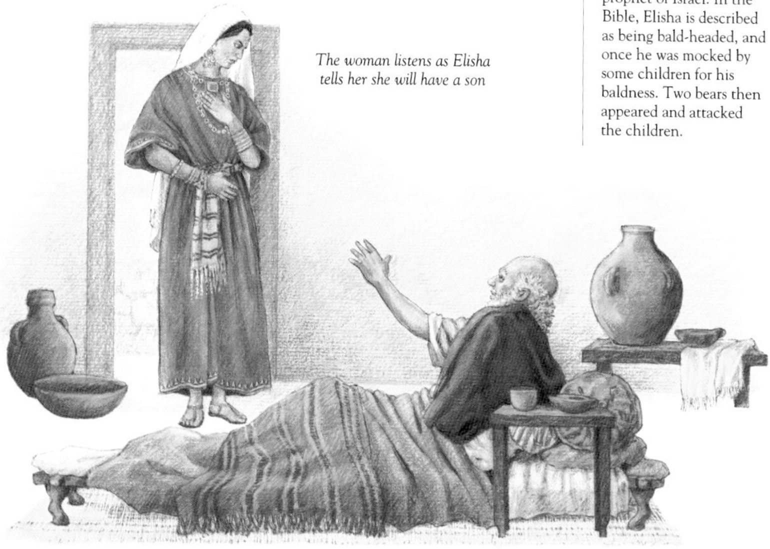

The woman listens as Elisha tells her she will have a son

The servant carries the sick boy back to the house and gives the child to his mother, but by midday he is dead

SHUNEM
The town of Shunem, present day Solem, lies in the fertile Jezreel Valley. The town is about 3 miles (5 km) north of the town of Jezreel, near Mount Gilboa. Shunem was situated on a well-used route, which explains why Elisha often visited the town.

When the boy was older, he went out one morning to find his father who was harvesting in the fields. "Father, help me! There is a pain in my head which I cannot bear!" Frightened by his son's appearance, his father told a servant to carry him at once to the house. There his mother took him and held him on her lap, but by midday he was dead. With tears running down her cheeks, she carried the lifeless body to Elisha's room, laid it on the bed, and closed the door.

"Quickly!" she said to her husband. "Fetch a donkey, and let me have a servant to accompany me. I am going to find Elisha."

Traveling as fast as they could, they soon caught up with the prophet at Mount Carmel. Dismounting, the woman clutched Elisha's feet, but Gehazi pushed her away. "Leave her alone," Elisha said. "She is in distress, and I must know what is wrong." As soon as the woman had spoken, Elisha said to Gehazi, "Take my staff and, girding your loins, run as fast as you can to Shunem. Go to the boy, and touch his face with the staff. I and the boy's mother will follow you."

Gehazi did as his master had said. On entering the house, he touched the boy's face with the staff, but the body remained still and cold. "The boy is dead," he whispered sadly as Elisha arrived. Elisha went alone to the room in which the body lay. Closing the door behind him, he knelt and prayed to God. Then very carefully he lay down on top of the child, putting his mouth to the boy's mouth, his eyes against his eyes, his hands against the dead boy's hands. As he did so he felt the flesh beneath him grow warm. Elisha stood up and watched as the color returned to the face of what only minutes ago had been a lifeless body. Suddenly the boy sneezed, and sneezed again. Then he opened his eyes and sat up.

"Come and embrace your son!" Elisha called. The woman ran into the room and gasped. Falling on her knees before the prophet, she thanked him with all her heart. Then, hand in hand, she and her son left the room together.

After the boy's mother has found Elisha, they travel back to Shunem together

Elisha's servant, Gehazi, runs on ahead with Elisha's staff in his hand

GIRDED LOINS
Gehazi "girded his loins" when he ran to Shunem. This means that he would have put his robe between his legs and tucked it into his belt, like the Syrian workman shown in the picture. Laborers often did this to give them greater freedom of movement when they were working.

ELISHA WENT UP, AND LAY UPON THE CHILD, AND PUT HIS MOUTH UPON HIS MOUTH, AND HIS EYES UPON HIS EYES, AND HIS HANDS UPON HIS HANDS: AND HE STRETCHED HIMSELF UPON THE CHILD; AND THE FLESH OF THE CHILD WAXED WARM.

II KINGS 4:34

Elisha brings the boy back to life

Elisha and Naaman

NAAMAN, THE COMMANDER OF THE SYRIAN ARMY, was a brave and clever soldier, but for some years he had suffered from the skin disease of leprosy. Namaan's wife had recently taken as a maid a young Israelite who had been captured in battle.

Naaman presents a letter to the king of Israel, asking to be cured of his leprosy

SYRIAN KING
This ivory figure of a Syrian king is thought to be Hazael, who fought against the Israelites around the time of Elisha.

The girl said to her mistress, "How I wish my master could go to the prophet Elisha, who is in Samaria, for I know he could cure him!"

This was repeated to Naaman, who went at once to the king of Syria. "Of course you must go," said the king. "I myself will write a letter on your behalf to the king of Israel, asking that your leprosy be treated." And so Naaman set off, taking with him the letter and a splendid collection of gifts: ten talents of silver, six thousand pieces of gold, and ten complete sets of richly embroidered clothing.

When Naaman presented the king of Syria's letter, the king of Israel was angry. "Am I expected to work miracles?" he demanded. "This is only an excuse for Syria to quarrel with us yet again!"

Naaman drives up to Elisha's door in his chariot

Elisha's messenger tells Naaman to go and bathe seven times in the River Jordan

RIVER JORDAN
The River Jordan was the longest and most important river in Canaan. "Jordan" means "flowing downward": the river begins at Lake Huleh in the north and flows down to the Sea of Galilee. From there it drops lower until it reaches the Dead Sea. The distance from the Sea of Galilee to the Dead Sea is 70 miles (113 km), but the river winds so much that it is more than twice that long.

Elisha heard what had happened and he sent word to the court. "Let Naaman come to me," he said, "and his wish shall be granted." When Naaman drove up to Elisha's door with his chariot and horses, Elisha remained inside, sending a messenger in his place. "The prophet says you must go down to the River Jordan and bathe seven times in the water. Then you will be cured."

Naaman was outraged. "Why did Elisha himself not speak to me? All he had to do was touch me with his hand and I would have been healed! And why the Jordan? We have greater rivers in my own land." In a fury he turned to leave, but one of his servants stopped him.

"Master," he said. "If the prophet had asked of you some difficult task, you would have done it without question. But all he requires is that you bathe in the River Jordan: should you not agree to this simple instruction?"

Realizing the sense in the man's words, Naaman went down to the river and immersed himself seven times in the water. When he stepped out on the bank after the seventh time, he saw that his skin, which had been covered in sores, was as smooth and clean as a child's.

Overcome with joy, he returned to Elisha to thank him. "Now I know that there is no god but the God of Israel!" He begged Elisha to accept the magnificent presents he had brought with him from Syria. Elisha refused his gifts, but blessed him and sent him on his way.

Naaman is healed in the River Jordan

Conquering Nations

IN THE 600 YEARS between 900 BC and 300 BC, the people of Israel and Judah were conquered by three powerful nations from the east: first the Assyrians, followed by the Babylonians and then the Persians.

The Assyrians

For many years the Assyrians had a powerful and very skilled army. From 750 BC they were a constant threat to Israel and Judah.

The Bible describes the attacks of the Assyrian king, Sennacherib, on the cities of Judah. Many carved stone panels, or "reliefs," have been found in Nineveh, the Assyrian capital city, showing their army, which was well equipped with chariots, bowmen, spearmen, and siege towers.

The Assyrians recorded their history on clay tablets and cylinders. In 1853, archaeologists at Nineveh found a clay tablet describing a great flood that destroyed all life. It is similar in many ways to the story in the Bible about Noah and the ark. The version found at Nineveh is called "The Epic of Gilgamesh," because one of the main characters is Gilgamesh, a hero-king.

THE SIEGE OF LACHISH
The limestone relief below is a detail of the Siege of Lachish, the city that was captured by the army of the Assyrian king, Sennacherib. The story of the battle is told in the wall reliefs, which are from Sennacherib's palace at Nineveh.

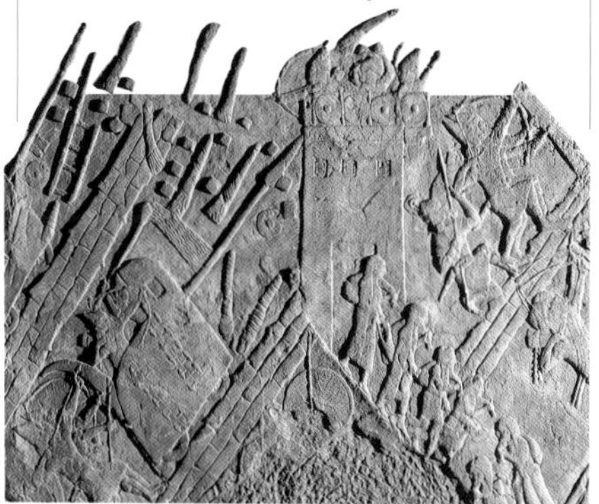

The Assyrians worshiped a god called Ashur, whose main temple was at Assur. The temple at Nineveh was for worship of Ishtar, the goddess of war and love. Other gods were linked to different aspects of life: Nabu with wisdom and Ninurta with hunting.

The Babylonians

Later the Assyrians became less powerful, until in 612 BC the Babylonians captured Nineveh and began to conquer the Assyrian empire. The Babylonian king, Nebuchadnezzar, soon ruled Judah, but when that area became rebellious, he ordered the temple in Jerusalem to be destroyed.

After the destruction of the temple, many people were taken to live in exile in Babylon.

This was in 586 BC. At the same time large numbers of people were forced to live in exile in Babylon. King Nebuchadnezzar made use of the finest craftsmen to rebuild the city of Babylon. The walls and the hanging gardens were among the Seven Wonders of the Ancient World.

The northern entrance to the city was guarded by the Ishtar Gate, which was covered in brilliant blue tiles, decorated with bulls and dragons. Two of the main buildings were a grand palace and a temple dedicated to Marduk. The temple was at the top of a ziggurat, or tower, that stood over 330 feet (around 100 m) high. Some people say that it was the building referred to in the story of the Tower of Babel.

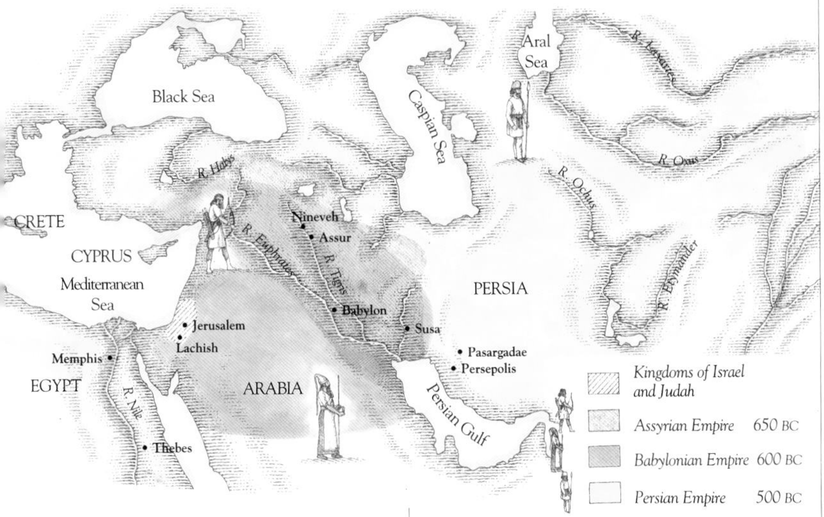

Aral Sea
Black Sea
Caspian Sea
R. Jaxartes
R. Oxus
R. Ochus
R. Halys
CRETE
CYPRUS
Mediterranean Sea
Nineveh
Assur
R. Euphrates
R. Tigris
PERSIA
R. Erymander
Babylon
Jerusalem
Lachish
Susa
Memphis
Pasargadae
Persepolis
EGYPT
ARABIA
R. Nile
Persian Gulf
Thebes
Kingdoms of Israel and Judah
Assyrian Empire 650 BC
Babylonian Empire 600 BC
Persian Empire 500 BC

The map above shows the three nations that conquered the people of Israel between 900 BC and 300 BC.

In spite of the beauty of the city, many of the people who had come from Judah longed for their homeland. They wrote about weeping for Jerusalem as they sat by the River Euphrates, the "waters of Babylon." While in exile, they began to meet together and worship God in buildings which came to be known as "synagogues." But the temple in Jerusalem remained the place where they most wanted to carry out their worship.

THE GATEWAY TO BABYLON

Hanging gardens
Nebuchadnezzar's palace, built around four courtyards
Ishtar Gate, decorated with enamel bricks of bulls and dragons
Walls of the city

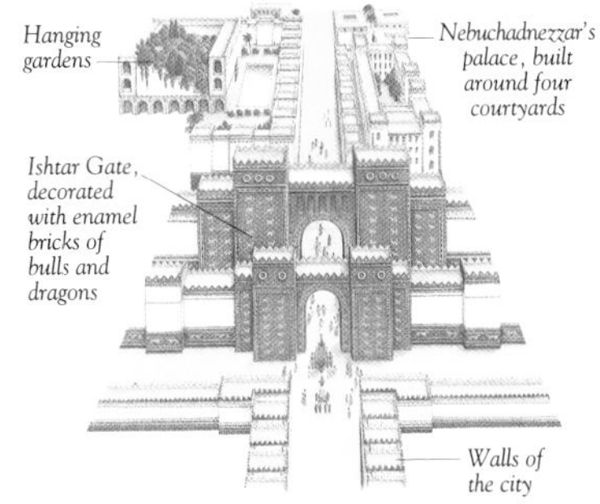

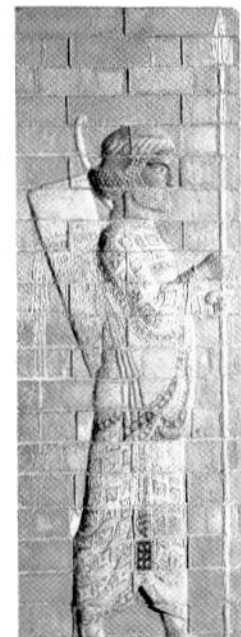

A brick frieze of a Persian guard.

The Persians

Babylonia's glory only lasted until 539 BC when Cyrus the Great, king of Persia, invaded the country and attacked the capital city. He entered it by diverting the River Euphrates and marching his soldiers along the dried-up riverbed. The "Cyrus cylinder" in the British Museum records his feelings: "As I entered Babylon peacefully, and took up my seat of government in the royal palace amid rejoicing and exultation, Marduk, the great lord, inclined the hearts of the Babylonians toward me."

Cyrus controlled an empire that stretched over an area of 3,000 miles (5,000 km) and was divided into 20 provinces. He made the Persian empire richer by avoiding war, and he sent exiles back to their homelands. So, after 50 years, the people of Judah (the Jews) returned to Jerusalem.

The Prophet Isaiah

ISAIAH WAS A PROPHET of the Lord. Through him God spoke to the people. Isaiah warned them what would happen if they failed to obey God's commandments; he told them, too, of the coming of the Messiah, who would bring hope and the chance of salvation to everyone on earth.

One day in the temple in Jerusalem, Isaiah had a vision. He saw God high up on a throne. God's robes were so vast that they swirled and billowed into every corner of the temple. Above were the seraphs: each had six wings, two to cover his face, two to cover his feet, and two to fly. Continuously they sang, "Holy, holy, holy is the Lord!" And at the sound of their voices the chamber shook to its foundations and the room was filled with smoke.

"When I hear these words," Isaiah cried, "I know how unclean are the words that come from my mouth!" As he spoke he saw one of the seraphs take a red-hot coal from the altar and fly toward him. The seraph touched Isaiah's lips with the burning coal, and said, "Now your guilt is burned away and you are without sin."

Then he heard God saying, "Who can I send?"

Isaiah replied, "Here am I: send me."

Isaiah sees a vision in the temple

"You must take my message to the people," said the Lord. "But you will find that at first they will not listen or understand, and they will refuse to be healed."

Isaiah was saddened by God's message. But throughout his life he continued to listen to the word of God. His spirits rose when he heard tell of the time to come, when happiness and joy will be everywhere. The desert will flower, the weak become strong, the lame man leap like a deer. The Lord will walk in the wilderness. God will come down to earth to tend to the people as lovingly as a shepherd tends his lambs, giving them food and water and protecting them from evil. Those who follow in the way of the Lord will be given new strength, and will be safe forever after.

HE SHALL FEED HIS FLOCK LIKE A SHEPHERD: HE SHALL GATHER THE LAMBS WITH HIS ARM, AND CARRY THEM IN HIS BOSOM, AND SHALL GENTLY LEAD THOSE THAT ARE WITH YOUNG.
ISAIAH 40:11

Hezekiah's Gold

THE KING OF ASSYRIA swept through Israel with his army, slaying all who stood in his way, burning crops, laying siege to cities, and taking prisoner anyone who did not escape.

This terrible punishment had fallen on the children of Israel because they had disobeyed the Lord. In recent years they had grown greedy and corrupt; they had ignored the warnings of the prophets, and returned to worshiping false gods. And now their country was occupied, and the ten tribes were forced to work as slaves.

In time a new king ascended the throne of Judah. Hezekiah was not only a wise ruler but a good man who obeyed God's laws. He destroyed the pagan altars and insisted that his people keep the ten commandments. A brave warrior, he had won many victories against his enemies, but not even he could withstand the might of King Sennacherib of Assyria.

HEZEKIAH'S TUNNEL
King Hezekiah once ordered that a tunnel be dug beneath Jerusalem, so that the city's water supply would not be cut off by the invading Assyrians. Today, water still flows through Hezekiah's Tunnel.

Desperate to stop the invaders, Hezekiah sent word to Sennacherib, begging him to withdraw his army. "If you agree to leave my land," he said, "I will pay any price you name."

The Assyrian king demanded huge sums in silver and gold, and in order to find them the precious metals were stripped from the very walls and pillars of the temple. Sennacherib kept the treasure, but broke his promise to go, ordering his soldiers to attack Jerusalem itself. Once the city was surrounded, he sent a message demanding that Hezekiah surrender.

Not knowing where else to turn, Hezekiah went to the temple to pray and ask for help from the prophet Isaiah. "Do not be afraid," said Isaiah. "God will defend you and save the city."

That night the angel of death flew low over the Assyrian camp, leaving many hundreds of thousands dead. In the morning instead of an army, Sennacherib saw only rows and rows of bodies. Turning his back on Jerusalem, he made his way home to Nineveh.

Silver and gold are stripped from the temple

Josiah and the Scroll of the Law

Josiah is only eight years old when he becomes king of Judah

ASHTORETH
This gold pendant (c1500 BC) represents Ashtoreth, or Astarte, the Canaanite goddess of love and fertility, and the partner of the god Baal. Josiah destroyed an altar dedicated to Ashtoreth.

JOSIAH, SON OF AMON, became king of Judah when he was only eight years old. From his earliest childhood he loved God, and when he was a man he gave orders for the temple in Jerusalem, God's house, to be repaired and put in order, for it had grown shabby over the years.

While the work was carried out, the high priest discovered in a corner of the temple the scroll containing God's law, the only copy that the Israelites had. This he took to the royal scribe, Shaphan, asking him to show it to the king. When Josiah heard the scribe read from the scroll, he fell into deep despair, tearing his clothes and weeping with sorrow. "We have forgotten God's law, and grown selfish and corrupt. How angry the Lord must be!" He told Shaphan to find out what fate was in store for his disobedient people.

Shaphan went to Jerusalem to consult Huldah, the prophetess.

"The Lord knows that the people have turned away from the law," said Huldah. "They will be punished for this, and Jerusalem will fall on hard times. But because King Josiah is a good man and has repented of the evil around him, all will be well while he lives."

Repairs on the temple are carried out

The high priest discovers the scroll of the law

Josiah reads the scroll of the law to the people

All the altars and statues of false gods are smashed and burned

THE KING WENT UP INTO THE HOUSE OF THE LORD, AND ALL THE MEN OF JUDAH AND ALL THE INHABITANTS OF JERUSALEM WITH HIM, AND THE PRIESTS, AND THE PROPHETS, AND ALL THE PEOPLE, BOTH SMALL AND GREAT: AND HE READ IN THEIR EARS ALL THE WORDS OF THE BOOK OF THE COVENANT.
II Kings 23:2

When Josiah heard this, he called his people together in the temple, and read to them the scroll of the law. He took an oath that from this day he would keep the word of God; and his people promised that they, too, would obey God's word.

Then Josiah commanded that all the altars and statues of false gods be smashed and burned. "Now my country is cleansed," he said, "and once again we may celebrate Passover." There was much rejoicing in Jerusalem that day, for the Lord was pleased by Josiah's repentance.

Kidron Valley
The Israelites burnt their altars and statues to false gods in the Kidron Valley, on the eastern slopes of Jerusalem. Later, idols were regularly destroyed and left here. The valley is also a place of burial.

Jeremiah and the Potter's Wheel

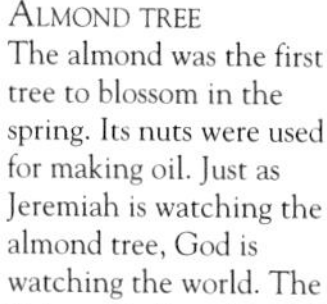

ALMOND TREE
The almond was the first tree to blossom in the spring. Its nuts were used for making oil. Just as Jeremiah is watching the almond tree, God is watching the world. The Hebrew for "watching" is similar to "almond tree."

GOD SPOKE TO A YOUNG MAN called Jeremiah, telling him that he had been chosen as a prophet. "But I am young," said Jeremiah, "and know nothing!"

"Do not be afraid," said the Lord, "for I am with you."

Then God's hand touched the man's mouth. "Now I have put words into your mouth. Tell me, what do you see?"

"I see the branch of an almond tree in bloom."

"Yes, you are right. I am watching to see that my word is fulfilled. What else do you see?"

"I see a boiling cauldron on the fire, tilted toward the north."

"It is from the north that disaster will come, a terrible punishment that will fall upon the land of Judah. For my people have forgotten me, and they worship false gods. You must speak to them, Jeremiah, tell them what I intend. They will turn on you, but you need fear nothing while I am with you!"

Then God sent Jeremiah to the house of a potter, who was at work at his wheel. Jeremiah watched the clay take shape; but the potter saw the shape was lopsided, and taking the wet clay in his hands, squeezed and molded it until he had made the jar perfect.

"Israel is like clay in my hands," said the Lord. "If my people persist in doing evil, they will be destroyed. But if they repent, I will make of them something good and strong. Go, Jeremiah, and tell them this."

The prophet did as God had said. He bought a clay jar; then he summoned the priests and wise men, and led them into the valley of Ben Hinnom.

"You will suffer war, famine, and plague unless you give up worshiping Baal and all your other false gods!" he told them.

In the silence that followed, Jeremiah lifted up the clay jar and hurled it to the ground so that it shattered into a thousand pieces. "Just as I have destroyed this jar, so will God

Jeremiah watches a potter shaping clay at his wheel

Jeremiah hurls a clay jar to the ground

He tells the priests and the wise men that just as he has destroyed the jar, so will God destroy the wicked Judeans

destroy the people of Judah if they do not listen to the Lord's word!"

But the Judeans did not listen, and the day soon came when Jeremiah's prophesy was fulfilled. Nebuchadnezzar, king of Babylon, sent a great army to attack Jerusalem. The city was taken and many of its people were led in chains to Babylon. Nebuchadnezzar chose a new king, Zedekiah, to rule Judah. Zedekiah had to obey the Babylonian king if Jerusalem were to be left in peace.

"Now what do you see?" the Lord asked Jeremiah.

"I see two baskets of figs set down outside the temple. One basket is full of figs that are ripe and juicy, the other full of bruised, rotten fruit that no one would want to eat."

"The Judeans in Babylon are like the ripe figs: they will repent of their sins, and I will bring them out of captivity and look after them well. But King Zedekiah and those Judeans who stayed in Jerusalem will not repent. They are rotten to the core, and nowhere shall they ever find rest or prosperity."

The ripe figs are like the repentant Judeans, while the rotten figs are like those who do not repent

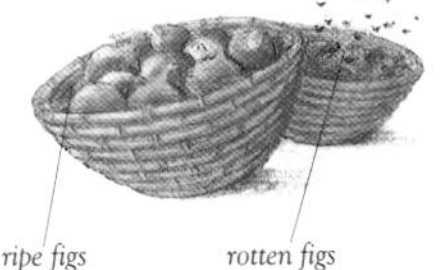

POTTER
Pottery is an ancient craft. This Egyptian figure of a potter at his wheel dates from around 2500 BC. Potters "threw" their clay pots on a wooden or stone wheel. They placed the clay on the wheel, then turned the wheel with their hand or feet as they molded the clay. God compared his control over people to the potter's control of clay.

The Israelites in Captivity

Jeremiah is lowered into a pit by King Zedekiah's men

YEARS PASSED, and the prophet Jeremiah, knowing that Jerusalem was in terrible danger, tried to warn the people. "You will die if you remain here," he said. "Soon the city will be in the hands of the Babylonians, and only those who leave now will survive."

Among those listening were some army officers, and they complained bitterly about Jeremiah to Zedekiah, king of Jerusalem. "It is not for me to interfere," said Zedekiah. "You must do with him as you choose." So the officers seized the prophet, and lowered him by a rope into a deep, dark pit, whose stone floor was thickly covered in mud. There was nothing in the pit either to eat or drink. Ebed-Melech, a member of the royal household, discovered what had happened, and knew that Jeremiah would die if left in captivity. He went at once to the king, who agreed to the prisoner's release.

Ebed-Melech went with thirty men to the dungeon with ropes and a pile of old rags. These he threw down to Jeremiah. "Put the ropes under your arms, and bind them with these rags so that the rope will

ZODIAC SIGNS
The Babylonians are thought to have invented the signs of the zodiac. The picture above shows part of a Babylonian boundary stone, built to honor the military services of a captain of chariots called Ritti-Marduk. The man firing the bow represents the ninth sign of the zodiac, Sagittarius, the archer.

The king relents, and Jeremiah is hauled to the surface

not hurt you." Then they hauled Jeremiah slowly to the surface.

But still Jeremiah's warnings were ignored. Within a short while Nebuchadnezzar, king of Babylon, laid siege to the city. For two years the enemy army surrounded the walls, so that no one could go in or out. The people were sick and starving, and at last in despair they threw open the gates, and Nebuchadnezzar took possession of Jerusalem.

Zedekiah, meanwhile, had fled with a small group of men, but he was soon captured. His sons were killed in front of him, Zedekiah's eyes were put out, and he was led in chains like a slave to Babylon.

On Nebuchadnezzar's orders, the temple and the royal palace and many houses were set on fire, and the city walls razed to the ground. People were rounded up and taken away – only the poor and weak were left behind to scratch what living they could from vineyards and fields.

ISHTAR GATE
This is a detail from the Ishtar Gate, built during King Nebuchadnezzar's reign of Babylon. Its enameled bricks were decorated with lions and bulls.

The Babylonians take possession of Jerusalem and King Zedekiah is led away in chains

Jerusalem is set on fire

The Israelites are rounded up and taken to Babylon

THEY SLEW THE SONS OF ZEDEKIAH BEFORE HIS EYES, AND PUT OUT THE EYES OF ZEDEKIAH, AND BOUND HIM WITH FETTERS OF BRASS, AND CARRIED HIM TO BABYLON.
II KINGS 25:7

The Golden Statue

Daniel tells King Nebuchadnezzar the meaning of his dreams, and in return the king gives Daniel and his three friends important posts

NEBUCHADNEZZAR, king of Babylon, was tormented by bad dreams. He consulted wise men, astrologers, and magicians, but none could tell him what his dreams conveyed. Eventually the king lost patience, and threatened them all with death, but still none was found who could interpret the terrible image of his nightmare.

Among the wise men was Daniel, a Judean who had been captured by the Babylonians. He was one of a group of young noblemen of exceptional intelligence, strength of character, and good looks who had been chosen for special training. They had been taught the language and history of Babylon, and after three years had been taken into the king's service. With Daniel were three others from Judah who were given new names by their captors: Shadrach, Meshach, and Abednego. The four men soon became good friends. They were all clever and quick to learn, but Daniel had a special gift: he was able to interpret dreams.

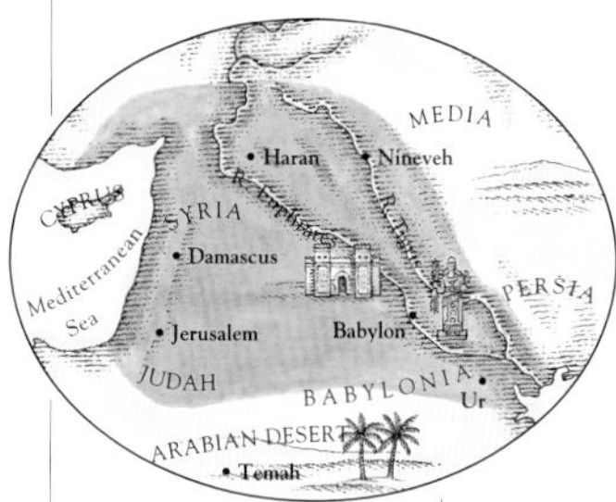

BABYLONIAN EMPIRE Under King Nebuchadnezzar II (605-562 BC), the Babylonian empire expanded until it dominated the ancient Middle East. The Judeans were one of the peoples that were conquered by the Babylonians and moved far from their homeland.

Having been sentenced to death with the others, Daniel went to see the king. "Please, sire, let us have more time. I am sure that I will soon be able to tell you the meaning of your dreams," To this Nebuchadnezzar assented, and Daniel and his three friends prayed to God for help. That night God revealed the secret of the king's dream.

Next day, Daniel went again to Nebuchadnezzar. "God has done what your wise men could not, and shown me the meaning of your dreams.

"As you slept, you saw a gigantic statue towering above you. Its head was sculpted of pure gold, its chest and arms of silver, its belly and thighs of bronze, its legs of iron, and its feet part iron, part clay. Suddenly a stone smashed against the statue's feet, and shattered them – whereupon the entire structure, gold, silver, and bronze, crashed to the ground, reduced to nothing but particles of dust. The wind blew the dust away, and the stone became a great mountain that covered the whole earth.

"I will tell you the meaning of this," said Daniel. "The statue's head of gold represents you, great King, and the parts made of silver, bronze, iron, and clay are the empires which shall come after yours, some strong, some weak and easily divided, none lasting forever. The stone is the kingdom of God; it is greater than any kingdom on Earth, and shall never be destroyed."

Nebuchadnezzar was so impressed with Daniel's wisdom that he knelt before him, swearing allegiance to his God. Loading him with treasure, he appointed Daniel governor of Babylon and chief of all his advisers. He also gave important posts to Daniel's friends, Shadrach, Meshach, and Abednego.

Later, the king gave orders for a statue to be built, ninety feet high, nine feet wide, and made of solid gold. He had it set upon the plain of Dura, and with great pomp and ceremony commanded all his officers, governors, captains, and counselors to come and worship the statue as a god. Only Daniel's three friends refused.

When Nebuchadnezzar learned that his order had been defied, he flew into a rage, and demanded that Shadrach, Meshach, and Abednego be brought before him. "If you do not worship as I tell you," shouted the king, "I will have you thrown into a fiery furnace and burnt to death!"

The king orders that a statue made of solid gold be built and commands everyone to worship the statue

The three men quietly replied, "We will not worship your statue, but our God will save us from the furnace, and protect us even from you, great King. We have nothing to fear."

Nebuchadnezzar, beside himself with rage, had the furnace heated to seven times its usual heat. Then the men, fully clothed, were thrown into the flames. But as he watched, Nebuchadnezzar saw to his astonishment that the three men walked through the fire unharmed, and that beside them stood an unknown fourth man.

"Shadrach, Meshach, and Abednego, come out of the furnace," said the king, his voice full of awe. As they stepped from the flames, everyone saw that not a hair was singed, not a thread of clothing was burnt. Nebuchadnezzar took each in turn by the hand. "From this day, the Jewish people may worship their God, who sent his angel to rescue these men," he vowed. "And I will decree that my people, too, shall worship only your God." Then he embraced the three friends, and gave them positions of great power in the government of Babylon.

THEN NEBUCHADNEZZAR CAME NEAR TO THE MOUTH OF THE BURNING FIERY FURNACE, AND SPAKE, AND SAID, "SHADRACH, MESHACH, AND ABEDNEGO, YE SERVANTS OF THE MOST HIGH GOD, COME FORTH, AND COME HITHER." THEN SHADRACH, MESHACH, AND ABEDNEGO CAME FORTH OF THE MIDST OF THE FIRE.

DANIEL 3:26

The three friends walk through the fire unharmed, while beside them stands an unknown fourth man

King Nebuchadnezzar calls to the three men to come out of the furnace

Belshazzar's Feast

King Belshazzar

King Belshazzar suddenly sees before him a hand, writing on the plaster of the wall

BELSHAZZAR, THE NEW KING OF BABYLON, gave a great feast. He gave orders that the gold and silver cups which his father, Nebuchadnezzar, had plundered from the temple in Jerusalem, should be used as goblets for wine.

As Belshazzar and his friends shouted and laughed and drank toasts to their gods, suddenly they saw before them a hand writing on the white plaster of the wall. The king turned pale, his knees shook, and in a faint voice he called for a wise man to tell him what the words meant. But no one could do so. Then the queen spoke. "Let Daniel be called: he will know what this means."

Daniel looked carefully at the writing on the wall: MENE, MENE, TEKEL, UPHARSIN. He said, "MENE means 'number': the days of your reign are numbered. TEKEL means 'weight': you have been weighed in the moral balance and found wanting. UPHARSIN means 'division': your kingdom will be divided between the Medes and the Persians."

That very night Belshazzar was put to death, and Darius, king of the Medes, took possession of the kingdom of Babylon.

IN THE SAME HOUR CAME FORTH FINGERS OF A MAN'S HAND, AND WROTE OVER AGAINST THE CANDLESTICK UPON THE PLAISTER OF THE WALL OF THE KING'S PALACE: AND THE KING SAW THE PART OF THE HAND THAT WROTE.
DANIEL 5:5

Daniel in the Lions' Den

MEDES
The Medes were closely related to the Persians, and joined forces with them in conquering Babylon. The gold plaque above dates from around 400-300 BC. It shows a Mede, possibly a priest, dressed in a tunic and trousers and wearing a soft, pointed cap.

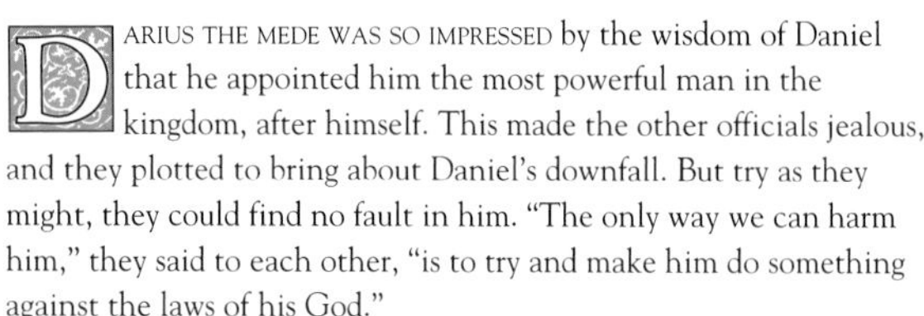

DARIUS THE MEDE WAS SO IMPRESSED by the wisdom of Daniel that he appointed him the most powerful man in the kingdom, after himself. This made the other officials jealous, and they plotted to bring about Daniel's downfall. But try as they might, they could find no fault in him. "The only way we can harm him," they said to each other, "is to try and make him do something against the laws of his God."

At their request, Darius issued a ruling that for the next thirty days no one should pray to any god, but only to the king himself. Any man found disobeying the new law would be thrown to the lions.

Daniel heard of this, but continued to pray to God three times a day before his open window, which looked toward Jerusalem and was in full view of the street. His enemies gathered outside to watch, then went off triumphantly to report him to the king.

Darius was dismayed that his favorite, Daniel, should have been made a victim of his law, but there was nothing he could do to save him. With a heavy heart, he gave the order for Daniel to be thrown into the lions' den. "Your God will save you," he said to Daniel, and turned away to hide his sorrow. The entrance was then sealed with a heavy stone. That evening Darius refused both food and drink, and lay all night unable to sleep.

Early the next morning the king hurried to where the lions were penned. "Daniel, Daniel," he called. "Has your God protected you?"

"The Lord sent his angel to stand beside me, and the lions have left me untouched."

Darius was overjoyed, and at once gave the order for Daniel's release. Daniel was lifted out of the lions' den unharmed and unafraid, for he knew that God was with him.

Then Darius had all the conspirators arrested, with their wives, and commanded them to be thrown to the lions. At once the beasts fell on them, savagely tearing them apart until there was nothing left of them but bones.

Daniel disobeys the new law by continuing to pray to God

King Darius goes to the lions' den and is overjoyed to find that Daniel is unharmed

MAN-EATING LION
This Phoenician ivory shows a lioness gripping a man by the neck. In the ancient Middle East, people were sometimes executed by being thrown to the lions.

Esther Becomes Queen

Many young women receive beauty treatments so that the king might choose a new queen

Esther comes before King Xerxes, and he chooses her to be his queen

COSMETICS
Esther may have used cosmetics such as the ones above. Mulberry juice was used to redden cheeks, kohl to outline the eyes, and henna to color the palms of the hands.

PERFUME MAKING
In ancient times, one way of making perfume was to drop flower petals and seeds into hot olive oil. The oil was strained and then left to cool.

XERXES, ALSO KNOWN AS AHASUERUS, was a powerful king who ruled over the entire Persian empire from India to Ethiopia. In the third year of his reign he gave a great feast, which lasted for over a hundred days. The marble pillars of his palace were hung with silk, and the floors covered in silken carpets, even the beds were made of silver and gold. His guests drank priceless wines from golden goblets studded with jewels.

One night, Xerxes sent for Vashti, his queen, for he wanted to show his guests how beautiful she was. But Vashti refused to appear. At this the king fell into a fury, and gave orders that Vashti should no longer be regarded as his wife. Messengers were sent in every direction to bring to the palace numbers of beautiful maidens so that the king might choose for himself a new queen.

Now in the royal household there was a Jewish man named Mordecai. He had brought up as his own daughter a cousin called Esther, a young girl of outstanding loveliness. When all the candidates were gathered together Esther was among them, and with her sweet nature she soon won favor with the keeper of the women's apartments. Mordecai visited her every day. He impressed on her the importance of never revealing that she was from Judah, for he was afraid that the king would not favor a Jewish girl.

For twelve months the women were tended with the greatest care, bathed in oil of myrrh, massaged with costly creams, their faces expertly painted, their hair brushed until it shone. One by one they were sent in to be inspected by the king. When it came to Esther's turn, he knew he had found the woman he wanted. Without wasting more time, Xerxes married her and crowned her queen.

One day, during the course of his duties, Mordecai overheard two men plotting to assassinate the king. He told Esther; she at once informed her husband, who had the culprits arrested and hanged.

Xerxes made one of his officials, Haman, chief of all his ministers, and commanded his subjects to bow before him. This Mordecai refused to do. Haman, enraged by the man's stubbornness, determined to take his revenge not only on Mordecai but on the entire Jewish people. He told the king that these people were different, they did not obey his laws, and should be destroyed. Xerxes told Haman to deal with them as he wished, and gave him his signet ring. Haman issued an order, sealed with the king's ring, that on an appointed day every Jewish person – man, woman, and child – should be put to death.

Mordecai, appalled and terrified, went to Esther and told her what was planned for their people. He begged her to plead with her husband to spare them. "It is for this purpose that you have become queen."

"Pray for me," said Esther. "I will go to the king, and if I die, I die."

XERXES I
The Persian king who married Esther was Xerxes I, called Ahasuerus in the Bible. His reign lasted from 486-463 BC. This Persian silver statue, probably of a king, dates from about this time.

Mordecai

Haman

Mordecai refuses to bow before Haman, chief of all the king's ministers

Haman is angry and decides to seek revenge

Esther Saves Her People

Xerxes, unable to sleep, asks that the book of records be read to him

DRESSED IN HER CEREMONIAL ROBES, Esther appeared in the audience hall before the king. From his throne, Xerxes stretched out to her his golden scepter as a sign of favor. "Whatever it is you desire, my queen, shall be yours."

"I ask that you and Haman dine with me tomorrow."

Haman was delighted by the queen's invitation, but meanwhile gave the order to build the gallows from which to hang Mordecai.

Xerxes, meanwhile, could not sleep, and to pass the hours until dawn asked that the book of records be read to him, from which he discovered that Mordecai had never been rewarded for uncovering the plot against his life. "How should I reward a man I wish to honor?" he asked Haman.

Haman, believing the king was referring to himself, replied, "Such a man should be proclaimed a hero. He should be dressed in royal robes, crowned with a golden crown, and led around the city on the king's own horse."

"Then in this way shall I reward Mordecai," said Xerxes, to Haman's dismay.

The next day both the king and Haman dined with Esther, who lost no time in begging a favor of her husband. "Speak, and it shall be granted," said Xerxes fondly.

"My people and I are to be destroyed: we have been bought as slaves, and now we are to be put to death like animals. I implore you to save our lives!"

Xerxes, appalled, demanded to know who was responsible for giving such an order.

"Someone you trusted but who has betrayed your trust," said Esther. "I am speaking of Haman, who is sitting beside you."

PRISONERS' FATE
This carving shows Judean prisoners being impaled on stakes. In the Bible it says that Haman was hanged on the gallows. As hanging was not common in Persia, it is possible that Haman met the same fate as these prisoners.

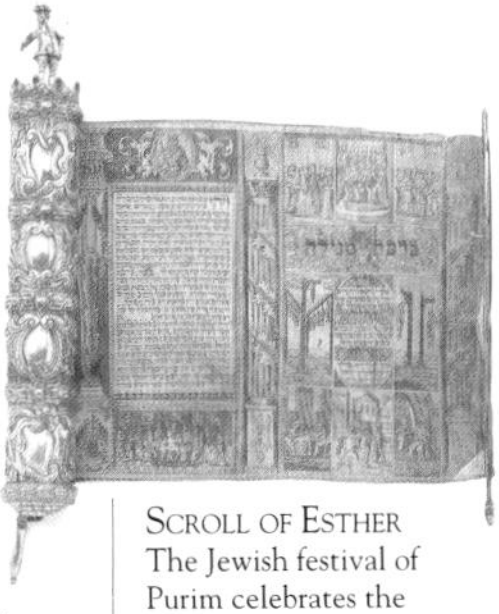

Xerxes was so shocked and angry he was unable to say a word. Leaving the table, he strode out into the garden. Haman, completely taken by surprise, went cold with horror. Suddenly realizing the danger he was in, he flung himself at Esther's feet to beg for mercy. The king came back into the room at that same moment, and believing that Haman was attacking his wife, had him arrested. Haman was hanged on the very same gallows that had been built for Mordecai.

Unable to reverse a royal proclamation, Xerxes sent out messengers to every city and province from India to Ethiopia to tell the people that the Jewish people everywhere must be honored and respected, and that they had the right to defend themselves as they saw fit on the day appointed for their destruction. Ever after the Jewish people have celebrated this deliverance, exchanging gifts and giving to the poor.

SCROLL OF ESTHER
The Jewish festival of Purim celebrates the story of Esther. A scroll containing the book of Esther is read in the synagogue. The scroll's case is often ornate, like the silver one above. Every time Haman's name is read, all the people boo and stamp their feet.

Xerxes is shocked and angry to hear what Haman has done

Haman goes cold with horror

Esther accuses Haman of giving the order to destroy her people

The Rebuilding of Jerusalem

King Artaxerxes notices that his cupbearer, Nehemiah, looks unhappy

SOMETIME EARLIER, Cyrus, king of Persia, had proclaimed that any captive Judeans who wished to return to Judah should be given their freedom. The king had also sent back the silver and gold treasure that had been plundered from the temple by the Babylonians.

The Jewish people who had returned to Jerusalem were saddened to see the state that the city had fallen into – the walls in many places reduced to rubble, the gates blackened by fire. Several of them went to see Nehemiah, cupbearer to Artaxerxes, who was now the king of Persia, to tell him of their damaged city. Nehemiah was so grieved at what he heard that he was unable to hide it from the king while serving wine that evening.

"Why do you look so unhappy?" Artaxerxes inquired. "Are you ill?"

"No, sire," said Nehemiah, "I am not ill, but my heart is breaking because I have been told that Jerusalem, the city of my ancestors, lies in ruins. I beg you to let me go there so that I may start the work of rebuilding." To this Artaxerxes gave his consent, sending with Nehemiah an escort of armed men and letters to the local governors asking them to give him any help he needed.

After Nehemiah had been in Jerusalem for three days, he rode on a donkey by night around the city to see for himself what needed to be repaired. Accompanied by only a few men, he inspected tumbled-down walls and gates that had been half destroyed by fire. Then he summoned the people. "Come, let us rebuild Jerusalem! The condition of our once-great city is a disgrace! Let us pray to God to help us in our work."

Nehemiah gathered together all the volunteers and organized parties of laborers, and gave them directions. But there were some who jeered at his efforts, and threatened to put a stop to the work.

"What do these Israelites think they are doing? Do they really believe that their feeble efforts will make walls out of rubble?"

Some of the men were discouraged, but Nehemiah reassured them.

SILVER CUP
As cupbearer, Nehemiah may have served wine in a silver, horn-shaped cup, such as this one, tasting the wine first to check for poison. A cupbearer held a position of trust, and Nehemiah would have been an influential friend of the king.

"Do not be afraid," Nehemiah told his men, "for the Lord is with us, and will protect us." Then he gave spears and shields to half his workforce, and they protected the other half while the repairs were made. And in fifty-two days the work was done.

Nehemiah rides on a donkey by night and inspects the ruined walls of Jerusalem

STONEMASON
Nehemiah would have employed skilled stonemasons to help rebuild Jerusalem. The mason hammered wooden pegs into holes in the rock, then poured water over the pegs. The wood then swelled, causing the stone to split. The mason sawed and trimmed the block with a pick. Stonemasons still practice in parts of the Middle East today.

Jonah and the Great Fish

SPERM WHALE
The "fish" that swallowed Jonah may have been a sperm whale. These whales are known to visit the eastern Mediterranean Sea. With their large throats, they can swallow the body of a man whole.

GOD TOLD HIS PROPHET, Jonah, to go to Nineveh, and warn the people there to turn away from their wickedness. But Jonah disliked the Ninevites and did not want them to hear God's message, so he went instead to Joppa. There he found a berth on a ship sailing to Tarshish. As soon as the ship put out to sea, God sent a great wind that whipped the water up into a storm, and it seemed that the ship would break apart. The sailors, terrified, threw everything they could overboard to lighten the load.

The captain went below, where he found Jonah fast asleep. "Wake up, and pray to your God to save us!" he cried. Meanwhile, the sailors on deck were drawing lots to discover who among them was the cause of the storm. The name drawn was Jonah's.

"Yes," he said. "I am the cause of the trouble. I am an Israelite, and I ran away from the Lord. Throw me over the side, and the storm will die down." At first the men hesitated, and tried to row the ship toward the shore, but the waves grew

The sailors throw Jonah overboard

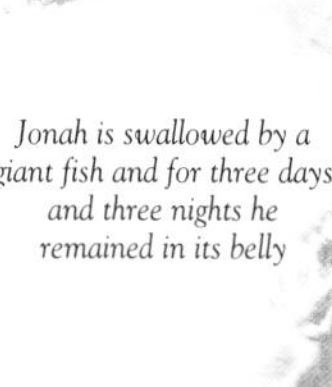

Jonah is swallowed by a giant fish and for three days and three nights he remained in its belly

higher and the wind screamed louder, and they took hold of Jonah and threw him into the sea. At once the wind dropped and the water grew calm.

As Jonah swam in the sea, he was swallowed by a giant fish. For three days and nights he remained in its belly, praying to God and thanking the Lord for keeping him alive, until the fish vomited Jonah onto dry land.

Again the Lord told Jonah to go to Nineveh, and this time he went, and warned the people that their city would be destroyed. The king and all his subjects, knowing that they had done wrong, begged God to spare them and promised that they would mend their ways. God heard their prayers and resolved not to harm them.

Jonah, however, was angry that the city was to be spared.

The fish vomits Jonah onto dry land

As Jonah watches over Nineveh, God makes a vine grow to shade him from the sun, but then causes it to wither and die

He built himself a shelter outside the city walls, meaning to stay there until Nineveh fell. God, watching over him, made a vine grow up to shade Jonah from the sun. But the next morning God sent a worm that fed on the roots of the vine until it withered and died. The sun grew hot, and a stifling wind blew from the east, until Jonah was suffering so much he wished himself dead. "Why are you angry that the vine has withered?" God asked him. "Why do you care about a vine that you neither planted nor watered, while you resent my care for the well-being of a city of thousands of souls?"

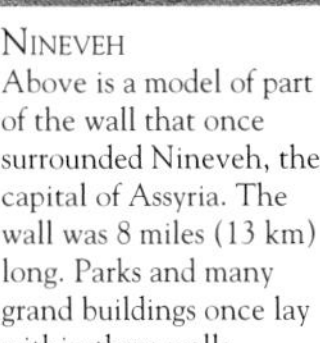

NINEVEH
Above is a model of part of the wall that once surrounded Nineveh, the capital of Assyria. The wall was 8 miles (13 km) long. Parks and many grand buildings once lay within these walls.

The Book of Psalms

King David is thought to have written many of the psalms

PSALMS ARE SONGS AND POEMS that praise and honor God. Many are thought to have been written by David, who was a poet, singer, and musician, and was known as the "sweet psalmist of Israel." The psalms cover a wide range of thought and feeling. They praise God as creator, as in psalm 8, and as protector, as in psalm 121 and psalm 23, which compares God to a shepherd, looking after his people in the same way that a shepherd watches over his sheep.

Psalm 8

O Lord our Lord, how excellent is thy name in all the Earth!
Who hast set thy glory above the heavens.
Out of the mouth of babes and sucklings hast thou ordained strength because of thine enemies,
That thou mightest still the enemy and the avenger.
When I consider thy heavens,
The work of thy fingers,
The moon and the stars,
Which thou hast ordained;
What is man, that thou art mindful of him?
And the son of man, that thou visitest him?
For thou hast made him a little lower than the angels,
And hast crowned him with glory and honor.
Thou madest him to have dominion over the works of thy hands;
Thou hast put all things under his feet,
All sheep and oxen,
Yea, and the beasts of the field;
The fowl of the air, and the fish of the sea,
And whatsoever passeth through the paths of the seas.
O Lord our Lord, how excellent is thy name in all the Earth!

Psalm 23

The Lord is my shepherd; I shall not want.
He maketh me to lie down in green pastures,
He leadeth me beside the still waters.
He restoreth my soul.
He leadeth me in the paths of righteousness for his name's sake.
Yea, though I walk through the valley of the shadow of death,
I will fear no evil, for thou art with me;
Thy rod and thy staff they comfort me.
Thou preparest a table before me in the presence of mine enemies,
Thou anointest my head with oil;
My cup runneth over.
Surely goodness and mercy shall follow me all the days of my life,
And I will dwell in the house of the Lord forever.

THE LORD IS MY SHEPHERD; I SHALL NOT WANT. HE MAKETH ME TO LIE DOWN IN GREEN PASTURES.
PSALMS 23:1-2

Psalm 121

I will lift up mine eyes unto the hills,
From whence cometh my help.
My help cometh from the Lord,
Which made Heaven and Earth.
He will not suffer thy foot to be moved,
He that keepeth thee will not slumber.
Behold, he that keepeth Israel shall neither slumber nor sleep.
The Lord is thy keeper: the Lord is thy shade upon thy right hand.
The sun shall not smite thee by day, nor the moon by night.
The Lord shall keep thee from all evil,
He shall keep thy soul.
The Lord shall guard thy going out,
And thy coming in from this time forth,
And even forevermore.

Psalm 23 compares God to a shepherd

THE NEW TESTAMENT

AND THERE CAME A VOICE
FROM HEAVEN, SAYING,
"THOU ART MY BELOVED SON
IN WHOM I AM WELL PLEASED."

MARK 1:11

THE NEW TESTAMENT

GALILEE, WHERE JESUS GREW UP, is a hilly area at the heart of which is the Sea of Galilee, a huge freshwater lake. In Jesus' time there were a number of thriving communities, such as Capernaum, Bethsaida, and Tiberias, around the shores of the lake. There were also several important trade routes through the area. This brought the Galileans into contact with people from many countries. Even those who lived in hill villages would have met foreign travelers in the lakeside towns.

Together with other Jewish people from Galilee, Jesus and his family traveled to Jerusalem in Judea for major festivals, such as Passover. The long journey, on foot or donkey, would have taken them south along the fertile Jordan valley, avoiding Samaria, to the low-lying area at the north end of the Dead Sea. They would have gone along a road that climbed, steeply in places, until they reached Jerusalem. The city would have been hidden from their view until, from across a valley, they would have seen the breathtaking sight of the city, dominated by the magnificent new temple. Alongside it was the Fortress of Antonia, which was the base for the Roman garrison.

Judea, the region in which Jerusalem was situated, was ruled when Jesus was older by a Roman governor called Pontius Pilate, who spent most of his time at a palace in the coastal town of Caesarea, only going to Jerusalem when necessary. Jerusalem was the most important Jewish religious center. It was very crowded during Jewish festivals, but it was always busy with merchants traveling there from different parts of the Roman empire. It was along the trade routes, which led to and from the city, that the first Christians traveled to tell people around the Mediterranean Sea about Jesus.

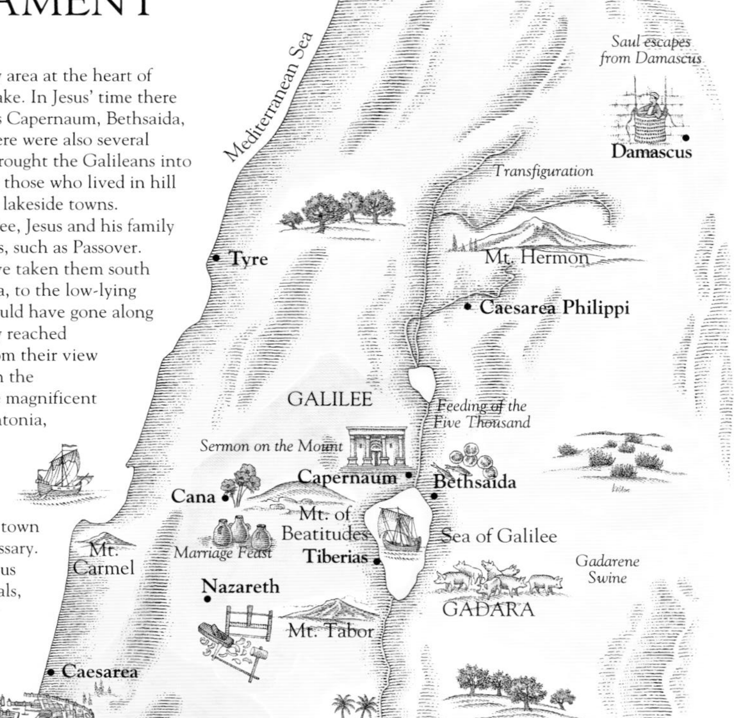

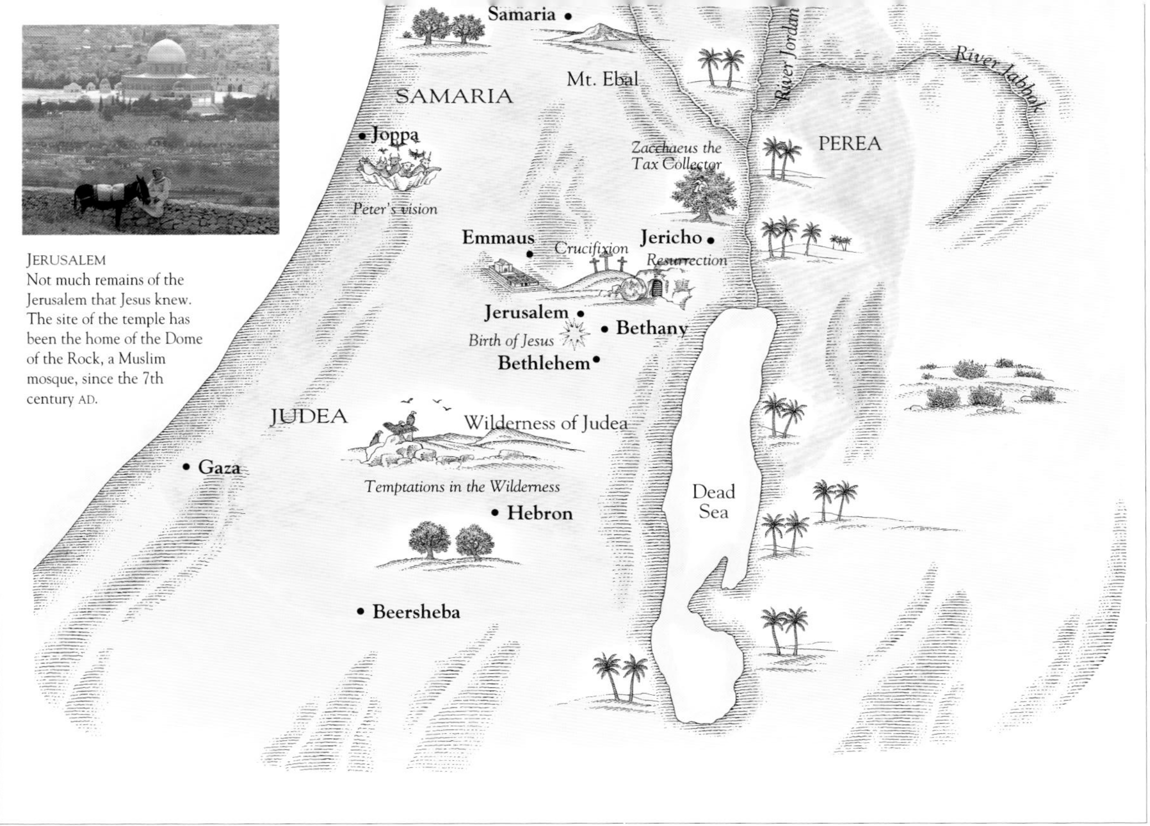

JERUSALEM
Not much remains of the Jerusalem that Jesus knew. The site of the temple has been the home of the Dome of the Rock, a Muslim mosque, since the 7th century AD.

WHEN JESUS WAS BORN, Palestine was part of the Roman empire, which was ruled by the emperor Augustus Caesar. He allowed a king named Herod the Great to rule the area. After Herod died in 4 BC, three of his sons – Antipas, Archelaus, and Philip – were made kings over parts of Palestine. Herod Antipas was given Galilee, where Jesus was brought up. He was the king who executed John the Baptist. Archelaus was given Judea and Samaria. Philip ruled in the northeast.

RULERS IN THE TIME OF JESUS

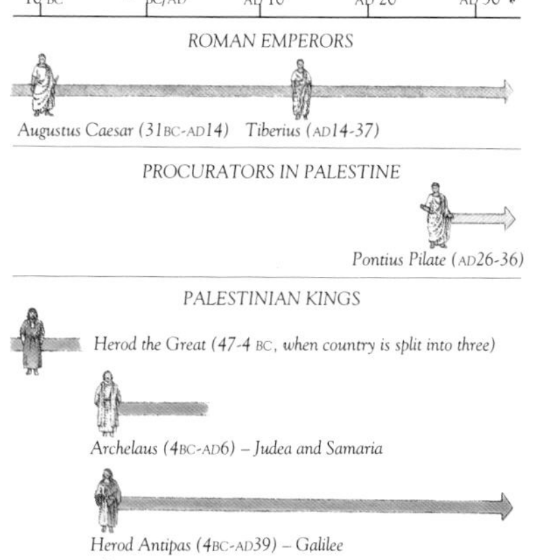

The chart shows the various rulers of Palestine during Jesus' lifetime. The procurators were Roman officers in an imperial province; the kings were appointed by the Romans to oversee smaller areas.

Herod the Great and his sons were not popular with the Jewish people; the Romans were even less popular because their soldiers occupied and ruled the land. Some groups, like the Zealots, tried to fight the Romans without success.

Worship At The Time Of Jesus

In most towns there was a synagogue, a building where Jewish people met for many reasons, but especially to worship God and to study the Torah, the Hebrew Testament. Children would go to the synagogue to be taught to read and write Hebrew in order to understand Jewish religious teachings. The synagogue served the social as well as religious needs of the community.

INSIDE THE SYNAGOGUE
By New Testament times the synagogue existed in many major cities throughout the Roman empire. It was run by an elected committee, and had no priests and offered no sacrifices. It was common practice to invite visitors to the synagogue to read from the Scriptures.

For example, funds were distributed by the synagogue committee to those in need.

When praying, men wore blue-striped shawls with knotted tassels to remind them of God's commands. When it wasn't the Sabbath or a holiday, they wore phylacteries on the head and left arm. These were leather devices to which were attached little boxes containing verses from the Bible. Phylacteries are still worn today by some Jews. One box is placed on the forehead, the other on the upper arm, near the heart. This is a sign that God's teachings are controlling the person's thoughts and feelings.

Phylacteries are worn on the head and left arm.

Jerusalem: The Religous Center

At festivals families would try to travel to Jerusalem. This was the most important place for Jewish worship because Herod's Temple was there. In the temple, priests offered sacrifices of animals, vegetables, or incense at the altar, especially at times of thanksgiving or sadness.

Some ceremonies could only be carried out by the high priest, the main religous leader. In the time of Jesus, the Romans took away some of the power of the high priest and even kept his special robes locked away for much of the year. In spite of this, the high priest and the Sanhedrin, a council of religious leaders, had great influence over the Jewish people.

The high priests were disliked by many Jewish people because they were appointed by the Romans, or by the king, who was also chosen by the Romans. To keep their positions, they had to do what the Romans wanted. The high priest who supervised the trial of Jesus was Caiaphas; also involved was his father-in-law, Annas, a former high priest.

PLAN OF THE CITY OF JERUSALEM

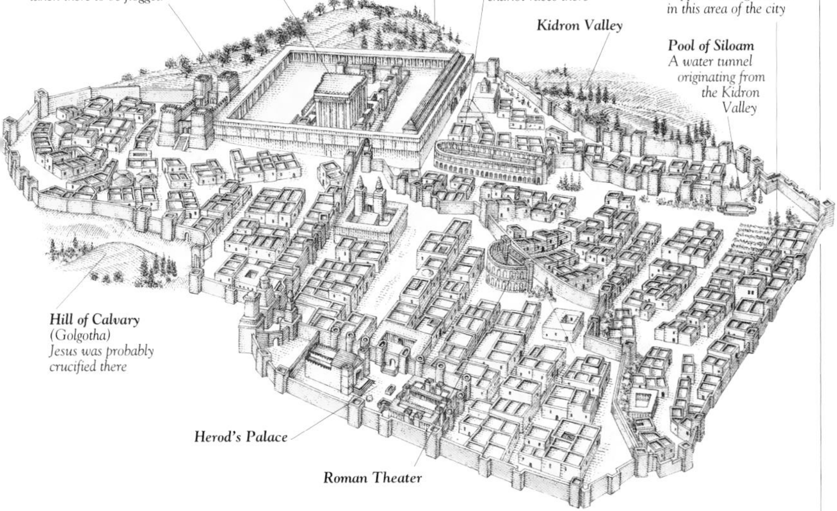

JERUSALEM FROM THE MOUNT OF OLIVES
The Mount of Olives, where Jesus went to pray in the Garden of Gethsemene, was outside the city walls. The Mount was opposite the eastern wall of the Temple, now the site of the Dome of the Rock.

The Temple
First built by Solomon, but destroyed. Rebuilt by Herod the Great. Jesus taught there

Garden of Gethsemane
Where Jesus was arrested

Fortress of Antonia
The Roman garrison next to Herod's temple. Paul was taken there to be flogged

Mount of Olives

Roman Hippodrome
The Romans held chariot races there

The Upper Room
The room of the Last Supper is thought to be in this area of the city

Kidron Valley

Pool of Siloam
A water tunnel originating from the Kidron Valley

Hill of Calvary
(Golgotha)
Jesus was probably crucified there

Herod's Palace

Roman Theater

A Son for Zechariah

ALTAR OF INCENSE
As a priest, Zechariah would probably have burnt the incense on a four-horned altar, such as the one above. These altars were also thought of as safe places. If a person grasped one of the horns, then the holiness of the altar protected them from harm. It was a great honor for Zechariah when he was chosen to offer incense. It would have been the only time he was allowed to enter the temple sanctuary, or holy place.

"FEAR NOT, ZECHARIAH: FOR THY PRAYER IS HEARD; AND THY WIFE ELIZABETH SHALL BEAR THEE A SON, AND THOU SHALT CALL HIS NAME JOHN. AND THOU SHALT HAVE JOY AND GLADNESS; AND MANY SHALL REJOICE AT HIS BIRTH."
LUKE 1:13-14

An angel appears before Zechariah and tells him he will have a son

Zechariah does not believe the angel, and is struck dumb

IN THE DAYS OF KING HEROD, there lived in Judea a priest named Zechariah. He and his wife Elizabeth were good people, who had always obeyed the word of God. Their one sorrow was that they were childless. Now they were growing old, and had given up all hope of ever having a family.

INCENSE SHOVEL
Zechariah may have used an incense shovel, such as the one above, to carry burning coals to the altar. Incense was sprinkled on the coals to produce a fragrant smoke. The rising smoke symbolized the prayers of the people going up to God.

There came a time when Zechariah, serving at the temple in Jerusalem, was chosen by lot to burn incense in the sanctuary. This was at an hour when the people were praying in an outer courtyard.

As Zechariah stood watching the fragrant smoke rise from the altar, he saw an angel standing before him. Frightened, he stumbled back, but the angel spoke to him gently.

"I am Gabriel," he said. "I have come from the Lord to bring you good news. Your prayers shall be answered, and your wife will give birth to a son, whose name shall be John. He will be a great joy to you both, and will bring much happiness and peace to the world. He will be great in the eyes of the Lord, and through him many people will turn to God."

"But how can this happen?" Zechariah exclaimed in disbelief. "After all, I am an old man, and my wife Elizabeth is past the age to bear children."

"I am an angel of the Lord," said Gabriel sternly. "I have been sent by God to speak to you and tell you this good news. Because you have doubted my word, which will be fulfilled in its own time, you will be unable to speak until what I have told you comes true."

Meanwhile, the crowd outside began to grow restless, wondering why the priest was so long in the temple before coming out to them. When Zechariah finally appeared, he could not say a word: all he could do was make gestures, and the people quickly realized that he must have seen a vision.

Having completed his duties, Zechariah returned home to his wife, and as the angel predicted, Elizabeth soon became pregnant. She stayed quietly at home, rejoicing that God had chosen her to bear this child.

Unable to speak, Zechariah makes gestures to the people

An Angel Appears to Mary

NAZARETH
Mary and Joseph lived in Nazareth, in the northern province of Galilee. This little town lay in a sheltered valley set in hills about 5 miles (8 km) from the important trading town of Sepphoris. Above is Nazareth today, with the Church of the Annunciation in the center of the picture. The Annunciation – the announcing – refers to the angel Gabriel's words to Mary, when he tells her that she will be the mother of Jesus.

AND THE ANGEL SAID UNTO HER, "FEAR NOT, MARY: FOR THOU HAST FOUND FAVOR WITH GOD. AND, BEHOLD, THOU SHALT CONCEIVE IN THY WOMB, AND BRING FORTH A SON, AND SHALT CALL HIS NAME JESUS."
LUKE 1:30-31

IN THE TOWN OF NAZARETH in Galilee, the angel Gabriel appeared to a young woman called Mary. Mary was promised in marriage to Joseph, who was descended from the family of David.

"The Lord is with you!" said Gabriel. "You are the most fortunate of women!"

Mary was troubled by the angel's greeting, and wondered why he had come to see her. "Do not be afraid," Gabriel reassured her. "God has chosen you to be the mother of a child, a son, who shall be called

Mary is troubled by the angel's greeting, and wonders why he has come to see her

Jesus. He will be great and his kingdom will never end."

"But how is this possible?" Mary asked. "I am still a girl, and not yet married."

"The Holy Spirit will come to you, and God's grace will be with you, for your child will be known as the Son of God."

At these words, Mary knelt before Gabriel, and with head bowed, replied, "I am obedient to God's will, and shall be prepared for whatever you wish me to do."

She looked up, but the angel had gone.

The angel Gabriel tells Mary that she will give birth to a son, who will be called Jesus

ANGEL GABRIEL
This page from an illuminated manuscript shows the angel Gabriel appearing to Mary. Gabriel was an archangel, or angel of high rank. He brought messages to God's people about the coming of the Messiah, the saviour promised by God. Gabriel is one of three angels, the others being Michael and Raphael, who are mentioned by name in the Bible.

The Birth of John

Mary visits Elizabeth at her home in Judea

MARY HURRIED INTO the hills of Judea to visit her cousin Elizabeth. As Mary entered the house and called out in greeting, Elizabeth felt the baby leap for joy in her womb. She felt the presence of God all around her, making her aware that the woman standing in front of her was the mother of the son of God.

"You are the most blessed of all women!" Elizabeth exclaimed. "When I heard your voice, I felt my baby move inside me. How honored I am that you have come here to be with me!"

Then Mary sang a song of praise:

"My soul sings of the glory of the Lord,
And my spirit rejoices in God who is my saviour.
He has looked with kindness on me, his devoted servant,
And because he has honored me, future generations will bless my name.
He is always merciful to those who love and obey him,
But he humbles the proud and the hard-hearted.
Always he feeds the hungry, but to the rich and greedy he gives nothing.
The Lord is great and holy is his name."

FLAT-ROOFED HOUSES
The houses in Judea and the surrounding area were built of mud bricks, or rough stones as in the picture above. People found the flat roofs of the houses useful. They could dry fruit and grain on them, as well as dry their clothes. In hot weather they might even sleep out on the roof.

Mary stayed with Elizabeth for three months, then returned home to Nazareth.

Soon afterward, Elizabeth gave birth to a son. There was great rejoicing by all her family and neighbors that God should have shown her such favor. On the eighth day, the time came for the baby to be circumcised.

"He must be called Zechariah, after his father," said her relations.

"No," said Elizabeth. "His name is John."

"But no one in your family is called John," they said, and they turned to Zechariah to ask what he wanted to call the child.

Zechariah, who still could not speak, signaled for writing materials. Then to the surprise of those around him, he wrote in large letters, HIS NAME IS JOHN. At that same moment he found he could talk, and at once started to thank God and to sing hymns of praise.

Soon the story had spread throughout the Judean hills that a holy child had been born to Elizabeth. All who heard knew that this was a great event, and that the Lord was with the child John.

Zechariah writes a message that they must call his son John

EN KEREM
The pretty little town of En Kerem, whose name means "vineyard spring," is set in the Judean hills. It is traditionally believed to be the hometown of Zechariah and Elizabeth, and the birthplace of John the Baptist.

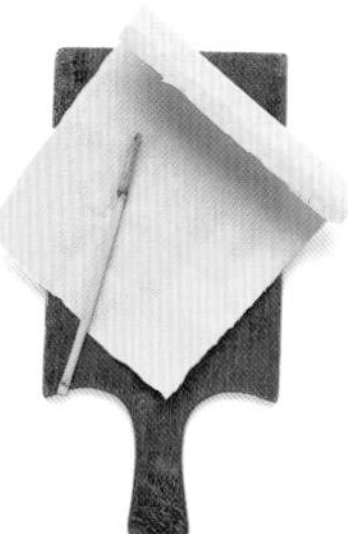

WRITING TOOLS
Zechariah may have written his message on paper made from the dried stems of the papyrus plant. He would have used a reed pen dipped in black ink to write with.

The Birth of Jesus

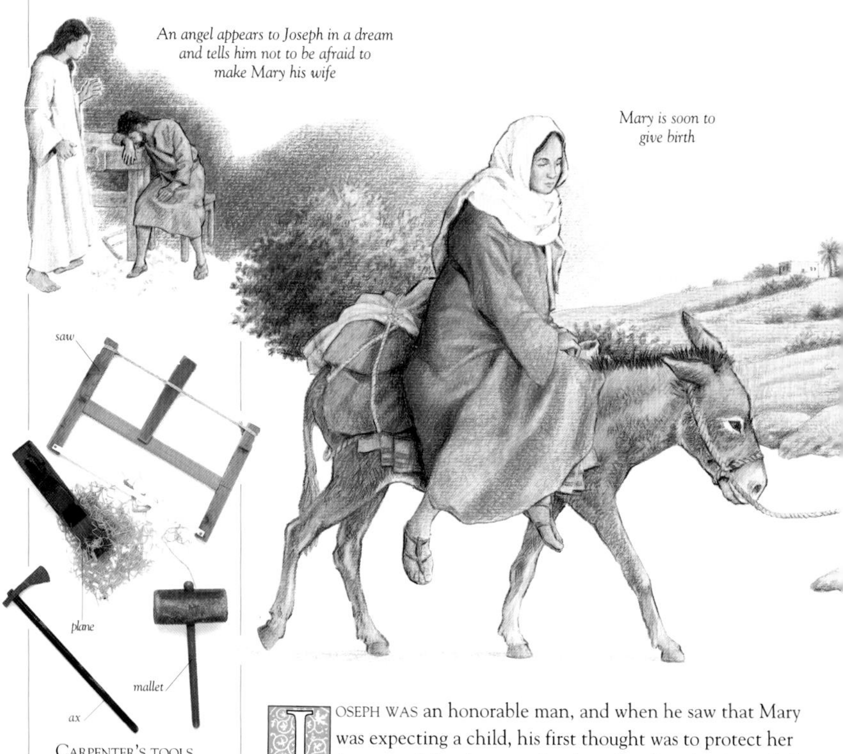

An angel appears to Joseph in a dream and tells him not to be afraid to make Mary his wife

Mary is soon to give birth

CARPENTER'S TOOLS
As a carpenter, Joseph would have used tools, such as the ones above, to make furniture, doors, farm tools, carts, and to repair houses. Joseph would have passed on the skills of his trade to Jesus.

JOSEPH WAS an honorable man, and when he saw that Mary was expecting a child, his first thought was to protect her from scandal and to quietly release her from her betrothal. But an angel came to him and said, "Do not be afraid to take Mary for your wife. She has conceived this child by the Holy Spirit. She will give birth to a son, whose name shall be Jesus."

Soon after Joseph and Mary were married, the Emperor Augustus passed a law that everyone should return to their hometown so that a count could be made of every person in the empire. Joseph went with

Joseph travels with Mary to Bethlehem in Judea

RIDING ON A DONKEY
Traditionally, Mary is thought to have ridden on a donkey from Nazareth to Bethlehem – a distance of about 70 miles (110 km). Donkeys were the most common form of transportation in Jesus' time, and were used by both rich and poor people.

SHE WRAPPED HIM IN SWADDLING CLOTHES, AND LAID HIM IN A MANGER; BECAUSE THERE WAS NO ROOM FOR THEM IN THE INN.
LUKE 2:7

Mary lays the baby Jesus in a manger

Mary, who was soon to give birth, to Bethlehem in Judea.

When at last they arrived, they found the city full of people. The streets were crowded, and every house and lodging already full. Joseph, anxious because he knew that the time of the baby's birth was near, searched and searched, but could find nowhere to stay. Eventually, worn out by their journey, they took shelter in a stable, and there during the night Mary's son was born. She wrapped him in strips of linen, as was the custom, and gently laid him in a manger, where the animals fed. There was nowhere else for the baby to sleep.

The Shepherds' Visit

SHEPHERD'S TOOLS
Shepherds would often have to stay out all night, keeping watch over their flocks. They kept warm by wearing camel-hair cloaks, or cloaks made from sheepskin, like this present-day shepherd's coat. A shepherd could use the hook on the end of his crook to pull or lift a sheep out of danger. His wooden rod had pieces of flint or nails driven into the end. He used this to drive away wild animals. He could use the wooden feeding bowl to bring water to an injured sheep.

THE ANGEL OF THE LORD CAME UPON THEM, AND THE GLORY OF THE LORD SHONE ROUND ABOUT THEM: AND THEY WERE SORE AFRAID
LUKE 2:9

IN THE FIELDS NEAR BETHLEHEM there were shepherds, tending their flocks. Suddenly a brilliant light blazed through the darkness, and an angel appeared. The shepherds, terrified, hid their eyes, but the angel reassured them. "I bring you good news, today in Bethlehem a child has been born, who will be the saviour of all people. You will find him in a manger." Then the night sky was filled with heavenly beings, and the angels sang in praise of God. They spoke of peace on earth and friendship between everyone.

"We must go at once to see the child," the shepherds said. They hurried to the town where they soon found Mary, Joseph, and the baby in the stable. Excitedly, they described what they had seen and heard, and went away praising God. Only Mary was silent, thinking quietly to herself of all that had happened.

Angels appear to the shepherds and bring news of Jesus' birth

AND THEY CAME WITH HASTE, AND FOUND MARY AND JOSEPH, AND THE BABE LYING IN A MANGER.
LUKE 2:16

The shepherds hurry to Bethlehem, where they find Mary and Joseph with the baby Jesus

The Presentation in the Temple

"LORD, NOW LETTEST THOU THY SERVANT DEPART IN PEACE, ACCORDING TO THY WORD: FOR MINE EYES HAVE SEEN THY SALVATION."
LUKE 2:29-30

Mary and Joseph watch as Simeon takes the baby Jesus in his arms

EIGHT DAYS AFTER HE WAS BORN, the baby was circumcised and given the name Jesus, as the angel had instructed. Mary and Joseph then took him to Jerusalem to present him to the Lord, and to make an offering, which according to custom could be either a pair of doves or two young pigeons.

In Jerusalem there lived a man called Simeon, a good man who had led a holy life. God had said to him that he would not die before he had set eyes on the Messiah. When Mary, carrying her child, and Joseph entered the temple, Simeon was already there. He had been guided by the Holy Spirit, and knew at once that he was in the presence of the saviour promised by God.

Taking Jesus gently in his arms, he gave grateful thanks to the Lord. "O Lord, now I may die in peace, for you have granted me what my heart most desired. Now I have seen with my own eyes the child who is to be a glory to all people!"

As he spoke, a very old woman came shuffling out from the shadows. Her name was Anna, and she had lived nearly all her life in the temple, spending every day and most of the night in fasting and prayers. She, too, thanked God that she had been allowed to see the child, and told all who could hear that Jesus would be the saviour of Jerusalem.

Mary and Joseph stood amazed as they listened to what was said about the child. Then, when all had been done, they left Jerusalem and returned home.

OLD AGE
Anna was an old prophetess who prayed and fasted in the temple day and night. Her holiness was rewarded when she saw Jesus in the temple. In the Bible, age is a sign of wisdom and goodness. To reach old age is seen as a blessing from God.

Anna comes forward to see Jesus

The Wise Men

> NOW WHEN JESUS WAS BORN IN BETHLEHEM OF JUDEA IN THE DAYS OF HEROD THE KING, BEHOLD, THERE CAME WISE MEN FROM THE EAST TO JERUSALEM, SAYING, "WHERE IS HE THAT IS BORN KING OF THE JEWS? FOR WE HAVE SEEN HIS STAR IN THE EAST, AND ARE COME TO WORSHIP HIM."
> **MATTHEW 2:1-2**

Wise men arrive from the east and are sent for by King Herod

Herod questions the wise men closely about the star they have seen over Bethlehem

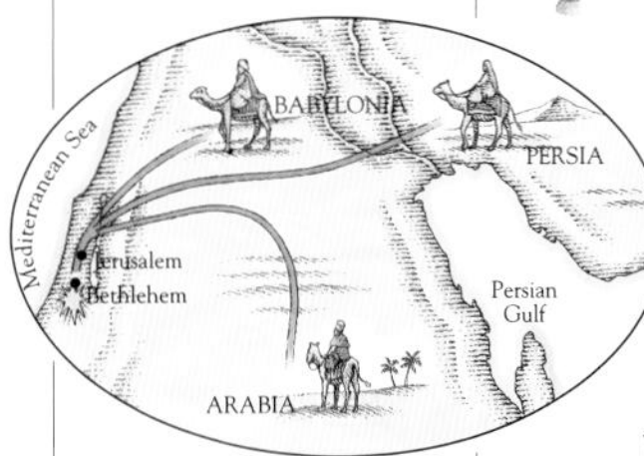

FROM THE EAST
It is not known where the wise men, or magi, came from. One idea is that they journeyed from Persia, Babylonia, and Arabia. They may have been astrologers, who read the stars for signs and omens. The wise men represented the Gentiles, or nonJewish people, who would worship Jesus.

EWS OF THE BIRTH of Jesus spread far and wide. A group of wise men traveled from the east to Jerusalem. When they arrived, they asked everyone, "Where is the child? Where is the one who has been born king of the Jews? We have seen his star and have come to worship him."

Now Herod was king of Judea, and stories soon reached his ears of the coming of the messiah, a child born to rule. Deeply troubled and determined to put to death any rival, he summoned together all the priests and lawyers of the Jewish people, and asked them in what city the child was to be born.

"In Bethlehem," they told him.

Then privately, Herod sent for the wise men, and pretending to be as religious as they, questioned them closely about the star: where they had seen it, what time it had appeared. "Go to Bethlehem," he said. "Make a thorough search for the child, and when you have found him, come and tell me, for I, too, wish to go and worship him."

So the wise men left Jerusalem and took the road for Bethlehem. The star guided them all the way, until, as they drew near the walls of the little town, it shone even brighter and stopped quite still over the place where Jesus was.

As they entered the house, they saw Mary and her small child, and falling to their knees, they worshiped him. Then they opened the heavy boxes they had carried with them, and spread out on the floor the magnificent gifts they had brought. They gave the baby Jesus gifts of gold, frankincense, and myrrh. Then, having been warned in a dream not to return to Herod, they went back to their own countries by another route.

THREE WISE MEN?
This mosaic showing the wise men is in Ravenna, Italy. The Bible does not say how many wise men there were, but the common belief is that there were three, because of the three gifts they carried with them.

The wise men bring gifts of gold, frankincense, and myrrh

They enter the house and see Mary and her child, Jesus

THREE GIFTS
The wise men brought gifts of gold, frankincense, and myrrh. Frankincense was a perfumed resin, burned in honor of God. Myrrh was a scented gum used to prepare the body for burial. The gifts had symbolic meanings. Gold honored Jesus as a king, frankincense honored Jesus as God, and myrrh was a sign that Jesus was a man and would die.

The Flight into Egypt

Joseph, Mary, and the child Jesus leave Bethlehem during the night and head for Egypt

SOON AFTER the wise men had left, an angel appeared to Joseph in a dream. "Take Mary and the child and go at once to Egypt. There is no time to lose. Herod's men are searching for the child, and if they find him, they will kill him."

At this Joseph awoke, and told Mary what they must do. Quietly they crept out of the house, and in the darkness made their way through the narrow streets of the town and out into open country. The journey took many days, but at last they arrived safely in Egypt; and there they stayed.

Herod, meanwhile, realized that the wise men had tricked him and would not be returning to tell him where Jesus was. He fell into a passionate rage, and screamed at anyone who dared come near, threatening with fearful punishment those who stood in his way. Summoning the officer of his guard, he gave an order that every male child in and near Bethlehem under the age of two years should be put to death. And this was done.

Soon after Herod himself died. Again the angel came to Joseph while he slept. "Your enemies are no more," he said. "It is now safe for you to return to your homeland." So the family left Egypt. But when Joseph learned that Herod had been succeeded by his son, Archelaus, as ruler of Judea, he was afraid. So they traveled farther north, and settled in the city of Nazareth in Galilee.

Mediterranean Sea
Nazareth
R. Jordan
Jerusalem
Bethlehem
EGYPT
NEGEV
SINAI

JOURNEY TO SAFETY
Mary and Joseph faced a difficult journey across 75 miles (121 km) of desert land before they reached Egypt, a country often used as a place of refuge. After Herod's death, the family went to Nazareth in Galilee.

On Herod's orders, every male child in Bethlehem under the age of two years is put to death

Jesus Is Found in the Temple

BAR MITZVAH
Jesus went to Jerusalem when he was 12, a time when he was preparing to become a Jewish adult. Today, a Jewish boy will celebrate his *bar mitzvah*, when, at the age of 13, he enters Jewish life as an adult.

EVERY YEAR AT THE FESTIVAL OF PASSOVER, Joseph and Mary went to Jerusalem, as was the custom. When Jesus was twelve, they took him with them. After the celebrations had finished, they set off for home, making the long journey, as they always did, with a party of friends and relatives. They had been on the road for a whole day before they realized that Jesus was not with them. At first they thought he must be with some of their friends' children; but he was nowhere to be seen.

Anxiously Mary and Joseph returned to Jerusalem, and for three days they searched the city without success. Desperate with worry they decided to go to the temple. And there they saw Jesus. He was sitting in the middle of a group of wise men and teachers, talking,

Jesus sits in the middle of a group of wise men, talking

listening, and answering questions. All these distinguished men were amazed at the wisdom and understanding of this child of twelve.

"How could you have left us like that?" his parents asked him. "Why did you not tell us where you were going to be? For three days we have been searching everywhere for you."

"But why did you need to search?" said Jesus, puzzled. "Did you not know that I would be in my father's house?"

Mary and Joseph did not understand what he meant by this. Then Jesus left the temple, and returned with his parents to Nazareth and was obedient to them.

HEROD'S TEMPLE
Herod's temple was the center of Jewish religious life. It was built by Herod the Great on the site of Solomon's temple. Herod, wishing to win favor with the Jewish people, had wanted the temple to be as splendid as Solomon's. Work began in 20 BC. The temple opened in 9 BC, but was not completely finished until AD 64. Six years later it was destroyed by the Romans. The temple was built of cream-colored stone, and had marble columns. It shone so brightly in the sun that people found it difficult to look at it directly (see page 17).

Mary and Joseph, who have been searching for Jesus, find him in the temple

The wise men and teachers are amazed at the wisdom and understanding of Jesus

AFTER THREE DAYS THEY FOUND HIM IN THE TEMPLE, SITTING IN THE MIDST OF THE DOCTORS, BOTH HEARING THEM, AND ASKING THEM QUESTIONS.
LUKE 2:46

John Baptizes Jesus

People flock to hear him

John preaches to the people to repent

DEEP IN THE WILDERNESS OF JUDEA, John the Baptist wandered from place to place, preaching. He wore only a rough coat made of camel's hair and a leather belt, and he lived on locusts and wild honey. "Repent! Repent!" he urged all who would listen. "Turn away from wickedness. The day of God's kingdom will soon be here!"

People flocked to hear him, pouring out in great crowds from Jerusalem and the Jordan Valley and all the towns of Judea. "What must we do?" they asked.

"Give as much as you can to others, do not hurt anyone, and never be false," he told them.

Group after group came to confess their sins, after which John baptized them in the River Jordan. "I baptize you with water," he told them. "But one will come after me who will baptize you with the fire of the Holy Spirit! He is a man so good and pure that I am unworthy even to unfasten his sandals."

"Are you Christ?" they asked him.

"No, I am the forerunner of Christ, the voice of one crying in the wilderness."

Jesus came from Galilee to hear the preacher, and to be baptized in

DESERT FOOD
John the Baptist ate locusts and wild honey in the desert. The honey would have been made by wild bees. They were common in Palestine, and nested in holes in rocks and trees. Locusts contain fat and protein, and are often eaten in areas where meat is scarce. They can be fried, boiled, dried, or eaten raw. Honey may be added to take away the bitterness.

The people come to John to be baptized in the River Jordan

John baptizes Jesus

the Jordan. But John said, "It is not right that I should do this. It is you who should baptize me."

"Let us do what God asks of us," Jesus replied, and he walked down to the banks of the river and into the water. As soon as John had baptized Jesus, the sky opened, and the Holy Spirit appeared in the form of a dove, and the voice of God was heard, saying, "This is my beloved son, in whom I am well pleased."

BAPTISM
Ritual cleansing was important to Jewish people. When John baptized people by lowering them into the water, he was obeying Jewish law, but giving it a new meaning. The purpose of John's baptisms was to rid people of wrongdoing, in expectation of Jesus' coming. Today, baptism is practiced by many Christians throughout the world upon entering into the Christian faith.

DOVE
At Jesus' baptism, the Holy Spirit took the form of a dove, and this bird has remained a symbol of the Holy Spirit. The dove also symbolizes peace, love, gentleness, and forgiveness.

The Temptations in the Wilderness

DEVIL
The devil has often been portrayed as a winged creature with horns, as in this ceiling painting. In the Bible, the devil, or Satan, opposes God in every way.

JESUS WENT INTO THE WILDERNESS for forty days to fast and pray, alone except for the wild beasts and birds of the desert. At the end of this time, he was exhausted and faint from hunger. Then the devil came to tempt him. "If, as you claim, you really are the son of God," said Satan, "then turn these stones into bread!"

"The scriptures say that man cannot live on bread alone, but must find strength from God's words," said Jesus.

Satan made a second attempt. Taking them to Jerusalem, he led

Jesus is alone, except for the wild beasts and birds of the desert

The devil tempts Jesus to turn stones into bread

Jesus up to the highest point on the temple roof. "Throw yourself down from here," he said. "The son of God, so we are told, is surrounded by angels, and cannot come to harm."

"Scripture says you shall not put God to the test," said Jesus.

Then the devil took Jesus to the top of a high mountain, and from there showed him all the kingdoms of the world. "I will make you lord of these lands," said the tempter, "if you will only kneel down and worship me!"

"Get behind me, Satan!" Jesus shouted. "It is God alone whom you should worship!"

At these words, the devil disappeared, knowing he was defeated. Angels then appeared from out of the sky to tend to Jesus.

JUDEAN WILDERNESS
The wilderness of Judea is a wild and lonely area west of the Jordan Valley. Alone in the desert, Jesus showed great strength in the face of temptation.

On the top of a mountain the devil tempts Jesus with the kingdoms of the world

The devil tempts Jesus to throw himself down from the temple roof

JESUS ANSWERED HIM, SAYING, "IT IS WRITTEN, THAT MAN SHALL NOT LIVE BY BREAD ALONE, BUT BY EVERY WORD OF GOD."
LUKE 4:4

Jesus of Galilee

JESUS GREW UP IN THE town of Nazareth, in a northern area of Palestine called Galilee. The people there had a reputation for being independent and strong-minded. They spoke with their own accent, which meant that in Jerusalem everybody could tell that Jesus and most of his friends came from Galilee.

Jesus was born in Judea, in the small town of Bethlehem, about 100 miles (160 km) to the south of Nazareth. However, most of the events of his adult life – healing the sick, the miracles, the sermon on the mount – took place in Galilee.

No one knows the exact date of Jesus' birth, but it was probably what we now call 5 or 4 BC, in the reign of the Roman emperor, Augustus.

The map of Galilee, above right, shows the area in which Jesus grew up and the main places connected with his ministry.

Jesus was brought up by his mother, Mary, and by her husband, Joseph, a carpenter. In their workshop in Nazareth they would have made and mended wooden items such as doors, carts, ladders, tools, and even bowls. They probably traveled around Galilee doing building work.

What was Jesus Like?

Down the centuries artists have shown Jesus in paintings, mosaics, carvings, and stained-glass windows. The way he appeared depended on the idea of Jesus the artists wanted to portray. For example, sometimes they emphasized his strength, sometimes his gentleness. In reality, he probably would have had dark hair and dark eyes. Because of his work as a carpenter, his shoulders would have been broad and his arms strong.

Jesus was Jewish. He and his family went to the synagogue at Nazareth, where each Sabbath (from dusk on Friday to dusk on Saturday) services were held and words were read from the

Torah, the first five books of the Bible. Jesus would have learnt about the rest of the Jewish Bible, what Christians call the Old Testament, together with other important Jewish writings. When he was 12 years old, he impressed the teachers in the temple in Jerusalem by his learning and wisdom.

At the age of 30, Jesus began to attract large crowds who came to hear him teach about God and to see him heal the sick. He mixed with all kinds of people, and could be serious and funny, blunt and kind.

The Son of God

Jesus made enemies because he claimed that he was the Son of God. However, many believed he was the Messiah, the special person whom God had promised to send into the world and whom the Hebrew prophets had predicted would lead Israel to greatness.The death of Jesus is important to Christians because they believe that, in dying, he was showing God's love for all people. For this reason the cross became the main symbol of Christianity. Christians believe, however, that death did not put an end to Jesus, but that his spirit lives on, especially through his followers.

SEA OF GALILEE

Many of the events of Jesus' life took place on the shores and in the towns around the Sea of Galilee. This freshwater lake, set between high hills, is called by several different names in the Bible, including the Lake of Gennesaret, and the Sea of Tiberias.

In Jesus' day, the Sea of Galilee was a rich source of fish. It was on the shores of the lake that Jesus found his first disciples – the fishermen Peter, Andrew, James, and John.

Friends and Followers

The first followers, or disciples, of Jesus were fishermen from Galilee. For three years these 12 men, who came to be known as his apostles, left their homes and jobs to travel with him to teach people about God. They were his close companions.

The first disciples called by Jesus were fishermen.

Three of Jesus' closest friends lived just outside Jerusalem, at Bethany. They were Martha, her sister Mary, and their brother Lazarus. When Jesus was in Jerusalem he often stayed at their house. Jesus had another friend called Mary, who came from Magdala on the western shore of the Sea of Galilee. She had led a life of which people disapproved, but Jesus helped her to make a fresh start. She was devoted to him and when he was crucified, she stayed near his cross with Mary, the mother of Jesus, and Mary, the mother of the disciple James.

There were several women among Jesus' close friends.

Jesus had followers from all walks of life: from tax collectors, such as Matthew, to wealthy, powerful people, such as Joseph of Arimathea, who was a member of the Sanhedrin, the Jewish council. It was Joseph who provided a tomb for Jesus to be buried in. Jesus turned no one away. He even showed compassion to Roman soldiers, who were hated by many for ruling over their land.

Jesus helped people from many different backgrounds.

Daily Life in Jesus' Time

MANY OF THE EVENTS of Jesus' life, and many of the stories – or parables – that he told, took place in and around the simple homes in which ordinary people lived.

Jesus used the parables to teach people about God in a way that they would understand and remember. His stories often reflected features of people's everyday lives, such as farming, fishing, working in the vineyards, shepherds and their flocks, and other things that would have been familiar to them.

SIMPLE HOUSES
There were different types of houses in Palestine at the time of Jesus. Many people lived in small one-room buildings like the ones shown above, which are in Judea.

Where and How People Lived
Galilean villagers often worked in their own houses, or in the fields and vineyards nearby. Many were fishermen on the Sea of Galilee. Although the houses of wealthier people would have had several rooms, ordinary mud-brick houses often had just one room downstairs with a raised section for cooking, eating, and sleeping. The cool, dark room, or rooms, inside the houses were lit by high, small windows, and by oil lamps. Animals were kept in a courtyard by those who could afford them, but household animals were often kept in the lower part of the house at night. Outside, stairs or a ladder led up to the flat roof where the family sometimes slept or spent time, and where they dried crops, such as grapes or flax. The roof was usually made of branches covered with a mixture of clay and straw. These could be cut away, as in the story of the men who break up the roof of a house to lower their friend down to Jesus.

In Jesus' story of the lost coin, the woman may have had trouble finding the coin in the straw spread for the animals in the house.

At the Festival of the Tabernacles (*Sukkoth*), families built shelters on the roof in thanksgiving to God for protecting them and fulfilling their needs. This festival came at harvest time and the shelter was decorated with leaves and fruit as a reminder of God's provision for his people.

Women and the Work They Did
It was a woman's duty to look after the home. She would prepare and cook the food, and bake the bread daily. She also spun, wove and made clothes, and worked in the fields at harvest time. Women made daily trips to the well for drinking water, which they carried back in large jars.

Larger houses with two floors had an outside staircase leading to the second floor.

The Farmer's Year

Jesus often referred to farming in his parables. For example, he compared the word of God to seed that a sower scatters on the ground; he once said that he was as close to his followers as a

PLOWING THE LAND
Jesus usually preached in the open air, so he may have been watching a farmer at work in the fields as he told his stories.

vine is to its branches; he also told people that God would decide who was in his Kingdom just as a farmer has to separate the wheat from the weeds, and the grain from the chaff.

The farmer's year started in October, when the fields were plowed for the two main cereal crops – barley and wheat. Farmers used wooden plows, sometimes drawn by oxen. After this, the seed was sown by hand over the plowed earth. In the new year, flax was harvested, followed by wheat and barley in April or May. The grain was cut with a sickle and tied into sheaves. Stalks were then beaten (threshed) with a stick to loosen the grain, and finally they were tossed in the air with a wooden fork – a process called winnowing.

Parable of the sower

Many of the Jewish festivals marked important times of the year for those who worked in the fields. The Feast of Passover was celebrated during the barley and flax harvest in March or April. Fifty days later, at the end of the grain harvest, the Feast of Pentecost was celebrated to thank God for the gifts of the harvest.

Winnowing fork

A Shepherd's Work

Shepherds often looked after both sheep and goats. Their job was to lead their flocks to fresh pasture and water, and to protect them from wild animals. In one parable Jesus tells of a shepherd who searches for his lost sheep. This story shows that God cares for people as a shepherd cares for his sheep.

Parable of the lost sheep

WORKERS IN THE VINEYARD
Vines were pruned from June through August. Then, in August and September, fruits, such as figs, pomegranates, and grapes, were picked.

MATTHEW 4, 9, 10; MARK 1, 2, 3; LUKE 5, 6

Jesus Calls His Disciples

Jesus tells Peter and Andrew to cast their nets into the water, and the nets fill with fish

JESUS WAS LIVING and teaching in Capernaum, a town by the Sea of Galilee. One day, as he was walking by the shore, he saw two fishing boats drawn up on land, their owners nearby, cleaning and mending their nets. Jesus stepped onto the nearest boat, and began talking to the crowds that soon gathered. After a while he said to the boat's owner, Simon Peter, "Let us go out a little way onto the lake."

When they were a short distance from land, Jesus told Simon Peter and his brother, Andrew, to throw their nets into the water. "But there are no fish," they said. "We have fished all night, and caught nothing."

However, they did as Jesus told them, and to their astonishment their nets filled instantly with such a weight of fish that they were unable to pull them up. They signaled to their partners in the other boat to help them, and together they hauled the nearly breaking nets on board.

When the two brothers saw the miraculous catch, they and their friends, James and John, the sons of Zebedee, fell down on their knees, terrified. But Jesus said, "Do not be afraid. Come, follow me, and I will make you fishers of men and women." So having brought their boats back to shore, they left their nets and the tools of their trade and followed Jesus.

Jesus traveled with his disciples throughout Galilee, preaching in the synagogues, spreading the word of God, and treating the sick. Men and women with every kind of illness and disease – some paralyzed, some epileptic, others racked with pain or tormented by horrific dreams – all came to be healed. People came from far and wide to hear him speak, not only from Galilee itself, but from Jerusalem, Judea, and from way beyond Jordan.

One day Jesus passed a man called Matthew, a collector of taxes.

FISHING
Fishing was an important industry around the Sea of Galilee. Lines and hooks were sometimes used, as above, but nets were more common. At least four of Jesus' 12 disciples were fishermen.

He worked for the ruling Romans and so was distrusted by the people. Jesus said to him, too, "Come, follow me." And Matthew, without a word, left his post and followed him.

When Jesus returned to his house and sat down to dinner with his companions, a throng of people came to join him, many of them well-known as sinners. The Pharisees, shocked to see this good man in such bad company, questioned some of his friends. "Why does your master mix with rascals like these?" But Jesus heard their sneering words, and replied, "It is not the healthy who need a doctor, but the sick: I have not come to ask good men to change their ways, but the sinners, for it is they who need me."

Jesus asks Matthew, a collector of taxes, to come and follow him

Jesus went alone to the top of a high mountain, where he stayed all night in prayer. The next day he called his followers together, and chose twelve of them to be his disciples. To each one he gave special powers of preaching and healing. The twelve were: Simon Peter and his brother, Andrew; James and John, the sons of Zebedee; Philip, Bartholomew, Thomas, Matthew the tax collector, James, Thaddaeus, Simon the Zealot, and Judas Iscariot.

AND HE SAITH UNTO THEM, "FOLLOW ME, AND I WILL MAKE YOU FISHERS OF MEN."
MATTHEW 4:19

Jesus chooses twelve disciples, to whom he gives special powers of preaching and healing

The Marriage Feast of Cana

WATER JARS
Stone jars, like the ones above, were used for carrying and storing water. The larger jars could hold up to 30 gallons (115 liters).

IN THE TOWN OF CANA in Galilee there was a wedding. Jesus and his mother, Mary, were invited, and so were the twelve disciples. The guests were sitting down to the feast when Mary noticed that the jugs were already empty. She whispered to her son, "There is no more wine." She then told a servant who was standing nearby to do whatever Jesus said.

Now standing against the wall were some huge stone water jars, used in the religious rituals of ceremonial washing, each so big that two men were needed to carry it. Jesus beckoned the servant to him. "Fill those jars with water," he told him; and when the jars had been

Mary and the disciples accompany Jesus to the wedding

Mary

bride

Jesus

servant

stone water jars

Jesus tells a servant to fill some stone jars with water and to take them to the guest of honor

filled to the brim, Jesus said, "Now take some to the guest of honor so that he may taste it."

The most important guest, sitting close to the bridegroom, did not know where this wine had come from, but at the first sip he knew it was exceptionally good. Rising to his feet, he drank a toast. "You are a generous man!" he said to the bridegroom. "Most people give good wine at the start of a banquet, then let us get drunk on the poor stuff. But you have kept the best till last!" And he threw his head back and happily swallowed a great mouthful of wine.

The miracle at the wedding in Cana was the first that Jesus worked. In this way he revealed his heavenly glory, and strengthened the disciples' faith in him.

CANA
The town of Cana is traditionally thought to be Kefar Kana, shown above. The town lies in a valley north of Nazareth, in Galilee. It is surrounded by olive and pomegranate trees. Two churches have been built there to commemorate Jesus' miracle.

The guest of honor toasts the bridegroom for keeping the best wine till last

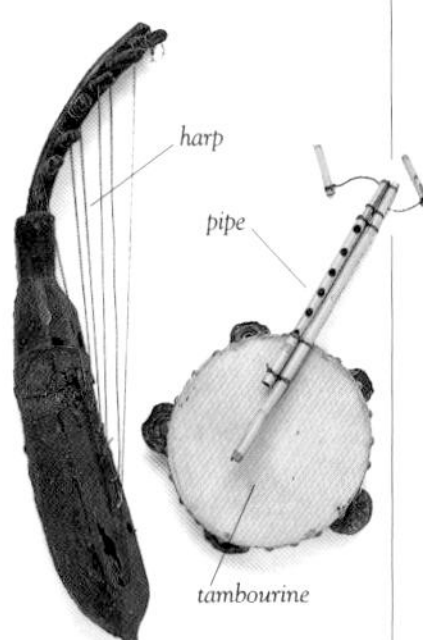

MAKING MUSIC
Musicians often played at Jewish wedding feasts. Harps were usually played with a plectrum, or pick. The musicians would play their pipes and tambourines as the women danced and sang.

The Sermon on the Mount

Jesus preaches on the mountainside

The crowds gather and listen to Jesus' words

BLESSED ARE THE POOR IN SPIRIT: FOR THEIRS IS THE KINGDOM OF HEAVEN. BLESSED ARE THEY THAT MOURN: FOR THEY SHALL BE COMFORTED. BLESSED ARE THE MEEK: FOR THEY SHALL INHERIT THE EARTH.
MATTHEW 5:4-5

THE CROWDS WHO CAME to hear Jesus were very great. So that everyone could see and hear him, he went a little way up the mountainside. This is what he said:

Blessed are the gentle, for they shall inherit the earth. Blessed are the merciful, for they shall be shown mercy. Blessed are the pure in heart, for they shall see God. Blessed are the peacemakers, for they shall be called the children of God. Blessed are those who are humble, those who are just, those who try to do right, those who suffer persecution – all of them will be rewarded in the kingdom of Heaven.

Do not keep your good qualities hidden, but let them shine out like a candle lighting up a dark house. When a lamp is lit, it is not put under a bowl, but placed where it can brighten the whole room.

I am not here to destroy the law, or contradict the words of the prophets. I am here to uphold them, for it is essential that the law be obeyed.

You have heard it said, you shall not kill. But those who keep murderous thoughts in their minds are also to blame. You must be able to forgive whoever has made you angry.

The old law speaks of an eye for an eye, and a tooth for a tooth, but if someone strikes you on the right cheek, it is better to turn the left cheek so that he may strike that, too.

It is easy to love your friends, but it is as important to love your enemies also, and be kind to those who turn against you.

You should never boast of your good deeds, but do them secretly.

You cannot value both God and money.

When you pray, do not do so in the open where everyone can see, but alone in your room. Talk directly to God, and say what is in your heart. Pray using these words: "Our Lord who is in Heaven, holy is your name. Your kingdom is coming. We will obey you on Earth as you are obeyed in Heaven. Give us our daily food. Forgive us our sins, as we forgive the sins of others. Do not lead us into temptation, but save us from evil."

Do not worry about what you wear or what you eat and drink. The birds in the air do not sow wheat or store it in barns, and yet the heavenly Lord feeds them; the lilies of the field do not spin or weave, and yet not even Solomon in all his glory was as magnificent as one of these.

Do not condemn: as you judge others, so will you yourself be judged. Before you criticize the speck of sawdust in another's eye, first remove the plank of wood in your own.

Ask, and it will be given to you; search, and you will find.

Avoid false prophets; beware of the wolf in sheep's clothing.

Anyone who hears my words and follows them is like the wise one who builds a house upon rock. When the rain comes, and the wind blows, and the floodwaters rise, the house will stand firm. But anyone who hears my words and ignores them is like the foolish one who builds a house upon sand. When the storm comes and the waters rise, the house will fall, because the foundations are built only on shifting sand.

MOUNT OF BEATITUDES
The Mount of Beatitudes is traditionally thought to be the place where Jesus gave his "sermon on the mount." The low hill is near Capernaum and overlooks the Sea of Galilee. The word "beatitude" means "blessed" and refers to the sayings of Jesus that begin "blessed are...." The beatitudes describe the qualities of the ideal follower of Jesus.

LILIES OF THE FIELD
When Jesus talked about the "lilies of the field" he may have been referring to anemones, shown above. In early spring these pretty flowers still cover the hills and fields of parts of the Middle East today.

Healing the Sick

LEPER
In the Bible, the word "leprosy" stands for a variety of skin diseases. Lepers lived apart from the community to prevent the spreading of infection. They had to wear torn clothes and cry "unclean, unclean" to insure that no one approached them. Yet Jesus was not afraid to touch the leper when he came to him to be cured.

NEWS OF JESUS' TEACHINGS had spread throughout the land, and wherever he went he was followed by vast crowds. One day in Capernaum a leper came up to Jesus, saying, "Lord, if you are willing, you can cure me." Moved by compassion, Jesus reached out his hand and touched him. "I am willing: be clean."

Instantly the man saw that his legs and arms were whole and his skin unmarked. "Go on your way," said Jesus, "Show yourself to a priest: he will offer sacrifices and declare you cured. But tell no one else about what has happened."

But the leper was so overjoyed at being cured that he described the miracle to everyone he met. Soon Jesus was unable to walk down the

Four friends lower an invalid through the roof of the house to be cured by Jesus

Jesus touches the leper and cures him

AND JESUS, MOVED WITH COMPASSION, PUT FORTH HIS HAND, AND TOUCHED HIM AND SAITH UNTO HIM, "I WILL; BE THOU CLEAN."
MARK 1:41

street without being surrounded by dozens of eager followers.

Later, Jesus was preaching in a house so full of people that there was hardly room to breathe. Four men arrived at the house, carrying a stretcher on which lay a man who was completely paralyzed. Realizing that they had no hope of entering by the door, they went up on the roof. There they made a hole, through which they lowered the invalid.

Jesus looked at the man and said, "My son, your sins are forgiven."

But some Pharisees and Jewish leaders overheard these words. Among themselves they accused Jesus of insulting God. They thought this man had no right to take upon himself such authority: only God could forgive sin.

Jesus, knowing what was in their minds, said, "Why do you think badly of me? Do you believe that I do not have the right to forgive sins? Which is easier, to forgive this man's sins, or to make him walk? But so that you will know that I have the power to forgive sins...." Pausing, he turned to the paralyzed man and said, "Get up, take your bed, and go home." Speechless, the man got up at once and returned to his house. The crowds who had seen the miracle talked excitedly and went away praising God. "We have never seen anything like this," they said.

REED-ROOFED HOUSES
In Jesus' time, most Galilean houses had flat roofs, similar to the ones above. The roofs were made from layers of reeds and mud laid on top of wooden beams. The surface was smoothed with a roller.

The man, now cured, takes up his mat and walks home

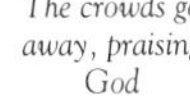

The crowds go away, praising God

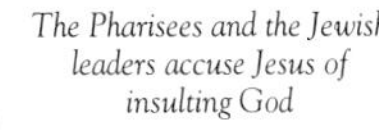

The Pharisees and the Jewish leaders accuse Jesus of insulting God

The Centurion's Servant

Jesus arrives in Capernaum and is met by Jewish elders and teachers

They tell Jesus that the centurion's servant is ill

THE CENTURION ANSWERED AND SAID, "LORD, I AM NOT WORTHY THAT THOU SHOULDST COME UNDER MY ROOF: BUT SPEAK THE WORD ONLY, AND MY SERVANT SHALL BE HEALED."
MATTHEW 8:8

JESUS PREACHED throughout the land for many days until he returned to the city of Capernaum. Here he was met by some Jewish elders, who told him of a man who was lying dangerously ill. He was the much-loved servant of a Roman soldier, a centurion. They told Jesus that the centurion had asked them to beg Jesus to come to him. "This centurion is a good man," said the elders. "He built a synagogue for us, and he has done much to help our people."

But as Jesus approached the house, the centurion himself came out to meet him. "Lord, I thank you for your trouble, but do not come any further. I know I am not fit to stand before you, nor am I worthy to ask you into my house. I am a man used to authority, to giving orders and having them obeyed – and in the same way I know that you have only to say the word, and my servant will be cured."

The elders are amazed when they find that the servant is cured

Jesus tells the centurion that his servant is healed

Jesus, astonished at the soldier's speech, turned to the people who were following him. "Look at this man, and listen to what I am about to say. I have not in the whole of Israel found a stronger nor a truer faith." Then to the centurion he said, "Go to your servant, for he is now healed."

The elders were amazed, even more so when they went to the house and found the servant completely cured.

ROMAN UNIFORM
Centurions were in charge of a troop of Roman soldiers. The soldiers wore sandals with iron hobnails on the soles, which were ideal for marching. They carried short swords, which were easy to wield in battle.

Jesus Calms the Storm

HIS DISCIPLES CAME TO HIM, AND AWOKE HIM, SAYING, "LORD, SAVE US: WE PERISH." AND HE SAITH UNTO THEM, "WHY ARE YE FEARFUL, O YE OF LITTLE FAITH?" THEN HE AROSE, AND REBUKED THE WINDS AND THE SEA; AND THERE WAS A GREAT CALM.
MATTHEW 8:25-26

JESUS AND HIS DISCIPLES were on the Sea of Galilee, aboard a small fishing boat. It was evening, and Jesus, tired from preaching all day, fell asleep on some cushions in the stern. Suddenly a violent storm blew up. The sky darkened, the wind howled and gigantic waves crashed over the little vessel.

Frightened, the disciples shook Jesus awake. "Save us, Lord!" they cried. "Our boat will sink, and we shall drown!"

"Why are you afraid?" said Jesus. "Have you no faith?" Stretching his hands out over the lake, he spoke to the wind and the waves: "Peace. Be calm." Instantly the storm died down and the lake grew still.

"How great a man he is," exclaimed the disciples. "Even the wind and the waves obey him!"

Jesus calls on the wind and waves to be calm

The disciples are frightened in the storm

The Gadarene Swine

AFTER THE STORM, Jesus and the disciples came safely to shore, to the country of the Gadarenes. As they stepped once more onto dry land, a man came running toward them. He was half naked and appeared to be possessed by evil spirits. His hair was long, his eyes wild, and he snapped and snarled like a beast. Many times he had been caught and chained, but he was so strong that each time he had broken free. No one was able to calm him. Now he lived among the tombstones in the surrounding hills, howling and crying day and night, and in his misery cutting himself with sharp stones.

He had seen Jesus from a long way off. "What do you want, Son of God?" he cried out in a loud voice, "Have you come to torment me?"

"What is your name?" Jesus asked.

"My name is Legion," replied the man. "Legion – for there are many demons within me."

Now feeding nearby was a large herd of nearly two thousand pigs. Jesus commanded the demons to leave the man. "Go!" he said. "Leave this man and enter instead the bodies of those pigs!"

So the evil spirits left the man and took possession of the herd of swine. Suddenly the pigs stopped feeding, looked up, and grunting and snorting, galloped to the cliff's edge and hurled themselves into the sea.

The men who were looking after the herd watched in horror as the pigs leapt to their deaths. They turned and ran back to the town to tell their story. A crowd gathered and came back to see for themselves. They were amazed to find the madman now cured of his madness. He was fully clothed, sitting quietly and talking to Jesus. The people were frightened by the extraordinary change in the man and begged Jesus to leave the country.

As Jesus was getting into the boat once more, the man who had been possessed by demons ran toward him. He pleaded with Jesus to let him go with him. Jesus said, "No, it is best that you return home. Tell your friends what the Lord has done, and how he has shown his mercy toward you."

Jesus commands the demons to leave the man and enter a herd of pigs

DEMON

The statue above is of an Assyrian demon. In the Bible, demons are evil spirits that join with the devil to oppose God and humans. In Jesus' time, it was believed that demons entered humans and caused disease and mental illnesses.

MATTHEW 9; MARK 5; LUKE 8

Jairus' Daughter

As Jesus goes to see Jairus' daughter, a woman touches the hem of Jesus' robe and is cured

Jairus, head of the synagogue, falls to his knees and asks Jesus to cure his daughter

SYNAGOGUE
A synagogue is a Jewish place of worship. Above are the ruins of a synagogue in Capernaum. Synagogues probably originated during the Jewish exile in Babylon, when the people were separated from the temple in Jerusalem. Synagogues came to be used as social, as well as religious, centers.

THE HEAD OF THE SYNAGOGUE came to Jesus, and falling on his knees, begged for his help. "My little daughter is dying," he said, weeping. "I implore you to lay your hands on her and make her well!"

As Jesus left with the man, a woman made her way through the crowd and timidly felt the hem of his robe. For twelve years she had suffered from internal bleeding, which no doctor could cure. She knew that Jesus would heal her, if she could only touch him.

Jesus stopped, and turned around. "Who touched me?" he asked.

Peter was puzzled by Jesus' question. "In such a crush of people," he said, "you ask who touched you?"

But Jesus looked straight at the woman, who shrank back trembling. "Do not be afraid, my daughter," he said. "Your faith in God has cured you. Go in peace, and be free from suffering." And from that moment the woman was well.

When Jesus reached the house where the young girl lay, he saw people wailing and wringing their hands, and pipers playing music for the dead. "Why do you come here?" they asked Jesus. "She is dead: there is nothing you can do."

"The girl is not dead: she is sleeping." said Jesus. No one believed him, and some laughed scornfully at his words. He went into the house, allowing only Peter, James, and John to come with him.

Jesus stood with the girl's mother and father beside the child. Gently taking her hand, he said, "Little girl, get up from your bed." The child opened her eyes, and as naturally as if she had indeed been asleep, got up from her bed, and hugged both her parents.

"Now give her something to eat," Jesus said to them. "But tell no one what has taken place in this room."

MOURNING SOUNDS
In Jesus' time, Jewish people used music to express sorrow as well as joy. The reed pipe had a sad, wailing tone and was often played at times of mourning, as at the death of Jairus' daughter.

Peter, James, and John enter Jairus' house

The girl's mother and father weep by her bed

Pipers play and people wail and wring their hands, as Jairus' daughter lies dead

Jesus gently takes the girl by the hand and she sits up, alive and well

The Sower

WHEREVER JESUS WENT, large numbers of men and women would follow. One day, Jesus was teaching by the Sea of Galilee. There were such crowds pressing around him that he got into a boat on the lake. All the people gathered by the water's edge to listen, and there he told them the parable of the sower.

There was a man sowing seed for the next year's harvest. As he walked along, scattering handfuls of wheat to the right and to the left, some of the seed fell on the beaten path, and this was quickly swooped on and eaten by birds. This is like the person who hears the word of God, but ignores its message. Satan, the evil one, will make sure they forget what they have heard.

SOWER'S BAG
A sower often carried his seed in a bag, like the one above. He sowed the seed by "broadcasting": he walked up and down the field and scattered seed along the way. Some seed was always lost, as in Jesus' parable.

As a man sows the seed, some falls on the beaten path and is eaten by birds

Some seed falls on shallow soil, so the wheat grows too quickly and is scorched by the sun

Some of the sower's seed fell where the soil lay very shallow, and because the earth was not deep enough for strong roots to take hold, the wheat grew too quickly. It was then scorched by the sun and withered and died. This is like the person who accepts the word of God, but who gives it little thought. When they are faced with any difficulty, their courage soon fails them, and they lose their faith.

Some seed fell among thistles, which grew tall and choked it. This is like the person who is lured by worldly pleasures, and whose heart is choked by ambition and a desire for wealth.

But some of the seed fell on good, fertile ground, and this seed ripened into a rich harvest. This is like the person who listens to the word of God, and loves and obeys the Lord. They will do much good in the world, and their efforts will be well rewarded.

SIFTING THE GRAIN
After harvesting, a woman would sift the grain. She held a sieve at an angle and shook it, while blowing across it to remove any husks. Stones collected at one end, and any broken pieces of grain fell through, leaving only the good grain.

The sower scatters handfuls of seed to the right and to the left

Some seed falls among thistles, which choke the wheat

Some seed falls on fertile ground and ripens into a rich harvest

The Death of John the Baptist

King Herod Antipas has John the Baptist thrown into prison

KING HEROD ANTIPAS had John the Baptist thrown into prison, because the prophet dared condemn him for having married his brother's wife, Herodias. Herod both feared and admired John, but Herodias hated him. She wanted to see him put to death. Her husband, however, knew that John was a good man, and often listened to the Baptist's words of wisdom. Herod did not wish John dead, and so kept him well guarded in jail.

On Herod's birthday, he gave a supper to which he invited his lords and captains and all the big landowners of Galilee. Herodias's daughter, Salome, a young girl of great beauty, danced before the king and his guests. Herod was so enchanted by her

GREEK DANCING
In Jesus' time, Palestine was influenced by Greek, as well as Roman, culture. The Greeks often hired women dancers to entertain at banquets and festivals. This detail from a Greek bowl shows a woman dancing while drumming her tambourine. When Herodias' daughter, Salome, danced before Herod Antipas, she probably would have danced in a similar way.

On Herod's birthday, Salome dances before the king, and he promises that she can have anything she wishes

performance that he said to her, "Ask me for anything you please – half my kingdom if you wish – and it shall be yours."

The girl went over to her mother. "What shall I ask for?" she whispered.

Now Herodias had never forgiven the prophet for his condemnation of her marriage, and realized that now she could have her revenge. "Ask that the Baptist's head be brought to you on a dish," she said to her daughter.

When Herod heard Salome's request, he was appalled, but his promise had been made in front of the entire company, and he had no choice but to keep his word.

The order was quickly given, and John the Baptist executed in his prison cell. Soon afterward the prophet's bleeding head was carried into the banqueting hall on a silver platter, and placed at Salome's

BUT WHEN HEROD'S BIRTHDAY WAS KEPT, THE DAUGHTER OF HERODIAS DANCED BEFORE THEM, AND PLEASED HEROD. WHEREUPON HE PROMISED WITH AN OATH TO GIVE HER WHATSOEVER SHE WOULD ASK.
MATTHEW 14:6-7

Herodias tells Salome to ask for the head of John the Baptist

Herodias

Salome

John the Baptist's head is carried in on a silver platter

feet. Silently she picked it up and carried it to her mother.

John's followers, meanwhile, took the headless body and buried it. Then they went to Jesus to tell him what had happened. Jesus was deeply saddened by the news of the Baptist's death. In order to mourn for his friend, he left the crowds for a little while, going by boat to a place where he could be by himself to think and to pray.

The Feeding of the Five Thousand

Jesus and his disciples cross the Sea of Galilee by boat

THEN HE TOOK THE FIVE LOAVES AND THE TWO FISHES, AND LOOKING UP TO HEAVEN, HE BLESSED THEM, AND BRAKE, AND GAVE TO THE DISCIPLES TO SET BEFORE THE MULTITUDE. AND THEY DID EAT, AND WERE ALL FILLED.
LUKE 9:16-17

LOAVES AND FISHES
The crowds were fed with unleavened bread made from barley. Barley was a common crop in Palestine because it could grow in poor soil. The fish would have been salted to preserve them.

JESUS WISHED TO SPEND A LITTLE TIME away from the crowds, so he, along with his twelve disciples, went by boat across the Sea of Galilee to a quiet desert region near Bethsaida. However, it soon became known where he was going, and thousands of people poured out of towns and cities to meet him there. When Jesus saw how greatly they needed him, he was moved, and walked among the crowd, talking, answering questions, and healing those who were ill.

Toward evening the disciples said, "Surely it is time for you to send these crowds away? You are tired and need to rest. Let them look after themselves, and find food where they can."

"No," said Jesus. "There is no need for them to go. And you can feed them here."

"But there are more than five thousand people!" exclaimed the disciples.

Then Andrew, the brother of Simon, said, "There is a boy here who has five loaves of barley bread and two small fish, but what use is so little divided among so many?"

Jesus told everyone to sit down on the grass, then he took the bread and the two fish from the boy, and blessed them. He told his disciples to give food to every man, woman, and child present. The disciples did as he asked them, and were astonished to find not only that there was plenty for all, but that afterward twelve baskets were filled with the food that remained.

A boy approaches Jesus carrying a basket of five loaves and two fish

The disciples give the food to all the people

Twelve baskets full of food are left over

Jesus Walks on the Water

JESUS TOLD HIS DISCIPLES to go ahead of him by boat across the Sea of Galilee, while he sent away the crowds that had come to hear him. When everyone had gone, Jesus went a little way up the mountain to pray by himself.

That evening a strong wind began to blow, and the boat carrying the disciples was tossed and buffeted by the waves. The harder they struggled to row toward shore, the more swiftly their little boat was swept off course. Knowing they were in distress, Jesus went to them, walking on the surface of the water. As they saw him approach through the dark, they thought he was a ghost, and cried out in fear.

Jesus goes up the mountain to pray by himself

The boat carrying the disciples is tossed and buffeted by the waves

SEA OF GALILEE
The Sea of Galilee is a large, freshwater lake that is fed by the River Jordan. It is about 13 miles (21 km) long and reaches a width of 8 miles (13 km). The lake is known for its sudden fierce winds and violent storms. When Jesus walked on the lake and calmed the storm, it was a sign of his control over nature.

"It is I," he said. "Do not be afraid."

"If it is you, Lord," said Peter, "let me walk to you on the water."

"Come," said Jesus.

Jumping over the side, Peter took several steps across the surface of the lake, but when he looked down at the swirling waves, his courage failed him, and he began to sink. "Save me, Lord!" he cried.

Jesus stretched out his hands and held on to him. "Why do you not have faith?" he asked. Then he went with Peter into the boat. At once, the wind died down, and the water grew calm. The disciples, filled with awe, said to Jesus, "Truly, you are the son of God."

IMMEDIATELY JESUS STRETCHED FORTH HIS HAND, AND CAUGHT HIM, AND SAID UNTO HIM, "O THOU OF LITTLE FAITH, WHEREFORE DIDST THOU DOUBT?"
MATTHEW 14:31

The disciples' boat is swept off course

Peter begins to sink as he walks on the water toward Jesus

Jesus, walking on the surface of the water, stretches out his hands to help Peter

The Good Samaritan

LAWLESS ROAD
Lone travelers on the road from Jerusalem to Jericho were easy prey for bandits. The quiet road drops steeply as it winds its way through rocky, desert land. It was ideal territory for robbers to hide in.

FIRST AID
The Samaritan put wine and oil on the wounds of the injured man. He would have applied wine first as an antiseptic. Then he would have soothed the wound by coating it with olive oil, before wrapping the cut in a linen bandage.

The thieves run away after attacking and robbing a man

A priest passes by the wounded man

A Levite passes by the wounded man

A Samaritan comes by and tends the man's wounds

NE DAY A LAWYER ASKED A QUESTION OF JESUS, thinking that he would trip him up. "What should I do," he asked, "to gain eternal life?"

"You know the law. What does that tell you?"

"You must love God with all your heart, and you must love your neighbor as you love yourself," said the lawyer.

"You have answered truly," Jesus said.

"But who is my neighbor?"

In reply, Jesus told the following story:

A man was traveling from Jerusalem to Jericho. On the way he was attacked by thieves, who stripped off his clothes, kicked and beat him, then left him half dead by the roadside. Not long afterward, a priest came by, and seeing the wounded man, crossed over to the other side. Next came a Levite, one of the men who assisted the priests in the temple. He, too, gave a quick look and then passed by on the far side of the road.

The third traveler to approach was a Samaritan. Seeing the man half conscious and covered in blood, he was filled with pity. Gently, he cleaned his wounds with wine and oil, before bandaging them with strips of linen. Then he put the stranger on his own donkey and took him to the nearest inn, where he looked after him all night. The following day before leaving, he gave the innkeeper money so that the invalid would have whatever he needed. "If you spend more than this, I will give you what is owed the next time I pass," he said.

"Now, which of these three men was the true neighbor?" Jesus asked the lawyer.

"The Samaritan."

"Just so. Remember this story, and behave to other people just as the good Samaritan did."

SAMARITAN
The picture above shows a Samaritan priest. Samaritans accept only the first five books of the Bible, the Torah, as the word of God. In Jesus' time the Samaritans lived in Samaria, in central Palestine. Many were descended from people who had settled in Israel after it was conquered by the Assyrians in 722 BC. The Samaritans and the Jews were sworn enemies. By using a Samaritan in his story, Jesus taught that one should be compassionate to everyone, to enemies as well as friends.

Samaritan

innkeeper

The Samaritan gives the innkeeper money and asks him to care for the wounded man

The Transfiguration

Jesus tells Peter that he will give him the keys of God's kingdom

PETER THE LEADER
This mosaic shows Peter, whose name means "rock." When Jesus said that he would give Peter the keys to the kingdom, he meant that Peter was to take a leading role in the church.

HAVING REACHED CAESAREA PHILIPPI, Jesus began to talk to his disciples. "Who do people say I am?" he asked them.

"Some say you are John the Baptist, others that you are one of the prophets, Jeremiah or Elijah," they told him.

"Who do you say that I am?"

"You are Christ, the son of God," Peter replied.

"You, Peter, are blessed, for God himself has revealed this to you. On you, as on a rock, I shall build my church, and to you will I give the keys of the kingdom of Heaven."

Then Jesus explained to his disciples that they must tell no one of his true identity. "The time will soon come when I must go to Jerusalem, and there I shall suffer at the hands of the chief priests and officers of the law. I shall be tried, condemned, and executed, but on the third day after my death, I shall rise again."

"This shall not happen to you!" Peter exclaimed. "It must never happen!"

"Do not deny the will of God. You are thinking of your own wishes, instead of God's."

Then Jesus said to his disciples, "Those who wish to follow me must, for my sake, give up all the comforts and riches of this life, but their reward in Heaven will be great. What are great possessions worth if, to win them, a man forfeits his soul and the chance of eternal happiness?"

A week later, Jesus took Peter, James, and John, the brother of James, up on a high mountain to pray. Suddenly the three men saw the appearance of Jesus change: his face shone like the sun and his clothes were as white as the purest snow. Then Moses and Elijah appeared and talked to Jesus. The disciples were terrified, and Peter, unsure what to do, said, "Lord, it is wonderful that we are all here. Let us put up three tents, one for you, one for Moses, and one for Elijah."

Then a bright cloud passed over, and the voice of God was heard, saying "This is my son, with whom I am well pleased. Listen to him."

The disciples fell on the ground in fear, covering their eyes. Jesus came to them and touched each on the shoulder. "Do not be afraid," he said. Timidly, they looked up, but saw only Jesus standing before them.

As they came down the mountain, Jesus said, "Tell no one what you have seen until after I have died and risen from the dead."

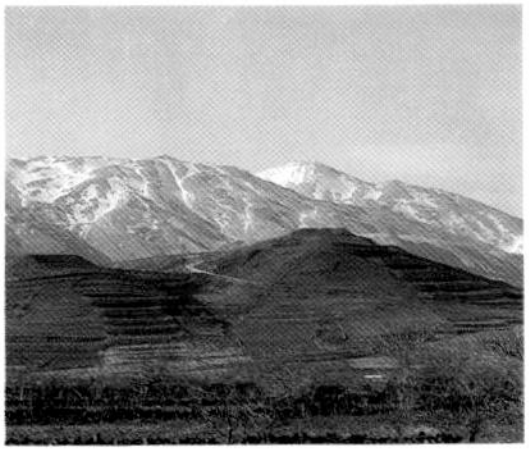

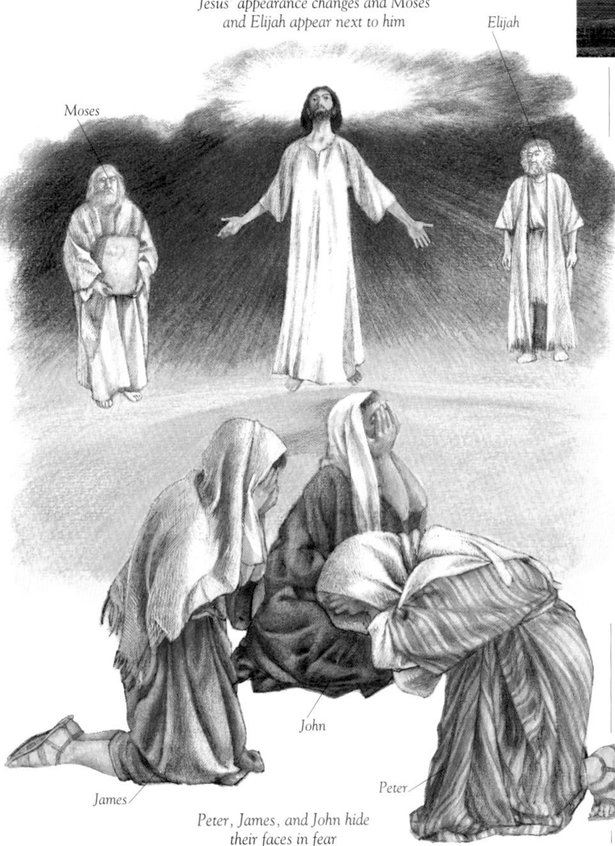

SACRED MOUNT
Mount Hermon, whose name means "sacred mountain," lies near Caesarea Philippi and is the most likely site of the transfiguration of Jesus. The snow-covered peaks reach a height of over 9,000 feet (2,700 m). When Jesus was transfigured, the glory of God shone through him and he was revealed as the son of God. Beside him were Moses, representing Jewish law, and Elijah, representing the prophets. This was to show that Jesus fulfilled the words of the law and the prophets.

Jesus' appearance changes and Moses and Elijah appear next to him

Peter, James, and John hide their faces in fear

BEHOLD, A BRIGHT CLOUD OVERSHADOWED THEM: AND BEHOLD A VOICE OUT OF THE CLOUD, WHICH SAID, "THIS IS MY BELOVED SON, IN WHOM I AM WELL PLEASED; HEAR YE HIM."
MATTHEW 17:5

Mary, Martha, and Lazarus

HOUSEHOLD TASKS
In Jesus' time, women like Martha worked hard in the home. Their household duties included making bread and preparing meals. Women rose at daybreak to begin breadmaking. Flour was mixed with water and salt, then kneaded into a dough. Sometimes yeast was added, to make the dough rise. The dough was pressed into a flat, rounded shape. One method of baking was to spread the dough on a hot, metal sheet, supported by stones and placed over a fire, as in the picture above.

JESUS ANSWERED AND SAID UNTO HER, "MARTHA, MARTHA, THOU ART CAREFUL AND TROUBLED ABOUT MANY THINGS: BUT ONE THING IS NEEDFUL; AND MARY HATH CHOSEN THAT GOOD PART, WHICH SHALL NOT BE TAKEN AWAY FROM HER."
LUKE 10:41-42

JESUS ARRIVED IN A VILLAGE CALLED BETHANY, not far from Jerusalem, and was invited to the house of Mary and Martha, who were sisters. Mary sat at Jesus' feet listening as he talked, while Martha hurried to and fro preparing the food. After a while she began to resent the fact that her sister was doing nothing to help. "It is not right, Lord, that Mary should sit at your feet, while I do all the work," she complained.

"But Mary is wise," he gently told her. "It is more important to listen to my teaching, as she does, than to worry, like you, about the affairs of the house."

The two sisters had a brother called Lazarus, and a little while after Jesus had left, Lazarus fell seriously ill. Mary and Martha sent word to Jesus, begging him to come and save their brother's life.

The message reached Jesus as he was talking to his disciples. "Lazarus is sleeping," he said. "I will go and awaken him." But he remained where he was for several days before returning to Bethany.

As he approached the sisters' house, Martha, in tears, ran out to meet him. "If only you had been here, Lord, my brother would not have died!"

"Your brother shall rise from death. You must have faith and believe

Martha works hard preparing the food

Jesus tells Martha not to worry about her work, but to listen to him, as Mary is doing

Jesus listens as Martha tells him that her brother, Lazarus, is dead

what I have taught you of the resurrection of the dead."

Mary, too, came out to Jesus, weeping as if her heart would break. When he saw the strength of her grief, he was deeply moved. "Where has Lazarus been laid?" he asked her. Accompanied by mourning relations, she led him to the tomb, which was in a cave, its mouth sealed by a heavy stone.

"Take away the stone," said Jesus. With difficulty, the stone was rolled to one side.

"Lazarus, arise!" To everyone's astonishment, Lazarus, his head and body covered in the white linen of his shroud, walked out of the cave. It was as Jesus had said: the dead man had been brought back to life, as if simply awakened from sleep.

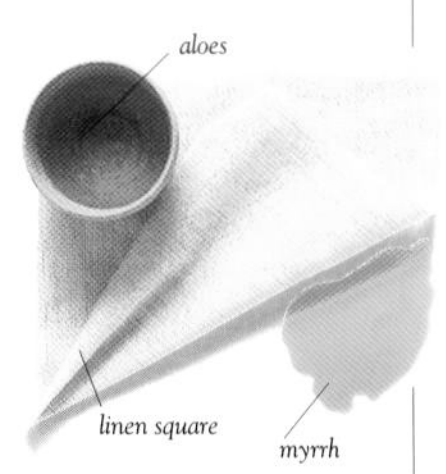

BURIAL

According to Jewish tradition, burials usually took place on the day of death. The body was washed then wrapped in a linen cloth. A linen square was wrapped around the head. Aloes and myrrh were often placed between the folds of linen. Myrrh was an expensive and fragrant gum from the bark of a tree. Aloes was juice from a medicinal plant.

Lazarus walks out of the cave at Jesus' bidding

Lost and Found

A shepherd loses one of his hundred sheep

A LARGE CROWD HAD SURROUNDED Jesus to hear him speak. Among them were the Pharisees, who strictly observed and upheld the Jewish law. The Pharisees were horrified to see tax collectors and people who were law-breakers gathered around Jesus. They muttered to each other against him. "This man even eats with these sinners," they said.

But Jesus welcomed everyone, explaining that he had come to care for outcasts and all these who needed him. Then he told a story, which compared God to a shepherd.

"God," he said, "is like a good shepherd with a flock of a hundred sheep. If he sees that one sheep is lost, that shepherd will leave the ninety-nine others and search the mountainside for his lost sheep. When he finds it, he will return home full of joy. He will rejoice more over the return of the one that had strayed than over all the rest of the flock that remained safe in the fold.

"For it is the will of God that no one, however humble, shall be lost."

THE GOOD SHEPHERD
God's care of the Israelites is often compared to that of a shepherd tending his sheep. In the New Testament, Jesus calls himself the Good Shepherd who cares, and finally dies, for his sheep.

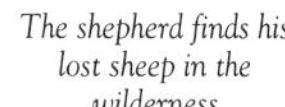

The shepherd finds his lost sheep in the wilderness

A woman sweeps the house searching for her lost coin

BROOM
The earth floors of houses had to be swept regularly to keep them free from dust and dirt. For this a woman would use a simple straw broom, such as the one above. The short handle meant that she had to stoop down.

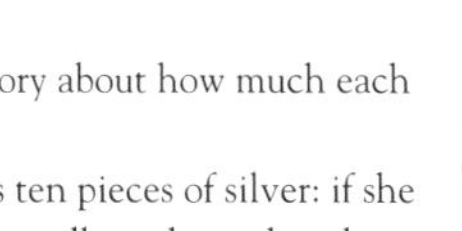

Jesus then told the people another story about how much each person matters to God.

"Again, think of the woman who has ten pieces of silver: if she discovers one is missing, she lights her candle and searches the house until she finds it. And when she has found it, she will call her friends and neighbors together so they may rejoice with her. 'Look,' she said to them. 'How happy I am to have found the coin that was lost!'

"Just so, there is great joy among the angels in heaven when even one person turns away from wrong-doing."

After finding the coin, the woman calls on her friends to rejoice with her

The Prodigal Son

After leaving home, the farmer's younger son is reduced to looking after pigs

PODS
The pigs would have eaten pods from the carob, or locust tree. The pods are filled with a dark, sweet syrup.

PIGS
Middle Eastern, domestic pigs originated from the wild boar, shown above. To Jewish people, pigs symbolize greed and filth and are "unclean."

THE THIRD STORY JESUS TOLD was of the prodigal son. A rich farmer had two sons, and the youngest said to him one day, "Father, will you give me now my share of the property that is due to me?" His father agreed, and the young man took his share of money and goods, and left home to settle in a far country. There he lived like a prince, gambling and spending his money on rich clothes and jewels. Night after night he entertained crowds of friends with dancing girls and the most expensive wines.

In time, he spent all his money, and as he grew poor, the country fell into famine. The young man's friends disappeared, his possessions were sold to pay his debts, and when he begged in the street for food, everyone he approached turned away. Eventually, he was hired by a farmer, who sent him into the fields to watch over the pigs. He was so hungry that he longed to eat the pods that he fed to the pigs.

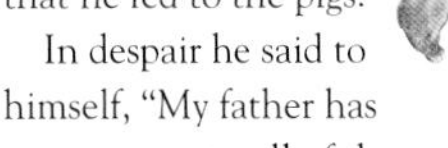

The youngest son returns home to his father, who embraces him joyfully

In despair he said to himself, "My father has many servants, all of them well clothed and fed, and here am I, his son, penniless and starving! I will go to him now and beg his forgiveness and see if I may work for him as a servant."

His father saw him coming from a long way off. Overjoyed, he ran to meet his son, threw his arms about his neck, and kissed him.

"Father, I have done wrong to God and to you. I am not worthy to be called your son." But immediately, his father gestured to him to be silent and called for his best robe to be brought out. "Put a ring on his hand, and soft shoes on his feet," he commanded. "And kill the fattest calf, for tonight we shall have a feast. My son, whom I believed to be dead, has come home!"

When the elder brother returned that evening from working in the fields, he was astonished to hear the sound of music and dancing. "What is the meaning of this?" he asked one of his men.

"Your brother has come home, and your father is holding a feast in his honor."

The elder brother was furious, and refused to enter the house. Soon his father came out to see what was wrong. "Father, how could you treat me like this? I, who have worked hard all these years, have never received anything from you. And yet for your other son, who left home and squandered his inheritance, you kill the fattest calf!"

"My son, you are very dear to me, and everything I have belongs to you. But your brother was lost, and now he is found, and it is right that we celebrate his return!"

So it is that God will forgive all who, having abandoned him, return. And, like the father in the parable, he will rejoice at their coming back.

A feast is held to celebrate the son's return

The elder son is angry: he has worked for his father for years, and has never received anything

His father tells his son that everything he has belongs to him

HARVEST
The farmer's elder son may have been helping his father with the harvest when the prodigal, or wasteful, son returned. Harvesting was a busy time and the farmer's whole family helped to gather the crops. The workers used a sickle to cut the grain. They held the stalks in one hand and cut them close to the ears of wheat with the sickle. It had a short handle and a rounded iron blade, like the one above. The cut stalks were laid on the ground, and the workers tied the stalks together into sheaves. The stalks were then taken away in carts for threshing.

"WE SHOULD MAKE MERRY, AND BE GLAD: FOR THIS THY BROTHER WAS DEAD, AND IS ALIVE AGAIN; AND WAS LOST, AND IS FOUND."
LUKE 15:31-32

The Unmerciful Servant

The servant falls on his knees in front of the king and begs for time to repay his debt

PETER CAME TO JESUS and asked him a question. "Lord, how many times should I forgive a man who has done me wrong? Up to seven times?"

"Not seven times, but seventy times seven: there should be no limit to forgiveness," said Jesus, and to show what he meant he told his disciples a story.

There was a king who was good to his servants, often lending them large sums of money.

THEN CAME PETER TO HIM, AND SAID, "LORD, HOW OFT SHALL MY BROTHER SIN AGAINST ME, AND I FORGIVE HIM? TILL SEVEN TIMES?" JESUS SAITH UNTO HIM, "I SAY NOT UNTO THEE, 'UNTIL SEVEN TIMES': BUT, 'UNTIL SEVENTY TIMES SEVEN'."
MATTHEW 18:21-22

The day came when the accounts had to be settled. There was one man who was brought before the king whose debt was so large that he had no hope of repaying it. "As you cannot pay," said the king, "I shall seize all your possessions and sell you and your wife and children into slavery."

The servant fell on his knees. "Sir, I beg you have pity on me! Give me time and I will raise the money and pay back everything!"

The king was moved by the man's despair, and raising him up told him that the whole of his huge debt was canceled, and that he was free to go.

Soon afterward this same man came across a fellow servant who owed him a small sum of money. He took him by the throat and demanded, "Pay me what you owe me now!" The fellow servant fell to his knees and begged the man for mercy.

The same man comes across a fellow servant and takes him by the throat

He demands that he repay the small sum of money he owes him

"I cannot pay this debt just now! Please have pity! Give me time and I will raise the money, I promise!"

But the servant showed no pity, and had the man thrown into prison, until he could pay back the debt.

The other servants were shocked by what they saw, and went to tell their master what had happened.

The king instantly summoned the man to come before him. "When you begged for mercy, I showed you mercy, and yet you had none for a man who owed you far less than you owed me. Now you shall be punished!"

And the king gave orders for his heartless servant to be taken away to jail.

"Just so," said Jesus, "this is how your heavenly Lord will treat each of you unless you forgive those who have done you wrong from the bottom of your heart."

SERVANT
This Roman carving dates from around AD 200 and shows a servant grinding spices. In Jesus' time a servant was either a slave or a hired worker who was paid for his work and was free to leave when he wished.

The king gives orders for his heartless servant to be jailed

Lazarus and the Rich Man

A rich man feasts every day

Lazarus longs to eat the scraps from the rich man's table

Dogs lick Lazarus' sores

ABRAHAM SAID, "SON, REMEMBER THAT THOU IN THY LIFETIME RECEIVEDST THY GOOD THINGS, AND LIKEWISE LAZARUS EVIL THINGS: BUT NOW HE IS COMFORTED, AND THOU ART TORMENTED."
LUKE 16:25

JESUS TOLD A STORY to warn people about God's judgment of the selfish.

There was once a rich man who dressed in the finest silks and linens. Every day he feasted off the most delicious dishes and drank the best wine. But at his gate lay a poor beggar called Lazarus. His body was thin and frail. He was covered in sores that would not heal, and wild dogs came and licked them. He longed to eat the scraps that fell from the rich man's table.

The day came when Lazarus died and was carried by the angels to Heaven. The rich man died soon after, but he went to Hell where he suffered in torment. Looking upward, he saw Lazarus in Heaven, and he cried out to Abraham, father of his people, "Help me! I am being burnt alive! Send Lazarus to dip his finger in water, so that he may cool my tongue!"

"No, Lazarus shall not come to you," Abraham replied. "On Earth he had nothing, while you were surrounded by luxury. It is right that he should now enjoy happiness while you are left to suffer punishment."

"Will you allow him then to go and warn my five brothers what may lie in store for them? If they saw a messenger from the dead, they would believe him and repent."

"They have the words of the prophets to guide them," said Abraham. "If they do not listen to them, then neither will they listen if someone returns from the dead."

The Pharisee and the Tax Collector

ESUS TOLD THE FOLLOWING STORY to show how important it is not to be conceited or to look down on others:

Two men went to the temple to pray. One was a Pharisee, the other a collector of taxes. The Pharisee stood in the middle of the court, and addressed God confidently. "I thank you, Lord, that I am so much better than other men, that I am not dishonest nor corrupt, that I am superior in every way to people like that little tax collector over there!"

The tax collector stood meekly in a corner, believing himself unworthy even to raise his eyes toward Heaven. Bowing his head, he whispered, "Please, Lord, show mercy to me, a sinner."

"Now," said Jesus, "it was the tax collector who went home with his sins forgiven. Everyone who thinks themselves higher than others will be humbled; everyone who is humble will be lifted high."

The tax collector prays in the corner

The Pharisee prays in the middle of the court

prayer shawl

phylactery

AT PRAYER

Jewish men wore prayer shawls and phylacteries during times of prayer. The shawl had a striped border. Phylacteries were small boxes made of black leather that held tiny strips of parchment. Four passages from the Torah, the first five books of the Bible, were written on the strips. One box was worn strapped to the forehead, and another was tied to the upper left arm, near the heart. This was a sign that God's teachings were controlling the person's thoughts and feelings and that both the head and the heart are used when seeing God. Many Jews still wear prayer shawls and phylacteries today.

"EVERY ONE THAT EXALTETH HIMSELF SHALL BE ABASED; AND HE THAT HUMBLETH HIMSELF SHALL BE EXALTED."

LUKE 18:14

Jesus and the Children

CHILDREN'S GAMES
Marbles were very popular with children in Jesus' time. Children also played with whistles, rattles, hoops, and spinning tops. Jesus said that to enter God's kingdom, people must be like children, innocent and trusting.

THE TWELVE DISCIPLES WERE ARGUING among themselves about who would be considered the most worthy in the eyes of God. Jesus, overhearing their discussion, called them to him and questioned them. But the disciples remained silent, because they were ashamed of what they had been saying. Jesus said to them, "In God's kingdom, he who wishes to be first, must be last: he who wishes to come first before God must live humbly while on Earth, and put others before himself."

A group of children came running up to Jesus and clustered around him. The disciples started to push them away, but Jesus was annoyed and stopped them. "These are my children," he told the disciples. "All children must be free to come to me when they wish, for the kingdom of Heaven belongs to all who are as innocent as they."

Then he picked up one child and set her on his knee. "Look at this little one," he said. "Unless you are as open and trusting as this child, you will have no chance of entering Heaven." Then he stretched out his hands and blessed the children.

Children come to be near Jesus

Jesus says to his disciples they must be like children if they are to enter Heaven

The Rich Young Man

YOUNG MAN from a rich family came running up to Jesus and knelt before him. "Lord, what must I do to gain eternal life?"

"Have you kept all the commandments?" Jesus asked him.

"I have, Lord."

"Then nothing remains but for you to sell everything you own, distribute your money among the poor, and follow me. Then you will find your treasure in Heaven."

The young man looked appalled, for he had great possessions, and sadly he turned away. Jesus looked at him with love, understanding how difficult it was for such a man to give up all that he owned. "You see," he said to the disciples, "it is easier for a camel to go through the eye of a needle than for a rich man to enter the kingdom of God."

"But what about us?" asked Peter. "We have left everything behind, our homes, our families, to follow you."

"Anyone who has done what you have done will be rewarded many times over on Earth and in Heaven," Jesus reassured him.

JESUS ANSWERETH AGAIN, AND SAITH UNTO THEM, "CHILDREN, HOW HARD IS IT FOR THEM THAT TRUST IN RICHES TO ENTER INTO THE KINGDOM OF GOD! IT IS EASIER FOR A CAMEL TO GO THROUGH THE EYE OF A NEEDLE, THAN FOR A RICH MAN TO ENTER INTO THE KINGDOM OF GOD."

MARK 10:24-25

On hearing he must give up everything he owns, the young man walks sadly away

A rich young man kneels before Jesus and asks what he should do to gain eternal life

Zacchaeus the Tax Collector

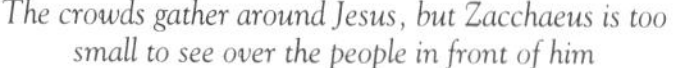

The crowds gather around Jesus, but Zacchaeus is too small to see over the people in front of him

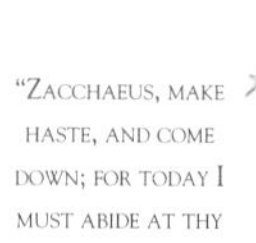

"ZACCHAEUS, MAKE HASTE, AND COME DOWN; FOR TODAY I MUST ABIDE AT THY HOUSE."
LUKE 19:5

Zacchaeus climbs a sycamore tree to see Jesus

Jesus calls to Zacchaeus to come down from the tree

SYCAMORE TREE
The sycamore tree was often planted along roadways in Palestine to provide shade for travelers. Zacchaeus would have found it easy to climb its low-lying branches.

JESUS HAD ARRIVED in Jericho. Pushing through the crowd was a rich man, a chief tax collector called Zacchaeus. He was eager to set eyes on Jesus, but because he was small, he could neither force his way through the crowd, nor see over the people in front of him. Finally, in desperation, he ran ahead, and climbed up into a sycamore tree that stood beside the road he knew Jesus would take.

As Jesus passed beneath the tree, he looked up and saw Zacchaeus sitting astride one of its branches. "Zacchaeus, come down from there! Take me to your house – I'd like to stay with you for a while."

Zacchaeus was overjoyed, and ran home as fast as he could to prepare a welcome. But others began to murmur resentfully. "How shocking," they said, "that he should stay with such a sinner!"

But when Jesus arrived at the house Zacchaeus said to him, "I will give to the poor half of everything I own. And if I have cheated anyone, I will repay that man with four times the amount I took from him dishonestly."

Jesus said, "Today a man has been saved!" And he blessed Zacchaeus, and went full of joy into his house.

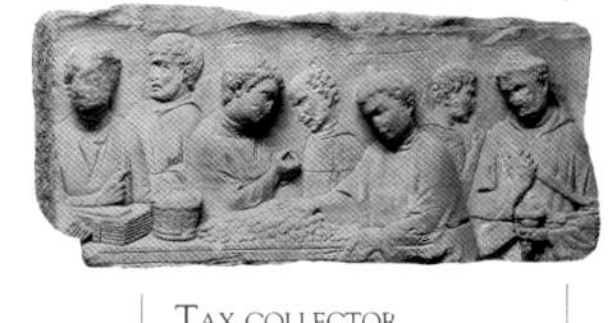

TAX COLLECTOR
In Jesus' time, tax collecting, banking, and money-changing were practiced in the open air, as in this stone carving from the 3rd century AD. Tax collectors set up simple wooden tables and people came to them to pay their taxes. People disliked tax collectors because they worked for the conquering Romans, and because they often swindled people. By being friendly with a tax collector, Jesus showed that his message was for all people.

Zacchaeus welcomes Jesus into his home and says that he will give half of everything he owns to the poor

Workers in the Vineyard

JESUS ONCE TOLD A PARABLE about a man who owned a big vineyard. One morning he went to the marketplace and hired some laborers, offering to pay each man one denarius for a day's work. A little later the same man saw a group standing by idly with nothing to do. "Go and work in my vineyard," he said. Delighted, the men accepted his offer.

Three more times the man hired more workers, until the sun was low in the sky and the day nearly over.

That evening the man told his steward to summon the laborers and pay them their wages. "Pay first those who started work last," he told him, "and give one denarius to each man."

However, when the men who had been toiling in the heat since early morning saw that they were to get no more than those who had started work at the very end of the day, they began to grumble. "We have worked longer hours, so we deserve more pay," they complained.

"No," said the man. "I offered to pay each of you one denarius, and to this you agreed. You are all equal in my eyes."

So, in the kingdom of Heaven those who come late to God are loved and valued as much as those who have always been with him.

VINEYARD
These women are sorting and packing grapes in a vineyard near Bethlehem. Vineyards were common throughout Palestine in Jesus' time. The vines were planted in rows and the branches were trained along sticks. Each vineyard had a watchtower, from which a worker could keep a look-out for thieves, animals, and birds. Wealthy farmers hired workers to help with the harvest.

The Wedding Feast

ONE EVENING, when dining at the house of a rich Pharisee, Jesus told this parable to explain the kingdom of Heaven:

There was a king who prepared a magnificent feast for his son's wedding. When everything was ready, he sent out his servants to summon the guests. But none of them would come. Again the servants went out to invite them, but each one had found an excuse for not attending.

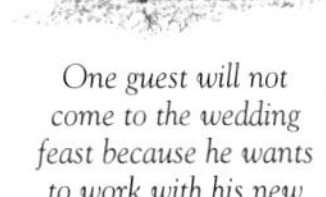

One guest will not come to the wedding feast because he wants to work with his new team of oxen

One said, "I have just bought a new team of oxen and want to work on my farm."

Another said, "I want to inspect my new piece of land."

A third said, "I am newly married, I cannot come."

Another guest wants to inspect his land

Angry, the king said, "Those who turned down my invitation were not worthy." He gave orders that all the beggars, the sick, and the blind should be asked in from the surrounding countryside. "They shall sit at my table and be entertained at my feast!" said the king.

Later that night, as the king wandered among his guests, he noticed one who was not dressed in wedding clothes. "Why do you come here to celebrate a wedding wearing such a garment?" he asked him. But the man remained speechless. "Throw him out into the darkness!" said the king.

Another guest says he is newly married

"So it is," said Jesus, "that many are invited to God's kingdom, but only those who come in the right spirit will be allowed in."

Beggars, the sick, and the blind are then invited to the wedding feast

The king throws out one guest for not wearing wedding clothes

The Wise and Foolish Maidens

TO EXPLAIN THE KINGDOM OF HEAVEN, Jesus told the following story:

There were ten young women at a wedding feast who went one evening to wait for the bridegroom's procession to arrive, all of them carrying lamps. Now five of the women were wise, five were foolish. The wise ones carried jars of extra oil for their lamps; but the foolish ones took nothing.

Ten maidens fall asleep while waiting for the bridegroom

Five wise maidens have extra oil for their lamps

Five foolish maidens have nothing

The bridegroom was late in arriving, so one by one the young women fell asleep. Then at midnight, a cry was heard: "The bridegroom is coming! Quickly, go out to meet him!" The maidens arose, and went to trim their lamps before going out into the darkness. The five foolish young women found that their lamps had gone out from lack of oil. "Please," they asked the others, "give us some of your oil."

"No," the wise maidens replied. "If we do that, there will not be enough to go around. You must buy some more oil for yourselves."

So the five foolish girls went to buy oil, and while they were gone the bridegroom arrived. The wise maidens welcomed him, and he took them with him into the wedding, shutting the door behind him.

When the foolish maidens returned, they beat with their fists on the closed door. "Sir, sir, please let us in!"

But the bridegroom answered, "I do not know you, therefore I cannot let you inside."

"So," said Jesus, "always be prepared, for you do not know when the son of God will come."

jar of oil

oil lamp

OIL LAMP
Lamps like the one above were common in Jesus' time. Oil was poured into the hole in the middle and a wick was placed in the end hole. The oil would last for about three hours, so it was important to have extra oil close by.

The five foolish maidens go to buy oil

While they are gone, the bridegroom arrives and takes the wise maidens to the wedding

The Parable of the Talents

To the first servant he gives five talents; to the second, two talents; and to the third, one talent

JESUS TOLD A PARABLE that compared the kingdom of Heaven to a man who, about to set out on a long journey, entrusted his servants with the care of his property. To each of them he gave a sum of money.

To the first and most senior he gave five talents; to the second servant, two talents; and to the third, one talent; so that each was paid according to his ability.

The first servant took his five talents and cleverly bought and sold so that before long he had doubled his money. The second servant did the same, returning with twice the sum he had been given. The third servant, however, went away and dug a hole in the ground and buried his talent.

BUT HE THAT HAD RECEIVED ONE TALENT WENT AND DIGGED IN THE EARTH, AND HID HIS LORD'S MONEY.
MATTHEW 25:18

After a while their master returned and he asked them what they had done with their money. He praised the first two for having made the most of what they were given. "You are good and faithful

The first servant buys and sells and doubles his five talents

The second servant buys and sells and doubles his two talents

The third servant digs a hole in the ground and buries his one talent

servants," he said, "You have been faithful with a few things – so I will put you in charge of many things."

But when the third servant came to him and returned his one talent, saying that he had simply hidden his coins in the ground, his master was very angry. "How stupid and ungrateful you are! At least you should have put the money in a bank where it would have earned interest." And he gave orders that the man should be thrown out of the house, and his one talent taken from him and given to the servant who now had ten.

So it is that we must make the most of what God gives us, and then we will be prepared to enter the kingdom of Heaven.

MONEY
The silver coins above are Roman denarii, which were commonly used in Jesus' time. Worth about a day's wage, each denarius had the head of the Roman emperor engraved on one side. A talent was not a coin, but a unit of weight equal to about 66 pounds (30 kg). In the parable it represents a large amount of money, the equivalent of several years' wages.

The first two servants are praised for making the most of what they were given

The third servant returns his one talent to his master

The man is angry with the third servant for not doing anything with his money

Jesus Enters Jerusalem

Two of Jesus' disciples find a donkey with its colt, and return with the little donkey

JESUS AND HIS DISCIPLES were on their way to Jerusalem. When they reached Bethphage on the Mount of Olives, which was only a short distance from the city, Jesus sent two of his followers into the village. "You will find a donkey with its colt tethered to a doorway," he said. "Untie the young donkey and bring it here. If anyone tries to stop you, say, 'The Lord has need of it,' and they will let you go in peace."

DONKEY AND COLT
In biblical times, royalty would ride on a donkey during periods of peace, rather than a horse, which was associated with war. When Jesus rode into Jerusalem on a colt, or young donkey, he fulfilled a prophecy that a king would come in peace and humility to Jerusalem.

Jesus rides toward Jerusalem on a donkey's colt

Crowds gather around Jesus, singing and shouting his praises to the sky

Palm leaves are laid in Jesus' path

The disciples did as Jesus had told them. Returning with the little colt, they put their cloaks on its back to act as a saddle. It had never been ridden before, but with Jesus it was docile and obedient. And so the Son of God rode into Jerusalem on a donkey.

When the people saw him coming, they covered the road with their garments and cut palm leaves and laid them in his path. Crowds gathered before him and behind him, singing, and shouting his praises to the sky. "Blessed is he, the son of David! Blessed is he who is coming in the name of the Lord! Peace in Heaven and glory in the highest!"

As Jesus drew nearer to Jerusalem he wept, for he knew that soon

Jesus and his followers pass through a gate into Jerusalem

great troubles would come to Jerusalem.

Jesus and his followers passed through the gate into the city and made their way toward the temple. The people of Jerusalem stared to see such a procession. "Who is this man?" they asked. "Why is he being honored in this way?"

"That is Jesus," the others replied. "He is the great prophet from Nazareth in Galilee."

PALM LEAVES
The people laid palm leaves in Jesus' path. These long, feathery leaves, which look like branches, grow from the top of the tall, slender trunk of the date palm. Palm leaves were a symbol of grace and of victory.

"BLESSED IS HE THAT COMETH IN THE NAME OF THE LORD; HOSANNA IN THE HIGHEST."
MATTHEW 21:9

THE HOLY CITY
Jerusalem is the Holy City to Jews, Christians, and Muslims, and pilgrims flock to the city every year. In the picture above, a Greek Orthodox priest walks along the Via Dolorosa in the Old City of Jerusalem where Jesus is believed to have carried the cross.

Jesus and the Temple Traders

WESTERN WALL
In front of the Dome of the Rock, a Muslim mosque, stands the Western Wall, the only remaining part of Herod's temple.

"MY HOUSE SHALL BE CALLED THE HOUSE OF PRAYER; BUT YE HAVE MADE IT A DEN OF THIEVES."
MATTHEW 21:13

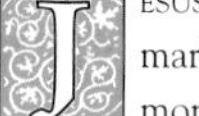

JESUS WENT TO THE TEMPLE in Jerusalem. Its courtyards were a marketplace, with people buying and selling, changing money and haggling over the price of cattle. In a fury Jesus threw over the tables of the money changers so that the coins poured on the ground, and drove out the traders with their oxen and sheep. "The house of God is a house of prayer," he thundered, "but you have turned it into a den of thieves!"

Once the temple had been cleared, people came to Jesus to be healed. But when some of the chief priests and the teachers of the law saw the eager crowds surrounding him, and when they heard the children singing, "Hosanna to the son of David!" they were uneasy. "Do you know what these children are saying?" they asked him.

"Yes," Jesus replied. "Have you never read the Scriptures that say that it is innocent children who praise God most sweetly?"

Then Jesus left for Bethany, where he stayed the

The traders gather in the temple courtyard

night, returning the next day with his disciples to begin teaching in the temple. Many chief priests and teachers of law were waiting for him. "Who gave you permission to teach here?" they demanded.

Jesus replied, "I will ask you one question, and if you can answer it, then I will tell you by whose authority I am here. The question is this: was it God or was it men who gave John the right to baptize?"

The priests were puzzled. "If we say God gave to him that right, he will ask, then why did you not believe him? And if we say, it was men, then the people will turn against us and stone us, for they look on John as a prophet."

So they said to Jesus, "We cannot tell." And Jesus said, "Then neither can I tell you by whose authority I am here."

SCALES
In Jesus' time money changers and traders used scales similar to these Roman bronze scales for weighing money and produce. The money changers changed people's foreign currency into shekels for use in the temple. They often made an unfair profit, and it was this that Jesus objected to when he drove them out of the temple.

Jesus drives the traders out of the temple

The chief priests and the teachers of the law are angered by Jesus

Matthew 26; Mark 14; Luke 22; John 12

Judas Plots to Betray Jesus

Spikenard
The spikenard, or ointment, that Mary used to anoint Jesus came from the fragrant oil produced by the dried roots and stems of the spikenard plant. The plant grows in the Himalayas in India.

Precious gift
Spikenard was imported from India into Palestine in alabaster jars, such as the one above. When Mary broke the jar and anointed Jesus with the valuable ointment, it was to honor him as a special guest. Spikenard was also used to anoint bodies before burial.

Martha

Martha serves dinner to Jesus and his disciples

Lazarus

Jesus

Mary

Mary pours precious spikenard over Jesus' feet, then wipes them clean with her hair

Judas is shocked that Mary used such expensive ointment

IT WAS SIX DAYS before the festival of Passover. Jesus and his disciples had traveled to Bethany, which lay just outside Jerusalem. They went to stay at the house of Jesus' friends, Mary, Martha, and their brother Lazarus, whom Jesus had earlier raised from the dead.

Martha made them very welcome and prepared a dinner in Jesus' honor. Jesus and his disciples sat down to the feast and Martha busily served them. Then Mary came up to Jesus, carrying an alabaster jar of precious spikenard. She broke the jar and gently rubbed his feet with the soothing ointment, afterward wiping them clean with her hair. Soon the whole house was filled with the spikenard's sweet-smelling perfume.

Judas Iscariot, one of the twelve disciples, was shocked that Mary should have used something so expensive. "You could have sold that ointment for a good sum and given the money to the poor! It is worth about the same as a year's wage to a laborer," he said to her angrily.

"Leave her alone," said Jesus. "She has done a beautiful thing for me. The poor you will always have with you, but you will not always have me with you. By anointing me with this perfume, she is preparing me for the day of my burial. What she has done will always be remembered."

Meanwhile the priests, scribes, and elders, who were members of the Jewish council, the Sanhedrin, assembled at the house of Caiaphas, the high priest. They were looking for an excuse to arrest Jesus and execute him, for they were afraid of his influence with the people. Judas went to them in secret and discussed with them how he might betray Jesus.

"What will you give me if I deliver Jesus into your hands?" he asked them.

"Thirty pieces of silver."

Judas agreed to this, and Caiaphas counted the thirty coins into his hand, one by one.

From then on Judas never left Jesus' side, watching and waiting for his opportunity to hand him over to the Jewish council.

THEN ONE OF THE TWELVE, CALLED JUDAS ISCARIOT, WENT UNTO THE CHIEF PRIESTS, AND SAID UNTO THEM, "WHAT WILL YE GIVE ME, AND I WILL DELIVER HIM UNTO YOU?" AND THEY CONVENANTED WITH HIM FOR THIRTY PIECES OF SILVER.
MATTHEW 26:14-15

Judas agrees to deliver Jesus into Caiaphas' hands for thirty pieces of silver

Preparing for the Passover

Peter and John follow a man carrying a jar of water

The man leads them to a certain house

Peter and John ask the owner of the house to show them the upstairs room where they are to celebrate Passover

UPPER ROOM
The site of the "upper room" is traditionally believed to be the Coenaculum, or "dining room," on Mount Zion in Jerusalem. Wealthy people often set aside their upstairs room for entertaining guests.

IT WAS A FEW DAYS before Passover, and Jesus knew that the time was near when he would leave this world and the people he loved, and join God in Heaven.

The disciples came to him to ask where they should prepare the Passover meal. Jesus told Peter and John to go into Jerusalem. "There you will see a man carrying a jar of water. Follow him, and speak to the owner of the house to which he goes. Ask him to show you the room in which your teacher will celebrate Passover with his disciples. He will take you to a large upstairs room, which will have in it everything you need. There you will stay and prepare for the feast."

The two men did exactly as Jesus told them, and when everything was ready, Jesus and the rest of the disciples arrived at the house and went into the room upstairs.

Jesus then took off his outer robe, and wrapped a towel around his waist. He poured water into a bowl and then knelt in front of each of the twelve disciples, washing their feet and drying them with his towel. But when it was Peter's turn, he objected. "Why do you do this, Lord?" he asked. "I cannot allow you to kneel and wash my feet."

Jesus said, "If you do not let me wash your feet, then you will not be part of me."

"Then, Lord, wash not only my feet, but my hands and my head as well!" said Peter.

When he had finished, Jesus put on his robe and sat down. "Now that I, your Lord, have washed your feet, you should wash one another's feet. I have set you an example, that you may learn that all of you are equal, that the master is not greater than his servant, and that you should behave humbly and kindly toward each other."

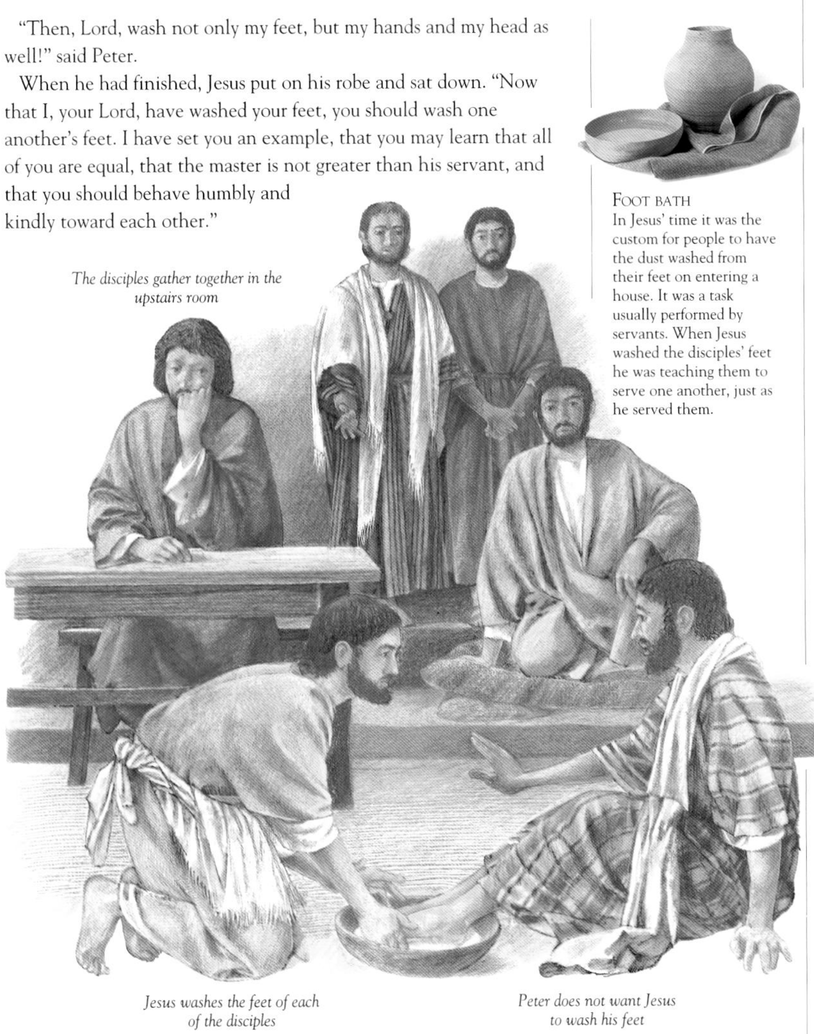

FOOT BATH
In Jesus' time it was the custom for people to have the dust washed from their feet on entering a house. It was a task usually performed by servants. When Jesus washed the disciples' feet he was teaching them to serve one another, just as he served them.

The disciples gather together in the upstairs room

Jesus washes the feet of each of the disciples

Peter does not want Jesus to wash his feet

MATTHEW 26; MARK 14; LUKE 22; JOHN 13

The Last Supper

Jesus blesses the bread, breaks it, and gives it to his disciples

AND AS THEY DID EAT, JESUS TOOK BREAD, AND BLESSED, AND BRAKE IT, AND GAVE TO THEM, AND SAID, "TAKE, EAT; THIS IS MY BODY." AND HE TOOK THE CUP, AND WHEN HE HAD GIVEN THANKS, HE GAVE IT TO THEM: AND THEY ALL DRANK OF IT.

MARK 14:22-23

The disciples are horrified when Jesus says that one of them will betray him

BREAD AND WINE
When Jesus shared the Passover bread and wine with his disciples he surprised them by making them picture his body and his blood. Today, Christians eat and drink in memory of Christ's death.

JESUS AND HIS DISCIPLES were reclining at their Passover meal. Jesus blessed the matzoh bread and broke it, saying to them, "Take this and eat it, for it is my body."

Then he blessed the wine and passed around his cup. "Drink this, for this is my blood."

Then Jesus looked at each man in turn, his face full of sorrow. "One of you sitting here will betray me."

The disciples were horrified, and looked at each other in dismay. "Is it you?" they asked each other. "Is it him? Is it me?"

Judas leaves the room and walks out into the night

Peter whispered to the disciple who was sitting next to Jesus, "Ask the Master which one he means." This disciple, whom Jesus loved dearly, leaned toward him and asked, "Lord, which one of us is it?"

"The one to whom I shall give this bread," replied Jesus. Then he took a piece from the loaf, dipped it in the dish in front of him, and handed it to Judas Iscariot. "Do whatever you have to do," said Jesus, "but do it quickly."

With a start, Judas got up from the table, left the room, and walked out into the night.

JOHN
The disciple who sat near Jesus during the meal is described in John's gospel as "the man whom Jesus loved." This may have been John himself.

The Garden of Gethsemane

MOUNT OF OLIVES
The Mount of Olives lies to the east of Jerusalem, across from the site of Herod's Temple, where the Dome of the Rock now stands. Jesus showed his human side when he came to the Mount of Olives to pray, and struggled to come to terms with his approaching death.

OLIVE GROVE
Olive trees have a long life and can produce fruit for hundreds of years. The Garden of Gethsemane lay in an olive grove on the Mount of Olives, but the exact site is not known.

JESUS AND HIS DISCIPLES walked to a garden called Gethsemane, a quiet place they knew and loved on the Mount of Olives. "Stay here for a little while," said Jesus, "while I go and pray." He took with him Peter, James, and John. "My heart is full of sadness," he told them. "Keep watch over me while I pray."

Peter, James, and John fall asleep while Jesus is praying

Jesus, full of grief, prays to God

Jesus moved a little farther off, where he lay down in prayer, his face to the ground in an agony of grief.

"Father, please take this cup of suffering from me. But I will always obey you. Let your will, not mine, be done."

He returned to the three men, only to find them fast asleep. "Could you not stay awake for just one hour?" he said. "Please keep watch while I pray." Again he went away to pray, and again the disciples fell asleep, for their eyes were heavy. A third time this happened, then Jesus said, "No matter: the hour has come. The traitor is here!"

As he spoke, Judas arrived, followed by a large number of men sent by the high priest, all armed with swords and clubs and carrying burning torches. Judas went up to Jesus and kissed him on the cheek. This was the prearranged signal. Immediately, two men seized Jesus and held him tightly. At once Peter drew his sword and struck off the ear of one of the guards. But Jesus rebuked him. "Put away your sword," he said. "If I need protection, it is my Father in Heaven who will protect me." He touched the man, and at once his ear was whole.

The disciples, terrified at what they saw happening, turned and ran for their lives. Among the crowd was a young man dressed only in a strip of linen. Armed soldiers tried to arrest him, but although they caught hold of his garment, he slipped from them and ran away naked.

MARK
In Mark's Gospel, a man runs away naked when Jesus is arrested. Scholars have suggested that the man may have been Mark himself, as only Mark tells this story.

A young man runs away naked

Soldiers come to arrest Jesus

Judas kisses Jesus on the cheek as a signal to the guards to arrest him

Peter draws his sword and strikes off the ear of one of the guards

Peter's Denial

IN THE STEPS OF JESUS
After Jesus was arrested he was probably led up these stone steps, which date from the 1st century AD. They lead to the traditional site of Caiaphas' house.

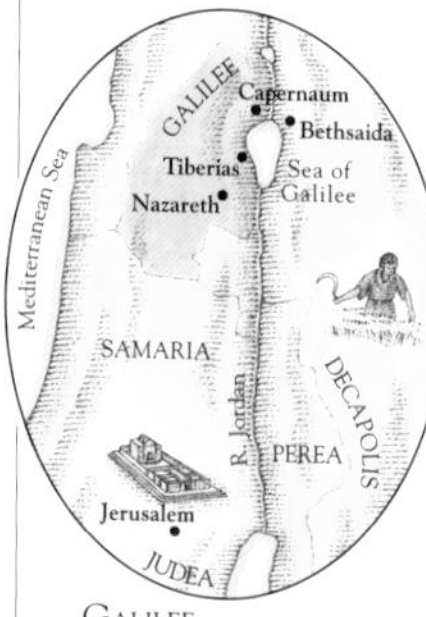

GALILEE
Jesus and all of his disciples, apart from Judas, came from Galilee, a province in the north of Palestine. Galileans spoke with a strong accent and were looked down on by the Judeans in the south.

Peter

Peter is asked three times if he knows Jesus, and three times he denies it

EARLIER, while on the Mount of Olives, Jesus had told his disciples that before the night was over, he would be betrayed by them. Peter had denied that this was possible, and Jesus had looked at him calmly, saying, "Before the cock crows at dawn, you will have disowned me three times." To this Peter had emphatically replied, "Never!"

Jesus was now under arrest, and was taken to the house of Caiaphas, the high priest. There, the scribes and elders and all the members of the Sanhedrin, the powerful Jewish council, had assembled and were waiting to interrogate him. Peter followed at a distance, watching to see what would happen. He went into the courtyard of Caiaphas' house and stood with the guards, who were warming themselves by the fire.

A servant girl came up to Peter and peered closely at him. "Were you not with Jesus of Galilee?" she asked him.

"I know no one of that name," said Peter, getting up and walking to the gateway.

A second girl approached him, saying to her companion, "This is one of the men who was with Jesus of Nazareth."

But Peter quickly denied it. "Not I," he said. "I swear I do not know the man."

By this time several people had gathered around, and were looking at him curiously. "Surely you are one of the disciples?" asked one. "You must be: you speak with a Galilean accent."

Peter turned on them angrily. "Have I not told you? I do not even know the man you are talking about!"

At these words a cock crowed and Peter suddenly remembered Jesus' words, foretelling how he would disown him. Peter walked out of the courtyard and broke down and wept.

COCK
Domesticated chickens were common in Palestine in Jesus' time. Cocks always crowed a few hours before dawn, and soldiers would use this as a signal to change the guard.

IMMEDIATELY THE COCK CREW. AND PETER REMEMBERED THE WORD OF JESUS, WHICH SAID UNTO HIM, "BEFORE THE COCK CROW, THOU SHALT DENY ME THRICE." AND HE WENT OUT, AND WEPT BITTERLY.
MATTHEW 26:74-75

The cock crows and Peter, remembering Jesus' words, goes out of the courtyard and weeps

Jesus Before the Sanhedrin

Jesus is brought before Caiaphas and the council of Jewish leaders

Caiaphas and the council accuse Jesus of insulting God

AGAIN THE HIGH PRIEST ASKED HIM, AND SAID UNTO HIM, "ART THOU THE CHRIST, THE SON OF THE BLESSED?" AND JESUS SAID, "I AM."
MARK 14:61-62

JESUS WAS BROUGHT BEFORE Caiaphas the high priest and the council of Jewish leaders, the Sanhedrin. Determined to find him guilty, they questioned a number of men who had been bribed to lie about Jesus, but none could produce convincing evidence against the prisoner. Eventually, two came forward who swore they had heard Jesus say he could single-handedly destroy the temple, then magically rebuild it within three days.

"What do you say to this?" Caiaphas demanded. Jesus remained silent. Caiaphas spoke to him again. "Are you the Son of God?"

"I am," Jesus quietly replied.

Caiaphas leapt to his feet. "We need no more evidence!" he shouted triumphantly. "No man can be the Son of God! It is insulting God to say so, and the punishment for blasphemy is death!" At this, the members of the council crowded around Jesus, jeering and jostling him and spitting in his face.

The next morning, Jesus, bound and blindfolded, was taken to Pontius Pilate, the Roman governor of Judea.

Judas, full of remorse for having betrayed Jesus, goes away and hangs himself

When Judas heard what had happened, he was overcome with remorse. He went to the priests with the thirty pieces of silver they had given him. "I cannot keep your money for I have betrayed an innocent man," he said, throwing the silver onto the floor of the temple. Then in an agony of shame he went away and hanged himself.

The priests picked up the coins. "This is blood money: we cannot put it into the temple treasury." Having consulted with each other, they decided to spend the sum on the purchase of a certain field belonging to a potter. It would be used as a burying place for foreigners, and became known as the Field of Blood.

The priests pick up the thirty pieces of silver that Judas had thrown down on the temple floor

THIRTY SILVER PIECES
Above is a bronze coin box with Tyrian and Jewish silver shekels, the coinage that Judas may have been paid in. Thirty silver pieces, traditionally the price of a slave, was not worth a large amount in Jesus' time.

JUDAS TREE
The Judas tree, above, is the type of tree that is traditionally believed that Judas hanged himself on. No one knows why Judas betrayed Jesus. One idea is that Judas thought that Jesus was a political leader who had come to overthrow Roman rule and seize power for the Jewish people. When he realized he was mistaken, he betrayed Jesus.

Jesus Before Pilate

PILATE'S COIN
Many new coins that were issued by Pontius Pilate, the Roman govenor of Judea, had a curved rod engraved on them, such as on the coin above. This was the symbol for a Roman augur, or fortune-teller, and replaced the Jewish symbols of palm branches and ears of wheat found on earlier coins. It was offensive to Jewish people, and showed Pilate's lack of sensitivity to Jewish feeling.

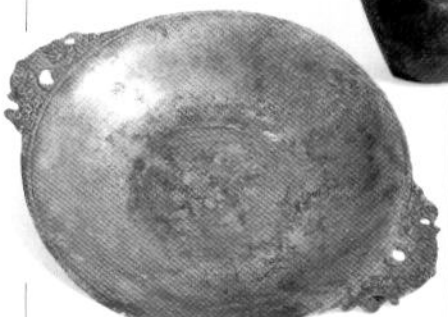

JESUS STOOD in the judgment hall before Pilate, the Roman governor, who questioned him closely. "Are you the king of the Jews?" he asked.

"It is as you say," Jesus replied.

To all other questions and charges Jesus remained silent, much to

Pilate gives the order for Barabbas to be released

Pilate washes his hands in front of the people

He gives the order for Jesus to be flogged

RITUAL WASHING
The bowl and jug shown above were found in a house in Pompeii, Italy, and date from Jesus' time. When Pilate washed his hands in front of the crowd, it symbolized that he wanted no part in condemning Jesus to death.

Pilate's amazement. He could not find any fault with Jesus, and thought that the council had brought Jesus to him out of envy.

It was the custom during the Passover festival for one prisoner, chosen by the people, to be released. Pilate went out and asked the crowd who had gathered, "Whom do you wish me to set free, Barabbas, the rebel and murderer, or Jesus Christ?" He thought that with this choice, the people would ask for Jesus.

But the chief priests and councilors, determined that Jesus should die, persuaded the crowd to ask for Barabbas.

"Then," said Pilate, "what shall I do with Jesus, who is called 'King of the Jews'?"

"Crucify him!" came the cry.

"Why? What crime has he committed?"

But the crowd only shouted all the louder, "Crucify him!"

Pilate shrugged. He called for a bowl of water and publicly washed his hands, saying, "Take note that I am innocent of this man's blood." He gave the order for Barabbas to be released, then he had Jesus flogged before handing him over to the guard.

The soldiers took him to their quarters where they stripped him, dressed him in a robe of royal purple, and placed on his head a crown of thorns. Mockingly they knelt before him. "Hail, King of the Jews!" they jeered, beating him and spitting at him. When they tired of this, they dressed him again in his own clothes, then led him away to be executed in the Roman way, by crucifixion.

CROWN OF THORNS
Crowns were a symbol of royalty and honor in Jesus' time. The Roman soldiers wove a crown out of thorny branches and placed it on Jesus' head to mock the idea of Jesus as a king.

AND WHEN THEY HAD PLAITED A CROWN OF THORNS, THEY PUT IT UPON HIS HEAD, AND A REED IN HIS RIGHT HAND: AND THEY BOWED THE KNEE BEFORE HIM, AND MOCKED HIM, SAYING, "HAIL, KING OF THE JEWS!"
MATTHEW 27:29

The soldiers mockingly kneel before Jesus and shout "Hail King of the Jews!"

The Crucifixion

VIA DOLOROSA
Jesus is believed to have carried the cross along the Via Dolorosa, which means "way of sorrows." The route is marked by 14 "stations of the cross," which recall the events of Jesus' crucifixion.

AS JESUS WAS LED AWAY to be crucified, he was met by Simon of Cyrene. At once the guards seized Simon and forced him to help carry the cross. When they reached Calvary, one of the soldiers offered Jesus a drink of wine mixed with myrrh, but he turned away his head. Then they raised him on the cross, placing above him the mocking inscription, "Jesus of Nazareth, King of the Jews."

The guards threw lots for his clothes before sitting down to keep watch. As people passed to and fro, they taunted the man hanging from the cross. "If you are indeed the Son of God, why don't you save yourself?" they jeered. Then Jesus said, "Father, forgive them, for they do not know what they are doing."

Two robbers are crucified, one on either side of Jesus

Simon of Cyrene helps Jesus carry the cross

The guards throw lots for his clothes

THEN SAID JESUS, "FATHER, FORGIVE THEM; FOR THEY KNOW NOT WHAT THEY DO."
LUKE 23:34

Two robbers were crucified, one on either side of Jesus. One of the criminals hurled insults, but the other defended Jesus. Jesus said to this man, "Today, you will be with me in paradise."

At noon darkness fell on the land, a darkness which lasted until the third hour of the afternoon. Then Jesus cried aloud, "My God, my

God, why have you abandoned me?" Hearing him cry out, one of the men standing at the foot of the cross ran to fetch a sponge soaked in vinegar, which he put on the end of a pole and held up to Jesus' lips. Jesus cried out, "Father, into your hands I commend my spirit." Then his head fell lifeless on his breast. At that same moment, the curtain in the temple was ripped from top to bottom, and a tremor was felt in the very depths of the Earth.

One of the centurions who had been keeping guard said, "Truly this man was the Son of God." And many of the people who were near began to feel afraid. At a little distance stood several women who had come with Jesus from Galilee, among them Mary, his mother, Mary Magdalene, and Mary, the mother of James. They had no fear, and remained where they were, waiting.

That evening Joseph, a rich man from Arimathea, arrived. He was a member of the Jewish council and was one of Jesus' followers. He had come to ask Pilate if he might take down the body from the cross. Pilate gave his permission, so Joseph, helped by a man called Nicodemus, anointed Jesus' body with myrrh and aloes, and wrapped it in a sheet of clean linen. They then laid the body in an unused tomb cut in the rock.

WAS THIS CALVARY? Some people believe that the rocky hill above is the site of Calvary (Golgotha), whose name means "skull." One reason for this is that the rocks form the shape of a human skull. The hill became known as Gordon's Calvary, after a British general, Charles Gordon, who was convinced that this was where Jesus was crucified and buried.

Jesus' body is laid in a tomb

Nicodemus

Several women remain near Jesus

Joseph

Joseph and Nicodemus prepare Jesus' body for burial

AN ALTERNATIVE SITE The other possibility for the site of Calvary (Golgotha) is the low hill on which the Church of the Holy Sepulcher now stands, within the Old City of Jerusalem.

The Resurrection

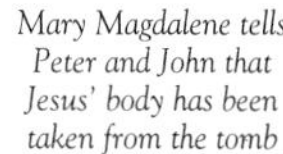

Mary Magdalene tells Peter and John that Jesus' body has been taken from the tomb

John hesitates to go inside the tomb

Peter goes right into the tomb

BURIAL PLACE
The Bible says that Jesus' body was laid in a tomb cut out of rock, which was sealed with a large rolling stone. This type of tomb was common in Jesus' time. Jesus' body would have been laid along one of the rocky ledges that were cut into the walls inside the tomb. The round stone would have been rolled into position along a groove, and held over the entrance by a small stone.

EARLY IN THE MORNING while it was still dark, Mary Magdalene arrived at the tomb. She found to her astonishment that the stone had been rolled away from the entrance. The body was gone. She ran to Peter and also John, the disciple whom Jesus particularly loved. "They have taken the Lord from the tomb," she told them.

The two men hurried to the tomb. John ran ahead and reached it first, but hesitated to go inside. Then Peter arrived, and went right into the tomb. He saw the strips of linen and the burial cloth that had been wrapped around Jesus' head lying on the ground. John joined Peter inside the tomb. They both wondered if Jesus'body had been stolen or if he had risen from the dead.

Peter and John returned home, but Mary stayed by the tomb weeping. Suddenly she looked up to see two angels sitting where the body of Jesus had lain. "Why are you weeping?" they asked her.

"Because they have taken my Lord away."

As she spoke, she turned around and saw a man standing behind her in the shadows. It was Jesus, although at first Mary failed to recognize him. "Why are you weeping?" he said. Believing him to be the gardener, she asked him if he knew where the body had been taken.

"Mary, it is I!"

"My Lord!" she cried, her face full of joy.

"Go now," he told her. "Tell my friends that you have seen me, and that soon I will be with my Father in Heaven."

Mary ran back to tell the disciples the news. "With my own eyes I have seen the Lord!" she said.

WEEPING WOMEN
In Jesus' time, people expressed their grief openly. They wept, tore their clothes, and put ashes on their heads.

Two angels are sitting inside the tomb

Mary turns around and sees Jesus standing behind her

On the Road to Emmaus

EMMAUS
No one knows the exact site of Emmaus, but some people think it was at the village of Amwas, shown above, which is about 20 miles (30 km) west of Jerusalem. The name "Emmaus" means "warm wells."

TWO OF JESUS' FORMER COMPANIONS were walking toward the village of Emmaus, discussing the tremendous events of the past days. As they went along, Jesus himself joined them, but neither man recognized him. "Why do you look so sad?" he asked them.

One of the two, Cleopas, gravely replied, "Where have you come from? Is it possible you have not heard the news?"

"What do you mean?" asked Jesus.

"We are sad because the great prophet, Jesus of Nazareth, has been crucified. We had believed him to be the saviour of our country, but when he died, all our hopes of salvation died with him."

"But do you not understand," said Jesus, "that Christ had to suffer first before he could be glorified?" And he explained what the prophets had foretold.

As they came near the village, the two companions persuaded him

Jesus joins two companions who are traveling to Emmaus

When the friends realize that the stranger is Jesus, he disappears from their sight

to stay the night and to eat with them. As they sat at the table, Jesus broke the bread, blessed it, and gave some to his companions. As he did so, suddenly their eyes were opened and the friends knew who he was, but at the same moment that they recognized him, Jesus disappeared from their sight. The two men were amazed, and asked each other, "Did you not feel something wonderful when he was walking with us on the road, when he explained what the prophets had foretold?" They lost no time in hurrying back to Jerusalem to tell the disciples that they had seen their Lord.

As they were speaking, Jesus again came among them. "Peace be with you," he said. The disciples were terrified, convinced that they saw a ghost. "Why are you frightened?" Jesus asked them. "I am no ghost. Come, touch me. Look at me. Feel the wounds on my hands and feet. Ghosts do not have flesh and bones, as I have." Then he asked them for food, and they gave him some grilled fish, which he ate in front of them.

One of the disciples, Thomas, was not present on this occasion, but he was told later what had happened. He could not believe that it was the Lord whom the others had seen.

"Unless I can feel for myself the wounds on his body I cannot accept that this man is Christ," he said.

A week later the disciples were together, Thomas with them, when Jesus entered.

"Thomas," said Jesus, "put your fingers on my side, touch the holes in my hands. Stop doubting and believe."

"My Lord and my God," said Thomas.

Jesus replied, "You believe because you have seen with your own eyes, but more blessed are those who have not seen and yet still believe."

DOUBTING THOMAS
This detail from a French illuminated manuscript shows Thomas looking at Jesus' wounds. Once Thomas had seen, he believed. Jesus said that a greater blessing awaits those who have faith without having seen him. Thomas' lack of belief earned him the name "Doubting Thomas."

Jesus tells Thomas to touch the wound in his side and the holes in his hands

The Ascension

At Jesus' bidding, the disciples let down their nets, and find them heavy with fish

Peter swims to the shore to see Jesus

CHRISTIAN SYMBOL
The fish was an early Christian symbol. It was used because the Greek word for fish is made up of the first letter of each word of the Greek phrase, "Jesus Christ, God's Son, Saviour."

ONE NIGHT several of the disciples, including Peter, Thomas, James, and John, went out fishing on the Sea of Galilee. All night they fished, but caught nothing. As dawn broke, Jesus, unrecognized, stood watching them on the shore nearby.

"Have you caught anything, my friends?" he called to them.

"Nothing," they tiredly replied.

"Let down your nets on the right side of the boat," he told them. And when they did so, they found the nets so heavy with fish they were barely able to pull them up.

At this sign John said to Peter, "It is the Lord." At once Peter threw

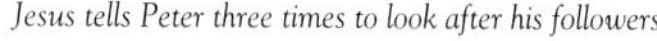

Jesus tells Peter three times to look after his followers

ASCENSION
Jesus ascended to Heaven, as shown in this stone carving, 40 days after he rose from the dead.

off his coat, leapt into the water, and began swimming for the shore. The others followed by boat, dragging their laden nets behind them.

Once on land, they saw fish cooking over a fire. "Come and eat," said Jesus. This was the third time that the Lord had appeared to his disciples since he had risen from the dead.

After they had eaten, Jesus turned to Peter. "Do you love me and have faith in me?"

"Yes, Lord," Peter replied.

"Then look after my flock, my followers."

Again Jesus said, "Do you love me?"

Peter answered, "Yes, Lord, you know that I love you."

"Look after my flock."

A third time Jesus said, "Peter, do you truly love me?"

This time Peter felt hurt that Jesus did not seem to believe him. "Lord, you know everything. You know that I love you."

"Take care of my flock."

Later, Jesus spoke to all of the disciples, telling them that once he had left them they would receive power from the Holy Spirit to help them spread the word of God throughout the world.

After he had spoken, Jesus was lifted up out of their sight, hidden from them in a cloud. As the disciples stood gazing up into the sky, two men dressed in white appeared beside them. "Jesus, who has been taken up into Heaven, will one day return to you in the same way."

Two men dressed in white appear beside the disciples

Jesus is lifted up out of the disciples' sight, hidden from them in a cloud

The Early Church

THE ACTS OF THE APOSTLES tells the story of the Church's early years, when the 12 apostles continued to preach Jesus' message to the people. Jesus chose 12 men to be his apostles: they were his close companions and he gave them authority to teach and heal in his name.

The word "apostle" means someone who is sent, a messenger. Paul is also called an apostle in the Bible, even though he was not one of the original 12 men whom Jesus chose to be his close companions. The apostles had special authority in the church.

Jesus' 12 original disciples became his apostles, or messengers, preaching his message to a wider audience.

The Apostles: Jesus' Original 12 Disciples

ANDREW – one of the first disciples called by Jesus, and a fisherman from Bethsaida in Galilee. He is said to have died on an X-shaped cross.

PETER – Andrew's brother, also a fisherman. Jesus called him "the rock" because of his firm faith.

JAMES – another fisherman. Jesus called him and his brother, John, "the sons of thunder."

JOHN – James' brother. In the Bible he is probably "the disciple Jesus loved."

PHILIP – also from Bethsaida. He spoke to Jesus when he miraculously fed a crowd of 5,000 people with loaves and fishes.

BARTHOLOMEW – sometimes called Nathanael. Little is known about him.

MATTHEW – worked in Capernaum, on the shores of the Sea of Galilee, as a despised collector of taxes for the Romans.

THOMAS – John's Gospel calls him "the twin." He is also known as "Doubting Thomas" because he did not at first believe in Jesus' resurrection.

JAMES – or "James the lesser," probably because he was shorter or younger than the other James.

SIMON – whose nickname was "the Zealot," either because he was a keen student of Jewish law or he belonged to a group of Galileans who fought the Romans when and where they could.

THADDAEUS – He is probably the same person as Judas son of James (not Iscariot) in Luke's Gospel.

JUDAS – his second name, Iscariot, is Hebrew for a person from Kerioth in Judea, suggesting that he came from this place. It was Judas Iscariot who looked after the disciples' money. After Judas betrayed Jesus and killed himself, Matthias took his place as an apostle.

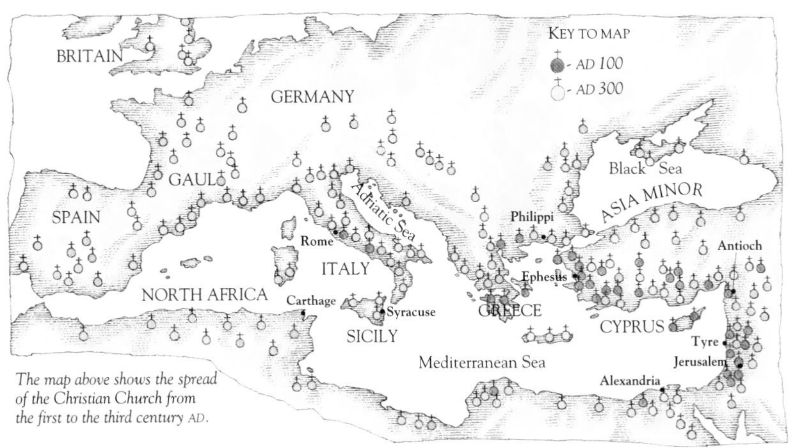

The map above shows the spread of the Christian Church from the first to the third century AD.

Pentecost

It is often said that Christianity began in Jerusalem, at the Jewish festival of Pentecost, 50 days after the death of Jesus. His followers, who had been frightened, became certain about their belief in Jesus and in his resurrection and boldly told other people about him. They said that God's Holy Spirit gave them a new courage. The apostle Peter was one of the main leaders.

Because they said that Jesus was the Son of God, Christians clashed with Jewish leaders, who did not believe this. The first martyr – the name given to someone who is killed for his or her beliefs – was Stephen. Among the people who stoned him to death was Paul, who later became a great Christian leader himself.

The First Christians

At first it was only Jewish men and women who became Christians. Later the apostles began to preach about Jesus to the Gentiles, people who were not Jews. Their message spread quickly, but they often faced opposition from the Roman authorities. The Emperor Nero, who ruled from AD 54 – 68, blamed Christians for the fire of Rome in AD 64, and put many of them to death.

The early Christians shared what they owned

FIGHTING THE LIONS
The Romans trained gladiators to fight wild beasts, but they also threw Christians to the lions for sport. This second-century Roman wall painting is from a Roman amphitheater.

and met to worship Jesus. The main service then, as now, was the Eucharist, which means "the thanksgiving." A small amount of bread and wine is eaten as a reminder of Jesus' death and the new life Christians believe he gives.

The cross became an important sign for Christians, but they also had a secret symbol, a fish. The letters of the Greek word for fish – "Ichthus" – also stood for "Jesus Christ, God's Son, Saviour." If people wanted to show that they were Christians, they drew the fish sign, perhaps with a stick in the dust or with a finger in the palm of the hand.

cross

fish

Tongues of Fire

SUDDENLY THERE CAME A SOUND FROM HEAVEN AS OF A RUSHING MIGHTY WIND, AND IT FILLED ALL THE HOUSE WHERE THEY WERE SITTING. AND THERE APPEARED UNTO THEM CLOVEN TONGUES LIKE AS OF FIRE, AND IT SAT UPON EACH OF THEM.
ACTS OF THE APOSTLES 2:2-3

A small flame flickers over the head of each apostle, a sign that the Holy Spirit is with them

THE DISCIPLES, as they continued in their work of spreading God's word, also became known as the apostles. In order to replace the traitor Judas, and bring their number again up to twelve, they put forward the names of two men, Joseph and Matthias. Having prayed for guidance, they all cast lots, and in this way Matthias was chosen.

Later, on the day of the Jewish harvest festival of Pentecost, the apostles were gathered in one room. Suddenly the sound of a mighty wind was heard rushing through the house, and over the head of each man flickered a small flame, a sign that the Holy Spirit was with them. As they turned in amazement and began to talk, they found they were able to speak in many different languages.

As the disciples walked through the streets of Jerusalem, news of their astonishing gift spread far and wide. Jewish people from many different countries had come to stay in Jerusalem for Pentecost. They came up to talk with the apostles, and were amazed because the apostles could speak and understand any language from any part of the world.

Eventually Peter started to preach to the crowd. He told them of Jesus of Nazareth and the miracles worked by him in God's name, and how Jesus had died on the cross and then rose from the dead, and was now in Heaven by God's right hand.

"But what should we do? How shall we be saved?" everyone anxiously asked one another.

"Turn away from sin," said Peter. "Repent and be baptized in the name of Jesus Christ and you will receive the gift of the Holy Spirit. This promise is for you and your children." Those who accepted what Peter said were baptized: about three thousand became followers of Jesus that day.

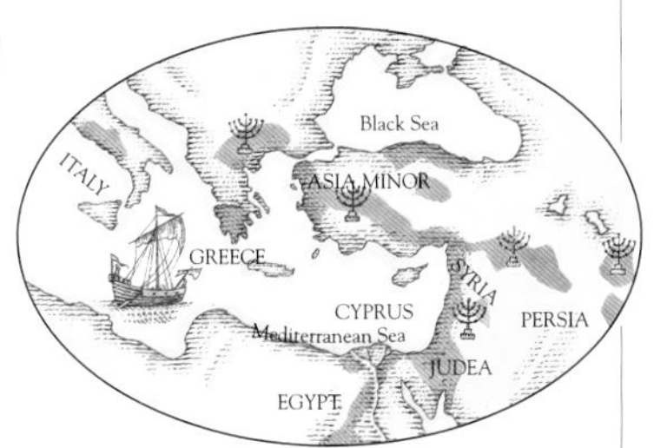

DIASPORA
Throughout much of their history, many Jewish people have lived in countries far from Judea. This is called the "Diaspora," a Greek word meaning "scattering." By the 1st century AD many Jewish people had settled in other countries, such as Italy and Egypt. Jerusalem was still thought of as the center of Jewish faith, and the Bible says that Jewish people came from many lands to celebrate the festival of Pentecost in the holy city.

Peter preaches to the crowd

Peter the Healer

Peter tells the beggar to get up and walk

ONE AFTERNOON Peter and John went to the temple to pray. Outside the gateway called Beautiful was a lame man who had been unable to walk from birth, and now begged for coins from passers-by. As the two apostles came toward him, he asked them for money. "Look at me," said Peter, holding out his hand to the beggar. "I do not have silver and gold, but what I have I give to you. In the name of Jesus of Nazareth, get up and walk!" At once the man leapt to his feet, and without any support went with Peter and John into the temple courtyard. He was overjoyed that he had been healed, and loudly sang songs of praise to God.

People were astonished to see the beggar walk, and soon a crowd had gathered around the three men. "Why are you amazed?" Peter asked them. "This is not our doing. It is by faith in Jesus that this man was made strong." Then Peter began to speak to the crowd about Jesus.

The priests and Sadducees and the captain of the temple guard were

THE WESTERN WALL
Above is a section of the Western Wall, the only remaining part of Herod's Temple. Jews come here to pray and to mourn the destruction of Jerusalem in AD 70. They tuck written prayers and requests in between the huge blocks of stone that make up the wall.

A crowd gathers around Peter, John, and the beggar, and Peter begins to preach

The priests and the Sadducees are angry

angry that Jesus' followers were preaching to the people. They had Peter and John arrested and thrown into jail.

The next day the prisoners were brought before the Jewish council, the Sanhedrin. "By whose authority do you preach in the temple?" the judges asked them.

Inspired by the Holy Spirit, Peter replied, "It is of Jesus of Nazareth that I preach, and through him that the lame man was healed."

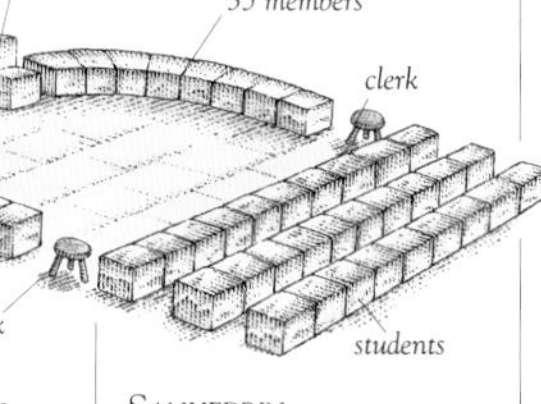

SANHEDRIN
The Sanhedrin, or council, was the highest court of justice among the Jewish people in Jesus' time. Its 71 members sat in a semi-circle, with the high priest – the leader of the council – in the middle. Two clerks sat on stools and took notes during meetings. The Sanhedrin was dominated by the Sadducees, who were a powerful group made up of priests and wealthy people. The other members included Pharisees, who were upholders of the Jewish law, and scribes, who were writers and specialists in the law. The Sanhedrin had the power to judge, punish, and imprison the Jewish people, but only the Romans could pass the death penalty.

Peter and John are arrested and brought before the Sanhedrin

When the council saw that the apostles were simple, uneducated men, they were astonished, and took note that these men had been friends of Jesus. They ordered Peter and John to leave, then discussed among themselves what they should do. They knew they could not deny that a miracle had happened, but they did not want the news spreading any farther. So they called the two men back and warned them not to preach in the name of Jesus any more. To this Peter and John replied, "Judge for yourselves whether it is right in God's eyes to obey you rather than God. We cannot help but speak of all we have seen and heard." The Sanhedrin could not decide how to punish them, so they reluctantly let them go.

AND THEY CALLED THEM, AND COMMANDED THEM NOT TO SPEAK AT ALL NOR TEACH IN THE NAME OF JESUS.
ACTS OF THE APOSTLES 4:18

The Death of Stephen

Stephen preaches to the people

AND STEPHEN, FULL OF FAITH AND POWER, DID GREAT WONDERS AND MIRACLES AMONG THE PEOPLE.
ACTS OF THE APOSTLES 6:8

MARTYRDOM
This painting is of Stephen, who was the first Christian martyr. Originally, "martyr" meant "witness," but because so many early Christians were killed for their beliefs, the word has come to mean someone who dies for their faith.

Stephen stays calm as the Jewish elders accuse him of speaking against God and Moses

AS THE WORK OF THE DISCIPLES INCREASED, so their number grew. One of them in particular, Stephen, worked many miracles, and preached with great fire and conviction. Some of the Jewish elders were angry at the following he had among the people. They had him brought before the council, where they produced false evidence that he had spoken against God and Moses. But as he listened to their lies, Stephen stayed calm, his face as beautiful as an angel's.

"We are told you say that Jesus of Nazareth intends to destroy Jerusalem," the elders claimed.

"Is this true?" the high priest asked him.

Stephen tried to persuade them that Jesus was the fulfilment of God's plan for his people, but they would not accept what he said.

"The truth," said Stephen, "is that you have betrayed and murdered Jesus, the righteous one."

The council members were enraged by the disciple's words, and ground their teeth with anger. But Stephen, looking upward, said, "I see the glory of God in Heaven, and Jesus standing by his right side."

LIONS' GATE
Traditionally, Stephen is believed to have been stoned near Lions' Gate, which is also known as Saint Stephen's Gate. It is on the eastern side of the wall that surrounds the Old City of Jerusalem.

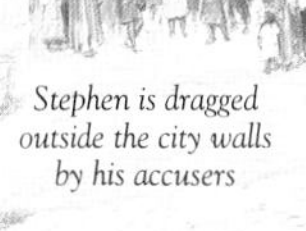

Stephen is dragged outside the city walls by his accusers

Stephen's accusers leave their cloaks with a young man called Saul

Stephen is stoned to death

At this his accusers, yelling with fury, covered their ears so they should hear no more. They seized Stephen, and dragged him outside the city walls. They left their cloaks with a young man called Saul, who watched as Stephen was stoned to death. As he died, Stephen prayed to God that his executioners should be forgiven.

This was the beginning of a terrible period of persecution for the Christians. Many, although not the apostles, had to flee for their lives, wandering homeless through foreign lands.

Saul's Journey to Damascus

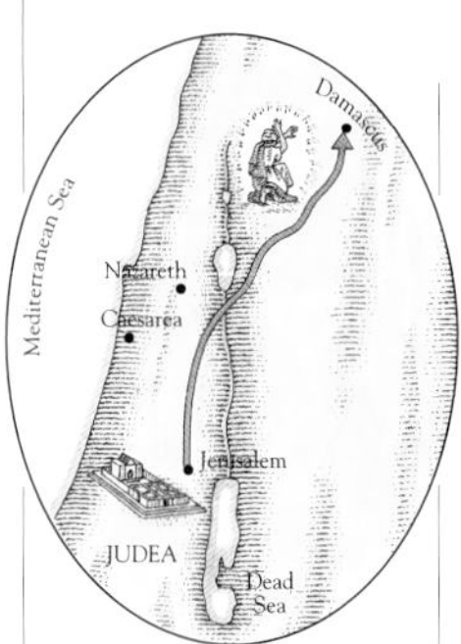

SAUL'S JOURNEY
Following Stephen's martyrdom, many Christians fled from Jerusalem and settled in Damascus. Saul set off from Jerusalem to arrest any Christians he could find. It is about 150 miles (240 km) from Jerusalem to Damascus, so Saul's journey, either on foot or by donkey, would have taken several days.

SAUL WAS ONE OF the great enemies of the early church. Due to leave Jerusalem for Damascus, he went to see the high priest and obtained from him the authority to have any man or woman arrested whom he suspected of being a follower of Jesus.

As he approached the city of Damascus, Saul was suddenly surrounded by a blinding white light. He staggered, and fell to the ground. Then a voice spoke in his ear. "Saul, Saul, why do you persecute me?"

Trembling and astonished, Saul said, "Who are you, Lord?"

And he heard the voice say, "I am Jesus, whom you are persecuting. Rise and go into the city and there you will be told what you must do."

Unsteadily, Saul got to his feet, but when he opened his eyes, he found he was unable to see. His companions led him into the city, and for three days he remained sightless, refusing both food and drink.

On the way to Damascus, Saul is blinded by a white light and falls to the ground

AS HE JOURNEYED, HE CAME NEAR DAMASCUS: AND SUDDENLY THERE SHINED ROUND ABOUT HIM A LIGHT FROM HEAVEN: AND HE FELL TO THE EARTH, AND HEARD A VOICE SAYING UNTO HIM, "SAUL, SAUL, WHY PERSECUTEST THOU ME?"
ACTS OF THE APOSTLES 9:3-4

Saul's sight is restored by Ananias

There lived in Damascus a disciple of Jesus called Ananias, and to him the Lord appeared in a vision. "Go to the house of Judas in Straight Street, and ask there for Saul of Tarsus. You must lay your hands on him and restore his sight, for I have chosen him to do great things for my people."

Anananias did as he had been instructed and went to Judas' house. "Brother," said Ananias to Saul, "the Lord has sent me so that you may see again and be filled with the Holy Spirit." He then laid his hands gently over Saul's eyes. Immediately his sight returned. Saul joyfully rose from his bed and was baptized. For the next few days he remained in Damascus to preach in the synagogues and spread the word of God. All who heard him were amazed at such a change of heart. "Is it possible," they asked each other, "that this is the same man who so fiercely persecuted the followers of Jesus?"

Some people, however, saw him as an enemy and planned to kill him. Saul heard of their plan, and with the help of some of the disciples he escaped at night in a basket lowered over the city wall. He then made his way to Jerusalem. At first, the disciples there were afraid of Saul and refused to accept him.

Saul escapes at night from Damascus in a basket lowered over the city wall

However, one of their number, Barnabas, believed Saul, and taking him to the apostles, explained what had happened on the road to Damascus. After this, Saul was welcomed as a true follower of Jesus.

STRAIGHT STREET
Above is Straight Street in Damascus, where Saul's sight was restored. It was one of the main routes through Damascus, a major trading center. It is called "straight" because it runs in a straight line through the city.

FROM SAUL TO PAUL
After Saul was converted, he became known by his Roman name, Paul. Shown in the mosaic above, Paul was a clear speaker and writer and played a vital role in the development of Christianity.

Peter and Cornelius

THERE LIVED IN CAESAREA a centurion called Cornelius, a good man who worshiped God and was generous to the poor. One day an angel appeared to him. "You must send men to Joppa to bring back Peter," said the angel. "He is lodging there with Simon, a tanner, in a house by the sea."

Cornelius is a good man who is generous to the poor

Once the angel had gone, Cornelius called two of his servants and a trusted soldier and sent them to Joppa.

The following day about noon, when Cornelius' men were approaching the city, Peter went up to the roof to pray. He was hungry, but while waiting for food to be prepared, he fell into a trance. He saw Heaven opening above him, and a great sheet descending to the Earth containing every sort of animal and bird. "Eat, Peter, eat," said a voice.

"Surely not Lord, I have never eaten anything that is unclean," Peter replied.

"Nothing is unclean that God has made clean," said the voice. Two more times Peter saw the same vision before the sheet was taken back to Heaven.

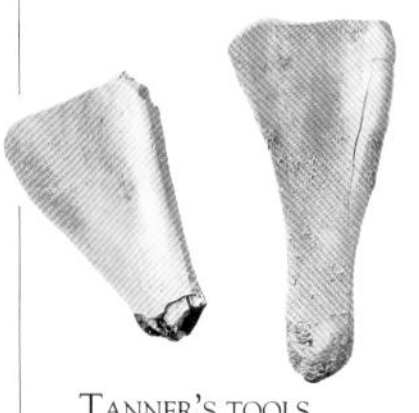

TANNER'S TOOLS
A tanner made leather from animal skins. He scraped hair and fat from the skins using a tool made of bone, like the ones above. He soaked the skins in lime and the juices of plants to soften them. The bad smell their work produced meant that tanners lived outside the towns and cities.

Peter is on the roof of Simon's house when he sees a great sheet descending containing every sort of animal and bird

Cornelius' men come to the house to ask Peter to return with them

As Peter enters the house, Cornelius falls down on his knees before him

JOPPA
Joppa, modern-day Jaffa, lies on the Mediterranean Sea and is one of the oldest seaports in the world. It is mentioned in both the Old and New Testaments. This attractive city, whose name means "beautiful," is built on a rocky hill about 116 ft (35 m) high. It was once the main port for Jerusalem, 35 miles (56 km) away. Today, only small fishing boats use the port.

Peter was puzzling over the meaning of the vision when the three men sent by Cornelius arrived at Simon's house, where they were invited to stay as guests.

The next day, Peter, understanding that it was God's will, returned with them to Caesarea. Cornelius, who was surrounded by his family and friends, was waiting to greet him. As Peter entered the house, he fell down on his knees before him. "Do not kneel," said Peter gently. "I, too, am a man, just as you are."

Peter then spoke to all who were gathered there. "God has shown me that all people, Jew and Gentile, are equal in his eyes, that none should be regarded as inferior or unclean."

After a few days Peter went on to Jerusalem. The apostles and other followers of Jesus criticized him for mixing with people of different beliefs, with Gentiles who had not been baptized. Peter told them of his vision. "All people are the same in the sight of God," he said.

AND AS PETER WAS COMING IN, CORNELIUS MET HIM, AND FELL DOWN AT HIS FEET, AND WORSHIPED HIM. BUT PETER TOOK HIM UP, SAYING, "STAND UP; I MYSELF ALSO AM A MAN."
ACTS OF THE APOSTLES 10:25-26

Peter in Prison

After the angel has led him out of prison, Peter finds himself alone in the city

Peter lies sleeping in prison, chained to two soldiers

An angel appears and tells Peter to get up quickly

AND, BEHOLD, THE ANGEL OF THE LORD CAME UPON HIM, AND A LIGHT SHINED IN THE PRISON: AND HE SMOTE PETER ON THE SIDE, AND RAISED HIM UP, SAYING, "ARISE UP QUICKLY." AND HIS CHAINS FELL OFF FROM HIS HANDS.
ACTS OF THE APOSTLES 12:7

KING HEROD AGRIPPA was a fierce enemy of the church. Having had several Christians executed, he arrested Peter during the Passover festival and threw him into prison. There he was heavily guarded throughout the four watches of the day and night by four squads of four soldiers each.

The night before his trial, Peter was sleeping, bound with two chains between two of the soldiers, while the remaining two stood guard at the door. Suddenly an angel appeared in a blaze of light and struck Peter on his side. "Get up quickly," he said. "Put on your cloak and sandals and follow me." As he spoke, Peter's chains fell away and he was free. As if in a dream, Peter followed the angel out of the prison. Silently, they passed the guards, and the gates of the prison opened as of their own accord.

Once out into the streets of the city, the angel disappeared and Peter found himself alone. Now he knew that this had not been a dream, but that God had rescued him from imprisonment and from King Herod's evil plans.

Peter went straight to the house of Mary, mother of Mark, where a number of people had gathered to pray for him. His knock was heard by Rhoda, a young servant girl. But when she heard Peter's voice, she was so overjoyed that instead of opening the door she ran back and told the company who it was standing outside. "It cannot be!" they exclaimed. "He is in prison: it cannot be him!

But Rhoda insisted that it was Peter at the door, so that they began to wonder if it could be his ghost. Peter kept on knocking until at last they went to open the door. When they saw it was indeed Peter, they were astonished.

The next morning panic broke out in the prison when it was discovered that Peter was gone. Herod was beside himself with rage and organized a thorough search, but Peter was nowhere to be found. No one could explain what had happened, and in his fury Herod commanded that all Peter's guards be put to death.

Rhoda

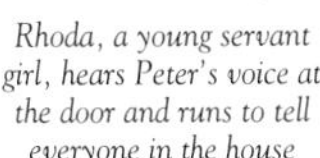

Rhoda, a young servant girl, hears Peter's voice at the door and runs to tell everyone in the house

The people are astonished when they open the door and see Peter standing there

ANGELS
In the Bible, angels are spiritual beings who are close to God and are immortal. Traditionally, angels were often depicted as having wings, similar to the angel in this stained-glass panel. Angels fulfilled a number of roles. They were sent by God as messengers of good news. They guided, instructed, and warned people. They were protectors – helping people in times of need. They carried out God's judgment. They praised God and obeyed him at all times.

Paul's Journeys

Paul traveled to see new groups of Christians.

AFTER PAUL BECAME a Christian, he traveled widely to spread the word about Jesus. He used the network of roads that the Romans had built throughout their empire. Paul was a Roman citizen and this gave him freedom of movement and some protection on his journeys. The fastest way to travel was on horseback and by ship, which was how letters were carried from place to place. When Paul could not be with new groups of Christians, he wrote letters to them about following Jesus.

Paul's First Journey

Paul traveled around the eastern part of the Mediterranean Sea to spread the message of Christianity. On his first journey he went to the island of Cyprus, where his companion Barnabas was born. They taught in the synagogues at Salamis and in other parts of the island. When they returned to the mainland they were welcomed in some places, but at others, such as Iconium and Lystra, the people refused to listen to their message.

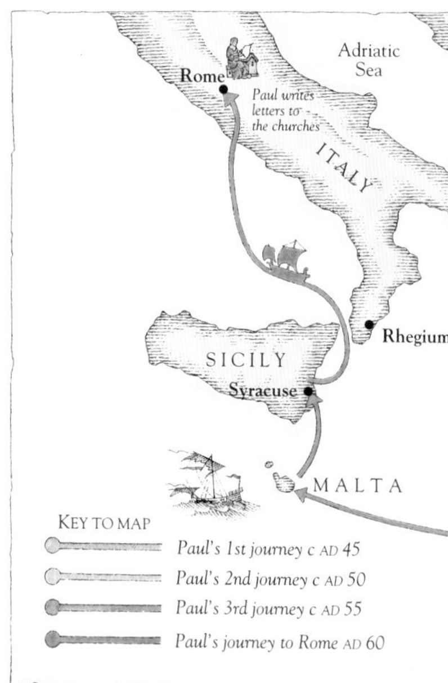

The map above shows the routes of Paul's three missionary journeys and his final journey to Rome.

CYPRUS
On his first journey Paul visited Cyprus, a beautiful Mediterranean island with a rocky coastline. A Jewish community had been on the island since the 4th century BC, and even before Paul arrived, there were some Christians living there. The purpose of Paul's journeys was to help more people become Christians, as well as to support and encourage those who had already become followers of Jesus.

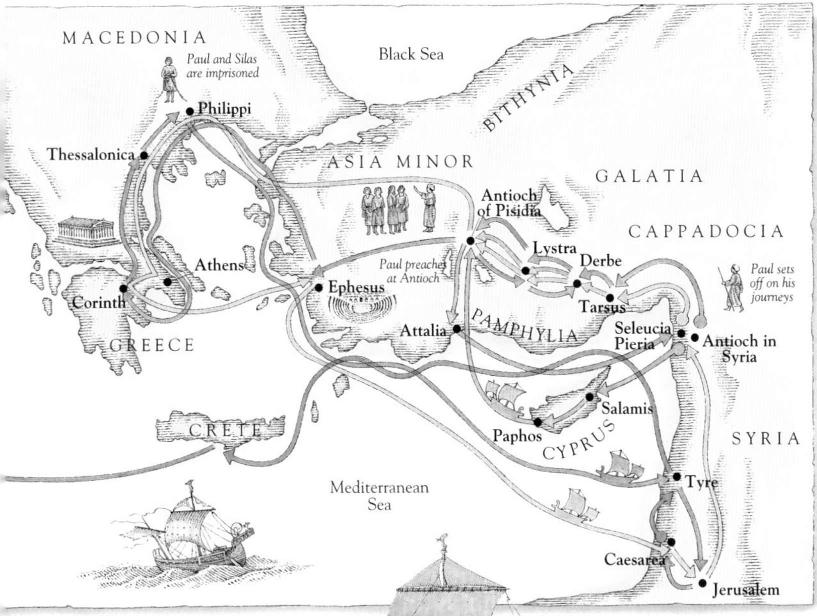

Paul's Second and Third Journeys
On his second journey, Paul, with a friend named Silas, traveled farther afield. He preached in the great cities of Philippi, Ephesus, and Athens and Corinth in Greece. On his third missionary journey, Paul stayed for some time at Ephesus. Travelers from east and west came by land and sea to this great city. In the massive theater a huge crowd demonstrated against Paul when he tried to prevent the worship of the goddess Artemis, who was called Diana by the Romans.

Grain ship

Paul's Last Journey
Paul was arrested when he returned to Jerusalem to care for the Christians there. His last long journey took place because he asked to be taken to Rome to state his case to the emperor. He traveled under guard on a grain ship, that was wrecked off the coast of Malta. When they eventually reached Rome, Paul was put under house arrest. During his imprisonment, he wrote many letters of encouragement to the Christian churches he had helped establish.

We do not know when and how Paul died, but it is thought that he may have been beheaded on the orders of the Emperor Nero in the year AD 64. In the 30 years between his conversion and his death, Paul founded churches in 20 cities of the Roman Empire.

Nero was emperor from AD54-68.

The Adventures of Paul

A man unable to walk from birth is cured by Paul

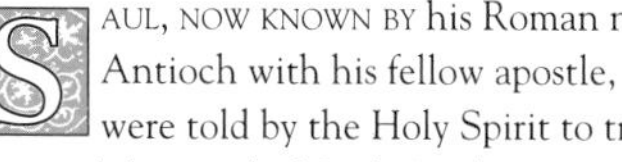

SAUL, NOW KNOWN BY his Roman name, Paul, was teaching in Antioch with his fellow apostle, Barnabas. The two men were told by the Holy Spirit to travel farther afield in order to spread the word of God. On this mission they went to Seleucia, to Cyprus, and to Pamphylia.

They came to Lystra, where there was a man in the crowd who had been unable to walk since birth. Paul, knowing that the man had faith, said to him, "Get up and walk." Immediately the man rose to his feet and walked. When the people saw this, they were astonished, and told each other that gods had come among them disguised as men. They hailed Barnabas as Zeus and Paul as Hermes.

The priest of the temple of Zeus, which lay just outside the city, heard of the miracle. He hurried to bring oxen and garlands of flowers so that he could offer sacrifices to Paul and Barnabas. But when they

ZEUS
The silver brooch above shows Zeus, the chief Greek god, who was known as Jupiter to the Romans. Zeus was the god of thunder and the ruler of heaven. The people hailed Barnabas as Zeus, and Paul as Hermes, or Mercury, the messenger god.

The priest of Zeus brings oxen covered in garlands of flowers to offer to Paul and Barnabas

At the river Paul and Silas meet Lydia, who invites them to stay at her house

A fortune-teller, possessed by an evil spirit, follows Paul and Silas

realized what was happening, they were horrified, and ran out into the crowd, tearing their clothes and urging the people to come to their senses. "We are ordinary men, just like you," they said. "We beg you to turn away from such foolishness and worship God!"

Some time after this Paul traveled with his companions to Philippi in Macedonia. On the Sabbath they went down to the river to speak to the women who were gathered there. One of these, Lydia, a seller of purple cloth, asked to be baptized. She then invited Paul, Silas, and the other disciples to stay in her house.

Paul and Silas returned regularly to the river to pray. One day they met a young slave girl whose owners made money out of her by exploiting her gifts as a fortune-teller. She followed the two men, talking and shouting wildly. Paul saw that she was possessed by an evil spirit, so he commanded the spirit in Jesus' name to leave her. At once the girl became calm, but when the spirit left her so did her powers of seeing into the future. This angered her owners, who were no longer able to make money from her.

They followed Paul and Silas into the marketplace, where they had the apostles arrested and brought before the magistrate for unlawfully disturbing the peace.

AND WHEN LYDIA WAS BAPTIZED, AND HER HOUSEHOLD, SHE BESOUGHT US, SAYING, "IF YE HAVE JUDGED ME TO BE FAITHFUL TO THE LORD, COME INTO MY HOUSE, AND ABIDE THERE."
ACTS OF THE APOSTLES 16:15

ARTEMIS
This statue of the Greek goddess, Artemis, known to the Romans as Diana, is in Ephesus, Turkey. Artemis was the goddess of fertility, hunting, and the moon. The Ephesians built a magnificent temple in her honor, and thousands of people flocked to Ephesus each year to worship there. Many of the visitors bought silver shrines to Artemis, and the silversmiths depended on this for their livelihood.

The prison door flies open, but Paul assures the jailer that he and Silas are still inside

On the magistrate's orders, the disciples were stripped, beaten, and thrown into jail, where they were fastened by their feet in the stocks.

At midnight, as Paul and Silas were praying and praising God, the prison was shaken to its foundations by a great earthquake: all the doors flew wide open, and everyone's chains were loosed. The jailer awoke with a start. Seeing every door standing open, he assumed the prisoners had escaped. Knowing the punishment he would receive for this, he drew his sword and he would have killed himself but Paul cried, "Put away your sword! We are all here!"

The jailer called for lights and rushed into the cell, then fell on his knees before the disciples. "What must I do to be saved?" he asked.

"Only have faith in Jesus," they told him.

The jailer washed and dressed their wounds and gave Paul and Silas clothes before taking them to his own house and giving them food. He and all his household were then baptized.

Next morning the magistrate ordered the two prisoners to be released, and Paul and Silas returned to the house of Lydia.

Some time later, Paul traveled to Ephesus to preach. In the city there was a silversmith called Demetrius who earned his living by making shrines used in worshiping the goddess Artemis. Demetrius was worried that Paul was turning people away from Artemis, and that soon no one would want to buy his silver shrines. "Not only is our livelihood in danger," he told his fellow craftsmen, "but this preacher is destroying people's faith in our goddess!"

Demetrius the silversmith tells his fellow craftsmen that Paul is threatening their livelihood

Soon an angry crowd had gathered in the city's theater. Paul wanted to speak to them, but the disciples banned him from entering the theater for his own safety. "Great is our goddess, Artemis of the Ephesians!" the crowd shouted defiantly. Eventually the city clerk restored order, and soon afterward Paul left Ephesus for Troas in Macedonia.

Paul and the disciples met to worship in the upstairs room of a house. Paul spoke until midnight, for he was leaving the following day. One of his audience was a young man named Eutychus; he was sitting on a windowsill, where he fell asleep. Suddenly he lost his balance and fell to his death three stories below. Paul ran down to the street, and taking the young man in his arms said to his friends, "Do not worry: his life has now returned to him."

Greatly comforted, they all returned with Eutychus to the house, and Paul continued preaching until dawn.

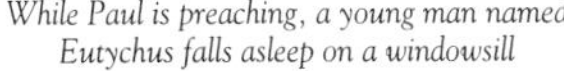

While Paul is preaching, a young man named Eutychus falls asleep on a windowsill

The disciples bar Paul from entering the theater

EPHESUS
In ancient times, the wealthy seaport of Ephesus was an important trading center. Its impressive theater was 495 ft. (151 meters) wide, and the marble seats held about 25,000 people. A wide road, flanked on both sides with columns, led from the theater to the city's natural harbor.

THERE SAT IN A WINDOW A CERTAIN YOUNG MAN NAMED EUTYCHUS, BEING FALLEN INTO A DEEP SLEEP.
ACTS OF THE APOSTLES 20:9

Paul Is Arrested

Agabus ties Paul's belt around his own hands and feet

PAUL AND HIS COMPANIONS arrived in Caesarea to stay at the house of Philip, one of the disciples. Here they were visited by Agabus, a prophet, who, to show the dangers that lay ahead, took Paul's belt and with it tied up his own hands and feet. "If you go to Jerusalem," he said, "this is how you will be treated by the people. They will seize you and hand you over to the Romans."

But Paul was unafraid. "I am prepared not only to be taken captive, but to die in the name of Jesus."

Soon after this, he and his friends left for Jerusalem. Paul went to the temple, where he was recognized by a group of Jews. "This is the

CAESAREA
The city of Caesarea, on the Mediterranean coast, was Judea's main seaport and the Roman's administrative center. Built by Herod the Great, the city was named in honor of the Roman emperor, Augustus Caesar. The most impressive feature at Caesarea was its huge, walled harbor, shown above. It was built to protect ships from the rough seas, and to prevent the harbor from becoming full of silt.

Paul faces the crowd on the fortress steps and tells them how he became a Christian

man who has spoken against us and our law!" they cried. Seizing hold of Paul they dragged him out of the temple. The uproar was so great that the Roman commander of the garrison was summoned. He and his centurions pushed their way through the crowd and rescued Paul from his attackers. They then led him away to the fortress. Paul turned and faced the crowd on the fortress steps. "I, a Jew, have persecuted many Christians in the past. But one day while on the road to Damascus I heard the voice of Jesus. Since then I have been baptized and have spread the word to both Jew and Gentile."

At this the crowd shouted even more. "Kill him! Kill him!" they yelled. The commander gave orders for the prisoner to be taken inside the castle and flogged. But while one of the soldiers was tying him down, Paul asked, "Is it lawful for you to flog me, a Roman citizen, and one who has not been accused of any crime?" The commander hesitated, for he knew he had no right to treat a citizen of Rome in this way. He commanded that they should untie Paul.

But this did not satisfy some of the crowd, who swore they would neither eat nor drink until they had killed Paul. They demanded that the commander bring Paul to be interrogated by their council, meaning to murder him on his way to the court. However, a nephew of Paul's heard of the plot and warned his uncle of the danger he was in. "You must tell the commander of this," said Paul.

When the young man had spoken, the commander swore him to secrecy. He then gave orders that his prisoner be taken by night to Caesarea with a large escort of heavily armed horsemen and infantry.

Paul is taken prisoner and is tied up, ready to be flogged

Herod's Temple

fortress of Antonia

FORT OF ANTONIA
The fortress of Antonia, where Paul would have been taken to be flogged, stood next to Herod's Temple. It reminded people of the Roman presence in Palestine.

Paul is taken by night to Caesarea with a large escort of heavily armed horsemen and infantry

Paul's Journey to Rome

Paul is shipwrecked off the coast of Malta

IT WAS FINALLY DECIDED that Paul should be taken to Rome and stand trial before Caesar himself. He and certain other prisoners were put in the charge of a centurion named Julius, and under his care they set sail from Adramyttium.

As they came near to the island of Crete, a strong wind began to blow, and soon a storm was howling round them. In fear of their lives, the sailors hauled down the sails, then strengthened the sides of the ship with ropes before finally throwing overboard anything they could lay their hands on. For three days and nights the storm raged and death seemed near.

AND WHEN NEITHER SUN NOR STARS IN MANY DAYS APPEARED, AND NO SMALL TEMPEST LAY ON US, ALL HOPE THAT WE SHOULD BE SAVED WAS THEN TAKEN AWAY.
ACTS OF THE APOSTLES 27:20

Paul, however, calmed their fears. "God has told me that although the ship will be wrecked, none of you will die," he said to them. Eventually the watch reported that they were running into shallow water. Paul repeated that they need not fear, that no harm would come to any of them. "Now you must eat," he said, "to keep up your strength and your spirits. Remember what I have told you: no one will lose his life, but you must have food to survive." Then Paul took some bread, broke it into pieces, and gave thanks to God. Everyone drew courage from this and began to eat.

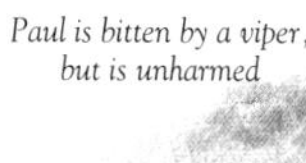

Paul is bitten by a viper, but is unharmed

At dawn they saw that they had drifted near the shore, and so by hoisting the mainsail they brought the ship onto a sandy bank where she ran aground before breaking up in the rough water. At first the soldiers wanted to kill the prisoners, fearing that they might in the confusion try to escape. Julius, however, anxious for Paul's safety, persuaded them to let the captives save themselves as best they could. He ordered all who could swim to jump into the sea, the rest to hang on to any broken plank or piece of rigging and propel themselves to land.

ST. PAUL'S BAY
Above is St. Paul's Bay, in Malta, where Paul is believed to have been shipwrecked. Paul's voyage took place in winter, when storms are most likely to arise on the Mediterranean Sea. In the Bible it says that as the ship approached Malta, it struck a sand bank. This detail fits St. Paul's Bay, which has a sandy ridge that runs out into the sea.

Paul cures Publius' father

The island to which they had come was Malta, and the inhabitants welcomed the shipwrecked survivors, lighting a fire to warm them, for it was raining and bitterly cold. Paul, who had been gathering sticks for the fire, was suddenly attacked by a viper, whose poisonous bite is known to be fatal. But Paul, unhurt, shook off the snake, which left not even a mark on his hand. The people were amazed. "This man must be a god," they said.

The governor of the island, Publius, gave them all lodging in his own quarters. Publius' father was dangerously ill with a fever, and Paul cured the sick man by laying his hands on him. After this, many others came to him to be healed, and Paul was treated with the greatest honor and respect.

Eventually they left Malta and sailed to Rome, where Paul and the other prisoners were handed over to the captain of the guard. Paul was allowed to live comfortably in his own rented house, but with a sentry to watch him day and night. Many came to hear him, and for two years Paul welcomed all comers, explaining the teaching of Jesus and spreading the word of God.

Paul leaves Malta and sets sail for Rome

I Corinthians 12, 13, 15; Galatians 5; Ephesians 6; Philippians 2; Philemon; II Timothy 2

Paul's Letters

Paul wrote many letters while he was living under arrest in Rome

WHILE PAUL WAS IN EPHESUS he wrote to the people of Corinth about the Church. "Compare the Church to the human body: our eyes and ears have different functions, but eyes and ears are equally important. The body has many parts, such as the eyes, the hands, and the ears; each part is different, but each is equally important to the whole body. In the Church there are many different people, who all play an important part in the life of the whole Church. Whether we are Jew or Gentile, we were all baptized into the one Church.

"Above all remember that without love you are nothing. However strong, however ambitious, however learned you are, all is worthless if you do not love. Love is patient, forgiving, and kind. Love is brave and true. Faith, hope, and love last forever, but the greatest of these by far is love.

"Christ rose from the dead. All who call themselves Christians must believe that this is so. Christ died to save us from our sins. He

INKPOT AND PEN
When writing his letters, Paul would have dipped his reed pen into black ink, made from soot mixed with water, gum, and oil. The ink would have been held in a pot similar to the one above, which is made of bronze.

rose from the dead, so that we, too, may be raised to new life. When the last trumpet sounds, the dead will rise. Our natural bodies will decay, but our spiritual bodies will live in glory ever after. When this day arrives, death itself, the final enemy, will die. Death shall be no more."

Paul knew how important it was to persuade people to follow the teachings of Jesus. "If you follow Jesus, you will find that you can overcome your worst instincts. Do as Jesus taught you, and instead of giving way to envy and anger, to jealousy, selfishness, and greed, you will be full of love and forgiveness. You will be patient, faithful, and kind. There is no earthly law to make you into a good person, but if you obey the laws of Jesus, you will not only do what is right, but also find true happiness and peace."

Paul wrote many letters while he was living under arrest in Rome. One was to the Ephesians. "Be strong in the Lord. Put on the whole armor of God in order to fight against wickedness. Arm yourself with the belt of truth, the shield of faith, the breastplate of honesty, the helmet of salvation, and the sword of the Spirit, which is the word of God. With these you will quench the flaming arrows of the evil one."

To the Philippians Paul wrote, "Do not give in to vanity and conceit. Instead regard others as better than yourselves. Remember that Christ came among you as an ordinary man, behaved humbly and obeyed God in everything. As he did, perform your duty without complaint. Do not bear grudges, but shine with goodness like a star on a dark night."

To his friend, Philemon, Paul wrote, "I beg you to be kind to Onesimus. He has run away from you, and now I am sending him back, much as I would like to keep him here with me. Although he is a slave, I ask you to regard him as a brother, as he became very dear to me. Treat him as you would treat me, for we are all brothers before Christ."

One of Paul's last letters was to his old friend, Timothy. "Be strong, and shoulder all hardships, like a good soldier of Christ. Remember the example set by Jesus. Do not be tempted away from what you know is right, but trust always in justice, honesty, peace, and love. With these as your goal you will remain pure in heart."

ROMAN HOUSE
This ancient house is in Rome, Italy. Paul probably wrote most of his letters while living in a rented house in Rome, where he lived for two years under Roman guard.

large paving stones
ditch for drainage of water
crushed stone
slabs of stone in cement
sand

ROMAN ROAD
Paul's letters were sent by messenger to fellow Christians who were scattered throughout the Roman empire. The messengers would have traveled on the straight, wide Roman roads that linked the provinces to Rome. The roads were made up of several layers.

REVELATION 1, 4, 5, 20, 21, 22

The Book of Revelation

WHILE ON THE ISLAND OF PATMOS, the disciple John heard a deep and beautiful voice speak to him. "I am the First and the Last. What I tell you now you must write in a book, and send the book to seven churches in seven different cities."

Alarmed, John looked up, and in the sky above him saw seven golden candlesticks, and standing still and radiant among them the Son of God. In terror John fell fainting at his feet. "Do not be afraid," said Jesus, holding out his hand. "I am he who died, but now I shall live forever."

Then John saw a door opening into Heaven. He saw God sitting on a throne made of precious jewels and encircled with an emerald rainbow. Around the throne were twenty-four elders clothed in white, with gold crowns upon their heads. Beside the throne were flaming torches, and in front of it a sea of glass, like crystal. At each of the four corners stood a strange beast, each with six wings and with eyes both in front and behind: one had the face of a lion, one of a calf, one of a man, and one of an eagle. The creatures chanted continually: "Holy, holy, holy, Lord God Almighty, who was, and is, and is to come!"

In his right hand God held a scroll sealed with seven seals. An angel asked in a loud voice, "Who is worthy to break the seals and open the scroll?" And John wept, for there was no one in Heaven or on Earth worthy to break the seals. But then at the very center of the circle of men and beasts, at the foot of the throne, he saw a lamb with seven horns that looked as though it had been slain. The lamb lifted the scroll from the hand of God. At this the beasts and elders fell on their knees before the lamb, who was the Son of God. They sang songs of thanksgiving and praise, and as their voices soared into the heights of Heaven, they were joined by the voices of thousands upon thousands of angels, also singing and praising God.

With a noise like thunder, the lamb broke the seals one by one, and

John hears a deep and beautiful voice speak to him

Revelations is about a vision John had of Heaven. The powerful images include the Four beasts around God's throne.

One has a lion's face *One has a calf's face*

One has a man's face *One has an eagle's face*

opened the scroll to reveal the future of the world: Satan and his army will roam the earth, tempting the souls of the weak into wickedness. But at the end of time, God will send fire from Heaven, and the devil and all his followers will be flung into a lake of flaming sulphur, where they will burn in agony forevermore.

On the day of judgment the dead will stand before the throne, and God will read from the Book of Life. Those whose names are written in the Book are saved, but those whose names are not inscribed will be condemned to burn with Satan in the fiery lake.

The lamb lifts the scroll from the hand of God

Then John saw a new Heaven and a new Earth. He heard a voice proclaiming: "I am the beginning and the end. I will make everything new once more so that God and the people shall live together. There shall be no more pain, nor sorrow, nor death, for all such things will have passed away."

Then an angel took John to the top of a high mountain, and showed him the holy city, the new Jerusalem, whose walls were of jasper and whose streets were made of gold. Through the city ran the River of Life, whose waters were as clear as crystal. Here there was no need of sun by day nor of moon by night, for in the city dwelled God and his Son, and all who came there walked in the light of their glory.

An angel takes John to the top of a high mountain and shows him the holy city

The walls of the new Jerusalem are made of jasper and the streets are made of gold

Who's Who in the Bible Stories

AARON Moses' brother, who was his spokesman when they met Pharaoh. *Pages* 71, 72-73, 74, 84-85, 90-91

ABEDNEGO One of Daniel's three friends. *Pages* 162-164

ABEL Adam and Eve's second son and Cain's brother. *Pages* 22-23

ABIGAIL King David's wife. *Pages* 124-125

ABRAHAM/ABRAM The first Patriarch of the Israelites. His faith in God made him a great leader. *Pages* 30-44

ABSALOM King David's son. *Pages* 132-133

ADAM The first man. *Pages* 20-21, 24

AGABUS A prophet who foretold Paul's imprisonment. *Page* 302

AHAB A king of Israel who lived at the time of Elijah. *Pages* 142-145

ANANIAS The Christian who restored Saul's sight. *Page* 291

ANDREW The fisherman brother of Simon Peter. One of the 12 disciples. *Pages* 210-211, 282

ANNA An elderly woman who saw Jesus when he was presented in the Temple. *Page* 195

ARTAXERXES The Persian king who allowed the cupbearer, Nehemiah, to return to Jerusalem. *Page* 172

AUGUSTUS The Roman emperor during the time of Jesus. *Pages* 182, 190

BALAAM A prophet called upon to curse the Israelites. *Pages* 86-87

BALAK The king of the Moabites who asked Balaam to curse the Israelites. *Pages* 86-87

BARABBAS The criminal who was set free instead of Jesus. *Page* 273

BARNABAS A Christian from Cyprus who briefly traveled with Paul. *Pages* 291, 296, 298-299

BARTHOLOMEW One of the 12 disciples. *Pages* 211, 282

BATHSHEBA King David's wife and Solomon's mother. *Pages* 130-131, 133

BELSHAZZAR The king of Babylon who saw mysterious writing on the wall during a feast. *Page* 165

BENJAMIN The youngest son of Jacob and Rachel. *Pages* 30, 62-65

BOAZ A Bethlehem farmer who married Ruth. *Pages* 106-107

CAIAPHAS The high priest at the time of Jesus' arrest and crucifixion. *Pages* 183, 261, 269, 270

CAIN The first son of Adam and Eve. He murdered his brother Abel. *Pages* 22-23

CALEB One of the spies sent to find out about the promised land. *Page* 90

CLEOPAS One of the two men who met Jesus on the road to Emmaus. *Page* 278

CORNELIUS The Roman centurion whom Peter visited. *Pages* 292-293

CYRUS The king of Babylon during whose reign the Israelites went back to Jerusalem. *Pages* 153, 172

DANIEL An Israelite who rose to an important position in Babylon. He had a gift for interpreting dreams. *Pages* 162-167

DARIUS A king of the Medes who ruled Babylon. *Pages* 165, 166, 167

DAVID The Bethlehem shepherd boy who became a king of Israel. *Pages* 117, 116-125, 128-133, 135, 176

DELILAH A Philistine woman who betrayed the secret of Samson's strength. *Pages* 102-103

DEMETRIUS A silversmith at Ephesus. *Page* 300

EBED-MELECH The servant who rescued Jeremiah from the pit. *Page* 160

ELI The high priest who raised Samuel. *Pages* 108-110

ELIJAH A great prophet of Israel who had a contest with the priests of Baal. *Pages* 140-146, 234-235

ELISHA The man who followed Elijah as God's prophet. *Pages* 146-151

ELIZABETH The cousin of Mary and the mother of John the Baptist. *Pages* 185, 188-189
ESAU Jacob's twin brother and the son of Isaac and Rebekah. *Pages* 46-48, 54-55
ESTHER The young Jewish queen in the court of King Xerxes who prevented the massacre of the Jewish people. *Pages* 168-171
EUTYCHUS The young man who fell out of a window when Paul was preaching. *Page* 301
EVE The first woman. *Pages* 20-22
GABRIEL The angel who announced to Mary that she would give birth to Jesus. *Pages* 185-187
GEHAZI Elisha's servant. *Pages* 147-149
GIDEON A judge who defeated the Midianites with a few soldiers. *Pages* 96-97
GOLIATH The great Philistine soldier killed by David. *Pages* 118-119
HAGAR The servant of Sarah and the mother of Ishmael. *Pages* 34-35, 40-41
HAM One of Noah's three sons. *Page* 24
HAMAN The man whose murderous plot Esther stopped. *Pages* 169-171
HANNAH Samuel's mother. *Page* 108
HEROD THE GREAT Ruler of Judea when Jesus was born. *Pages* 182, 196, 198, 302
HEROD AGRIPPA A fierce enemy of the early Church. *Pages* 182, 294-295
HEROD ANTIPAS Son of Herod the Great. Ordered John the Baptist's execution. *Pages* 182, 226-227
HEROD ARCHELAUS Son of Herod the Great, and a ruler of Judea. *Pages* 182, 198
HERODIAS Wife of Herod Antipas. She told Salome to ask for John the Baptist's head. *Pages* 226-227
HEZEKIAH A king of Judah during the time of Isaiah. *Page* 155
HULDAH Prophetess at the time of Josiah. *Page* 156
ISAAC Son of Abraham and Sarah and the father of Jacob and Esau. *Pages* 30-31, 35, 40, 42-48
ISAIAH A prophet who foretold the coming of the Messiah. *Pages* 154-155
ISHMAEL Son of Abraham and Hagar, Sarah's servant. *Pages* 35, 40-41
ISRAEL The name later given to Jacob and his descendants. *Page* 31, 55
JACOB One of Isaac's sons who stole Esau's inheritance. Father of the 12 tribes of Israel. *Pages* 30-31, 46-55, 56, 62-65
JAIRUS The leader of the synagogue whose daughter Jesus healed. *Pages* 222-223
JAMES The name of two of the 12 disciples. *Pages* 210-211, 223, 234, 266, 280, 282
JAPHETH One of Noah's three sons. *Page* 24
JEPHTHAH A general who sacrificed his daughter because of a vow he made. *Pages* 98-99
JEREMIAH A prophet in Judah who foretold great misfortunes. *Pages* 158-161
JESSE King David's father. *Page* 116-117
JESUS CHRIST Regarded by Christians as the son of God, and the Messiah predicted in the Old Testament. The main focus of Christian faith and the central figure in the New Testament. *Pages* 190-283
JETHRO Moses' father-in-law. *Pages* 70, 72
JEZEBEL Ahab's cruel wife. *Pages* 144-145
JOAB The commander of King David's army. *Pages* 131, 133
JOHN One of the 12 disciples, the brother of James. He wrote the fourth Gospel. *Pages* 10, 210-211, 223, 234, 262, 265, 266, 276, 280, 282, 286-287, 308-309
JOHN THE BAPTIST Jesus' cousin who prepared people for his coming. *Pages* 184-187,202-203, 226-227
JONAH The prophet whose disobedience led to his being swallowed by a great fish. *Pages* 174-175
JONATHAN The son of King Saul who became David's close friend. *Pages* 120, 122-123, 127
JOSEPH Jacob's favorite son. He was sold into slavery in Egypt, then rose to a position of power. *Pages* 30, 53, 56-65, 89
JOSEPH The husband of Mary. *Pages* 186, 190-195, 198, 200-201

JOSEPH OF ARIMATHEA The man who provided a tomb for Jesus' body. *Pages* 207, 275

JOSEPH One of the men put forward to replace Judas. *Page* 285

JOSHUA The leader of the Israelites after Moses. *Pages* 91, 93-95

JOSIAH A man who became king of Judah at a young age. *Pages* 156-157

JUDAH One of Jacob's 12 sons. *Pages* 30, 57, 64-65

JUDAS ISCARIOT The disciple who betrayed Jesus. *Pages* 211, 260-261, 265, 267, 271, 282

JULIUS The centurion who escorted Paul on the journey to Rome. *Pages* 304-305

LABAN Rebekah's brother. Father of Rachel and Leah. *Pages* 30, 45, 48, 51-53, 54

LAZARUS The brother of Mary and Martha. Jesus raised him from the dead. *Pages* 207, 236-237, 260-261

LAZARUS The poor man in Jesus' parable. *Pages* 244-245

LEAH Daughter of Laban and Jacob's wife. *Pages* 51-53

LOT Abraham's nephew who lived in Sodom. *Pages* 32-33, 37-39, 98

LUKE A doctor who wrote one of the Gospels. *Page* 10

LYDIA A Christian from Thyatira. *Pages* 299-300

MARK The writer of one of the four Gospels. His mother's house in Jerusalem was a meeting place for the early Church. *Pages* 10, 267

MARTHA The sister of Lazarus and Mary, and close friend of Jesus. *Pages* 207, 236-237, 260-261

MARY The mother of the disciple James. *Page* 275

MARY The mother of Jesus. *Pages* 186-188, 190-195, 197, 198, 200-201, 212, 275

MARY The sister of Martha and Lazarus, and close friend of Jesus. *Pages* 207, 236-237, 260-261

MARY MAGDALENE The first witness of the resurrection. *Pages* 207, 275, 276

MATTHEW A tax collector who became one of the 12 disciples. The writer of one of the Gospels. *Pages* 10, 207, 210-11, 282

MATTHIAS He became one of the 12 disciples after the death of Judas Iscariot. *Pages* 282, 285

MESHACH One of Daniel's three friends. *Pages* 162-164

MICHAL Saul's daughter who became David's wife. *Pages* 120-121, 129

MIRIAM The sister of Moses and Aaron. *Page* 78

MORDECAI The cousin of Esther. *Pages* 169-171

MOSES The man who led the Israelites out of Egypt to search for the promised land. *Pages* 67-85, 90-92, 234-235

NAAMAN An army general whose leprosy was healed by Elisha. *Pages* 150-151

NABAL Abigail's husband. *Pages* 124-125

NABOTH A farmer who was killed for his vineyard by King Ahab. *Pages* 144-145

NAOMI The mother-in-law of the devoted Ruth. *Pages* 106-107

NATHAN The prophet who delivered God's word to David. *Page* 131

NEBUCHADNEZZAR The king of Babylon who captured Jerusalem and took the people of Judah into exile. *Pages* 152, 159, 161-164

NEHEMIAH After the Jewish exile in Babylon, he returned to rebuild Jerusalem. *Pages* 172-173

NERO The Roman Emperor before whom Paul stood trial. *Pages* 283, 297

NICODEMUS The Jewish leader who helped prepare Jesus' body for burial. *Page* 275

NOAH He and his family were saved from death in the great flood by building a boat. *Pages* 24-27

ONESIMUS The slave who ran away from his master, Philemon. Paul wrote a letter about him. *Page* 307

ORPAH Naomi's daughter-in-law. *Page* 106

PAUL/SAUL At first a persecutor of Christians, he became one of the greatest Christian leaders after he saw a vision of Jesus. In his travels he helped build up the early Church. *Pages* 282-283, 289-291, 296-307

PETER A fisherman who became one of the 12 disciples and a close friend of Jesus. *Pages* 211, 222, 231, 234, 242, 262-269, 276, 280-282, 285-287, 292-295

PHILIP One of the 12 disciples. *Pages* 211, 282, 302

PHILEMON Owner of the slave Onesimus. *Page* 307

PONTIUS PILATE The Roman governor who ordered the crucifixion of Jesus. *Pages* 180, 270, 272-273, 275

POTIPHAR The Egyptian courtier for whom Joseph worked. *Pages* 58-59

PUBLIUS The governor of Malta whose father Paul healed. *Page* 305

RACHEL Jacob's favorite wife. The mother of Joseph and Benjamin. *Pages* 30, 50-53, 56

RAHAB A Jericho woman who hid two Israelite spies in her house. *Pages* 93, 95

REBEKAH Isaac's wife, the mother of Jacob and Esau. *Pages* 30, 44-48

REHOBOAM Solomon's son, who caused the kingdom to be split in two. *Pages* 89, 140

REUBEN Jacob's eldest son. *Pages* 30, 57

RHODA An early Christian who answered the door to Peter after he had escaped from prison. *Page* 295

RUTH The devoted daughter-in-law of Naomi, who traveled with her to Bethlehem. *Pages* 106-107

SALOME The daughter of Herodias who danced in front of King Herod and asked for the head of John the Baptist. (Not referred to by name in the Bible.) *Pages* 226-227

SAMSON An Israelite man of great strength who fought against the Philistines. *Pages* 100-105

SAMUEL The prophet who annointed Saul and David, Israel's first two kings. *Pages* 108-109, 112-113, 115-117, 126-127

SARAH/SARAI Abraham's wife and the mother of Isaac. *Pages* 32-36, 40

SATAN The name sometimes given to the devil, who is thought to be the source of all sin and evil. *Pages* 20, 204-205, 221, 224

SAUL The first king of Israel. *Pages* 89, 112-115, 118-123, 126-127

SAUL see PAUL

SENNACHERIB King of Assyria whose army trapped Hezekiah in Jerusalem. *Pages* 152, 155

SHADRACH One of Daniel's three friends. *Pages* 162-164

SHAPMAN Scribe to Josiah. *Page* 155

SHEBA, QUEEN OF The queen who visited Solomon. *Pages* 138-139.

SHEM One of Noah's three sons. *Page* 24

SILAS He traveled with Paul on some of his missionary journeys. *Pages* 297, 299, 300

SIMEON The elderly man who saw Jesus presented in the temple. *Pages* 194-195

SIMON One of the 12 disciples. *Pages* 211, 282

SIMON The tanner at whose house Peter had a vision. *Pages* 292-293

SIMON OF CYRENE The man from Cyrene who carried Jesus' cross. *Page* 274

SOLOMON King David's son. The king who built the Temple in Jerusalem. *Pages* 132, 134-139

STEPHEN One of the first Christian leaders and the first martyr. *Pages* 283, 288-289

THADDAEUS One of the 12 disciples. Pages 211, 282

THOMAS One of the 12 disciples. He doubted at first that Jesus had risen from the dead. *Pages* 211, 279, 282

TIMOTHY One of Paul's traveling companions. *Page* 307

URIAH Bathsheba's husband who was sent to his death by King David. *Pages* 130-131

VASHTI The queen who Xerxes deposed. *Page* 168

XERXES The Persian king who married Esther. Also known as Ahasuerus. *Pages* 168-171

ZACCHAEUS The tax collector who climbed a tree to see Jesus. *Pages* 248-249

ZECHARIAH The father of John the Baptist. *Pages* 184-187

ZEDEKIAH The last king of Judah. *Pages* 159-161

INDEX

A

Aaron, 71, 72-73, 74, 84-85, 90-91
Abednego, 162-164
Abel, 22-23
Abigail, 124-125
Abraham/Abram, 16; as Patriarch, 30-31; and Hagar, 34-35; and three strangers, 36; and Sodom and Gomorrah, 37-39; and Isaac and Ishmael, 40-41; and sacrifice of Isaac, 42-43; and a wife for Isaac, 44
Absalom, 132-133
Acts of the Apostles, 10, 282
Adam, 20-21, 24
Agabus, 302
Ahab, 142-143, 144-145
almond tree, 158
aloes, 237
altars, 115, 184
Ammonites, 98-99, 114
Ananias, 291
Andrew, 210-211, 282
anemones, 215
angels, 37-39, 41, 43, 49, 154, 192-193, 198, 205, 276-277, 294-295, 308-309, *see also* archangels
Anna, 195
Annas, 183
anointment, 112, 117, 260, 275
Antioch, 297, 298
Antipas, *see* Herod Antipas
Antonia, Fortress of, 183, 303
apostles, 207, 282; *see also* disciples
Ararat, Mount, 14, 26, 27
archangels, 185-187; *see also* angels
Archelaus, *see* Herod Archelaus
ark, Noah's, 24-27
Ark of the Covenant, 16-17, 91, 94-95, 108, 110-111, 128-129, 136
Artaxerxes, 172
Artemis, 297, 300-301
Ashdod, 110
Asher, son of Jacob, 30, 89
Ashtoreth/Astarte, 156
Ashur, 152
Assur, 152
Assyria/Assyrians, 152-153, 155, 233
Augustus, emperor, 182, 190
Authorized Bible, 11

B

Baal, 88, 96, 143, 158
Babel, tower of, 28-29
Babylon/Babylonians, 15, 28, 152-153, 159, 160-161, 164, 165; empire, 162
Balaam, 86-87
Balak, King, 86-87
baptism, 202-203, 285
Bar-/Bat-Mitzvah, 9, 201
Barabbas, 273
barley, 209, 228
Barnabas, 291, 296, 298-299
Bartholomew, 211, 282
baskets, 68
bathing, 130
Bathsheba, 130-131, 133
Beatitudes, Mount of, 180, 215
Bedouin, 33, 34, 80
Beersheba, 15, 31, 41, 42, 181
Belshazzar's feast, 165
Ben Hinnom, 158
Benjamin, 30, 62, 64-65, 89
Bethany, 181, 236
Bethel, 15, 48, 49
Bethlehem, 15, 106, 116, 181; and birth of Jesus, 191-193, 196, 198
Bethphage, 256
Bethsaida, 180, 228
Bible, 8-9, 10-11
Bilhah, 30
boat building, 24, 25
Boaz, 106-107
Book of Proverbs, 135
Book of Revelation, 10, 308-309
bows, 122
bread, 228, 264; making, 236
breastpiece, 108
bricks, mud, 29, 72, 188
broom, 239
burial, 237

C

Caesarea, 180, 297, 302
Caesarea Philippi, 234
Caiaphas, 183, 261, 269, 270
Cain, 22-23
Caleb, 90
Calvary, 183, 274, 275
camels, 33, 45, 138; caravan of, 31
Cana (Kefar Kana), 212, 213
Canaan, 14, 32, 33, 54, 90, 91, 132; life in, 88-89
Canaanites, 66, 115
Capernaum, 180, 210, 216, 218
Carmel, Mount, 15, 124, 125, 142, 143, 148, 180
carob, 240
carpenter's tools, 190
carts, 111
cedars of Lebanon, 136
centurion, 219
chariot, 61, 78, 146
cherubim, 20, 21, 136, 137
children, 35; games, 246
children of Israel, *see* Israelites
Christians/Christianity, 207, 280, 282-283, 296
Church, early, 282-283, 306
circumcision, 40
Cleopas, 278
coat of many colors, 56
cock, 269
codex, 10
Codex Sinaiticus, 11
Coenaculum, 262
coffins, 119
coins, 255, 272; *see also* silver
Corinth, 297
Corinthians, Paul's letters to, 306
Cornelius, 292-293
cosmetics, 168
council, 270, 287, 288
count, 190

covenant, 16, 30
Creation, 18-19
crops, 22
cross, 207, 274, 283
crown of thorns, 273
cupbearer, 59, 172
cypress tree, 24
Cyprus, 296, 298
Cyrus cylinder, 153
Cyrus, King, 153, 172

D

Dagon, 105, 110, 111
Damascus, 180, 290, 291
Dan, 30, 89
dancers/dancing, 78, 99, 128, 226
Daniel, and Nebuchadnezzar, 162-164; and Belshazzar, 165; in the lions' den, 166-167
Darius, King, 165, 166-167
David, chosen as king, 117; and Goliath, 118-119; and Saul, 120-121; and Jonathan, 122-123; and Abigail, 124-125; becomes king, 128-129; and Bathsheba, 130-131; and Absalom, 132-133; death of, 135; and the Psalms, 176
Dead Sea, 14, 15, 38, 39, 181
Dead Sea Scrolls, 9
Delilah, 102-103
Demetrius, 300
demons, 221
denarius, 255
desert, life in the, 33, 34
Devil, *see* Satan
Diana, 297, 300-301
Dinah, 30
Diaspora, 285
disciples, 207, 210-211, 220, 228, 230-231, 262-263, 264-265, 266-267, 279, 280-281, 284-285; *see also* apostles
diviner, 87
Dome of the Rock, 42, 128
donkey, 87, 191, 256
Doubting Thomas, 211, 279, 282
dove, 27, 203
dyes, 56

E

Ebed-Melech, 160
Ebal, Mount, 180
Eden, Garden of, 20-21, 23
Edom, 15
Egypt, 15, 66-67; in the time of Joseph, 58-65; in the time of Moses, 68-79; flight of Joseph, Mary, and Jesus to, 198
Eli, 108-109, 110
Elijah, in the wilderness, 140-141; and Baal, 142; and Ahab, 145; and Elisha, 146; and transfiguration of Jesus, 234-235
Elisha, and Elijah, 146; and the woman of Shunem, 147-149; and Naaman, 150-151
Elizabeth, 185, 188-189
Elkanah, 108
Emmaus, 180, 278
En-gedi, 15, 89, 123
En Kerem, 189
Endor, witch of, 126-127
Ephesians, Paul's letters to, 307
Ephesus, 297, 300, 301
Epistles, 10; *see also* letters
Ephraim, 30, 89
Esau, 46-48, 54-55
Essenes, 9
Esther, 168-171
Eucharist, 283
Euphrates, River, 153
Eutychus, 301
Eve, 20-21, 22
Exodus from Egypt, 67, 76

F

faith, 31
false gods, 84, 155, 157, 158
famine, 62
fans, 69
farming, 209
feasts, 64; *see also* meals
fertile crescent, 14
Festival of Tabernacles, 208
Field of Blood, 271
fig cakes, 124
fire, tongues of, 284-285
fish, as Christian symbol, 280, 283
fishers of men, 210
fishing, 210
flax, 93
flood, the, 26-27
food, 202; *see also* feasts, hospitality, meals
foot bath, 263
fortune-teller, 87, 299
frankincense, 197

G

Gabriel, 185, 186-187
Gad, 30, 89
Gadara, 180
Gadarenes, 221
Galilee, 198, 206, 210, 268; life in, 180, 208, 209; Sea of, 206, 207, 210, 220, 224, 230
Garden of Eden, 20-21, 23
Garden of Gethsemane, 183, 266- 267
Gaza, 103, 181
Gehazi, 147-149
Genesis, 20
Gennesaret, Lake of, 207
Gethsemane, Garden of, 183, 266-267
Gideon, 96-97
Gilboa, Mount, 15, 127
Gilgamesh, The Epic of, 152
girded loins, 149
gladiators, 283
gleaning, 107
goats, wild, 46
gold, 197
golden calf, 84-85
Golgotha, 183; *see also* Calvary
Goliath, 118-119
Gomorrah, 15, 37-39
Good Samaritan, 232-233
Good Shepherd, 238
Gordon, Charles, 275
Goshen, 15, 66
Gospels, 10; *see also* John, Luke, Mark, Matthew
grapes, 90

H

Hagar, 30, 34-35, 40-41
hair/hair styles, 101, 103, 132

Ham, 24
Haman, 169-171
Hanging Gardens of Babylon, 153
Hannah, 108
Haran, 15, 32, 48, 50, 51
Harod, spring of, 97
harp, 120, 213
harvest/harvesting, 107, 209, 241; recording, 63
Hebrews, 14, 16; *see also* Israelites
Hebron, 15, 128, 132, 181
Hermes, 298
Hermon, Mount, 235
Herod, Agrippa, 294, 295; Antipas, 182, 226, 227; Archelaus, 182, 198; the Great, 182, 196, 198, 302; *see also* Herod's Temple
Herodias, 226, 227
Herod's Temple, 17, 42, 185, 258; and Jesus, 195, 200, 201, 258
Hezekiah, 155
Hezekiah's Tunnel, 155
high priests, 16-17, 108, 156, 183
Hiram, 136
hired workers, 243
Holy City, *see* Jerusalem
Holy of Holies, 16
Holy Spirit, 187, 195, 203, 281, 285
honey, 90-91, 202
Horeb, Mount, 83
horns, animal, 95, 112
hospitality, 36
houses, 188, 208, 217, 307
Huldah, 156

I

ibex, 46
incense, 184, 185
ink, 306
Isaac, 35, 40; as Patriarch, 30-31; and Abraham, 42-43; and Rebekah, 44-45; and Esau and Jacob, 46-48
Isaiah, 154, 155
Ishmael, 30, 35, 40-41
Ishmaelites, 57
Ishtar, 152; Gate, 152, 160
Israel, 31; *see also* Jacob
Israel, land of, 89, 140, 152
Israelites, 88; in Egypt/crossing of the Red Sea, 67, 68, 72, 77, 78-79; in the Sinai Desert, 80-81; and the Promised Land, 90-91; in captivity, 160-161
Issachar, 30, 89

J

Jabbok River, 54, 55
Jabesh, 114
Jacob, as Patriarch, 30-31; and Esau, 46-48, 54-55; and his dream, 49; and Rachel, 50-51, 52-53; and Leah, 52-53; and Joseph, 56, 65; and famine, 62, 63, 64;
James, 211, 282
James, brother of John, 210-211, 223, 234, 266, 280, 282
Japheth, 24
Jebel Musa, 83
Jebusites, 128
Jephthah, 98-99
Jeremiah, 158-159, 160-161
Jericho, 15, 93, 181; battle of, 94-95
Jericho, king of, 93
Jeroboam, 89
Jerusalem, 15, 128, 257; destruction of, 157, 159, 160-161; rebuilding of, 172-173; in Jesus' time, 180, 181, 182-183; *see also* Dome of the Rock, Herod's Temple, Jesus, Lion's Gate, Solomon's Temple
Jesse, 116-117
Jesus, 206-207; birth and childhood, 190-191, 194-195, 197, 198, 200-201; and John the Baptist, 202-203, 227; and temptations in the wilderness, 204-205; calls his disciples, 210-211; and sermon on the mount, 214-215; transfiguration of, 234-235; and Mary, Martha, and Lazarus, 236-237, 260-261; and the children, 246; and the rich young man, 247; and Zacchaeus the tax collector, 248-249; enters Jerusalem, 256-257; and the Temple traders, 258-259; and the disciples, 262-263; and the Last Supper, 264-265; in the Garden of Gethsemane, 266-267; under arrest, 269, 270-271, 272-273; Crucifixion of, 274-275; Resurrection of, 276-277; on the road to Emmaus, 278-279; Ascension of, 280-281; *see also* miracles, parables
Jethro, 70, 72
Jewish people, 153, 245, 285; and Diaspora, 285
Jezebel, 144-145
Jezreel, 15, 143; Valley of, 91, 143, 148
Joab, 131, 133
John, 210-211, 223, 234, 262, 265, 266, 276, 280, 282, 286-287; and book of Revelation, 308-309; Gospel of, 10, 265
John the Baptist, 184-187, 202-203, 226-227
Jonah, 174-175
Jonathan, 120, 122-123, 127
Joppa (Jaffa), 180, 293
Jordan, 15, 33; Valley, 88
Jordan, River, 15, 93, 94, 151, 181; and baptism of Jesus, 202-203
Joseph, husband of Mary, 186, 190-193, 194-195, 198, 200-201
Joseph, 30, son of Jacob, birth of, 53; and coat of many colors, 56; sold to the Ishmaelites, 57; as slave to Potiphar, 58-59; and Pharaoh's dreams, 60-61; as Minister of Egypt, 61-65
Joseph of Arimathea, 207, 275
Joshua, 91, 93, 94-95
Josiah, 156-157
Judah, brother of Joseph, 30, 57, 64, 65
Judah, kingdom of/Judea/Judeans, 89, 140, 152, 155, 158, 159, 172, 181, 202, 205; *see also* Jewish people
Judas Iscariot, 211, 260-261, 265,

267, 271, 282
Judas tree, 271
Julius, 304-305
Jupiter, 298

K

Kidron Valley, 157
King James' Bible, 11
Kingdom of Heaven, 214, 234, 246, 252, 254; keys of, 234
King's Highway, 138
kinnor, 120

L

Laban, 30, 45, 48, 51, 52-53, 54
Lachish, Siege of, 152
lamb, 131; *see also* sheep
Lamb, the, 308
Last Supper, the, 264-265
laws, Jewish, 16, 108
Lazarus, 207, 236-237, 260-261
Lazarus, the beggar, 244-245
Leah, 30, 51-53
Lebanon, cedars of, 136; mountains, 15
Legion, 221
lepers/leprosy, 150, 216
letters, by Paul, 10, 296, 297, 306-307
Levi, tribe of/Levites, 30, 68, 84, 89
lilies of the field, 215
linen, 93
lions, 100, 166, 167, 283
Lions' Gate, 289
locust tree, *see* carob
locusts, 75, 202
Lot, 32-33, 37-39, 98
Lot's wife, 39
Luke's Gospel, 10
Lydia, 299, 300
Lystra, 296, 298

M

Magdala, 206
magi, 196
Malta, 297, 305
Mamre, 36
manna, 80-81
Manasseh, kingdom of, 89
marbles, 246
Marduk, 152
Mark, 267; Gospel, 10, 267
Martha, 207, 236-237, 260-261
martyr/martyrdom, 283, 288
Mary, mother of James, 207, 275
Mary, mother of Jesus; and Gabriel, 186-187; and birth of John the Baptist, 188; and birth/childhood of Jesus, 190-193, 194-195, 197, 198, 200-201, 207; and marriage feast of Cana, 212; and the Crucifixion, 275
Mary, sister of Martha, 207, 236-237, 260-261
Mary of Magdala (Mary Magdalene), 207, 275, 276
Matthew, 207, 210-211, 282; Gospel, 10
Matthias, 282, 285
meals, 36, 47; *see also* feasts
Medes, 165, 166
menorah, 16
Mercury, 298
Meshach, 162-164
Mesopotamia, 14
mess of pottage, 47
Messiah, 10, 154, 187, 195, 207
Michael, 187
Michal, 120-121, 129
Midian/Midianites, 15, 70, 96-97
milk and honey, land flowing with, 88, 90, 91
miracles: calming the storm, 220; the centurion's servant, 218-219; feeding of the five thousand, 228-229; the Gadarene swine, 221; healing the sick, 216-217, 222; Jairus' daughter, 222-223; the marriage feast of Cana, 212-213; walking on the water, 230-31
Miriam, 78
Moab, 15, 86, 106
money, 255, 272; *see also* silver
moneychangers/money changing, 249, 258, 259
Mordecai, 169-171
Moriah, 42
Moriah, Mount, 42
Moses, 8; in Egypt, 67; in the bulrushes, 68-69; and the burning bush, 70-71; and Pharaoh, 72-73; and plagues, 74-77; and crossing of Red Sea, 78-79; in the Sinai Desert, 80-81; and the Ten Commandments, 82-83; and the golden calf, 84-85; and the Promised Land, 90-92; and transfiguration of Jesus, 234-235
mosque, 42, 128
Mount Ararat, 27
Mount of Beatitudes, 180, 215
Mount Carmel, 15, 124, 125, 142, 143, 148, 180
Mount Ebal, 180
Mount Gilboa, 15, 127
Mount Hermon, 235
Mount Horeb, 83
Mount Moriah, 42
Mount Nebo, 15
Mount of Olives, 183, 256, 266
Mount Pisgah, 91
Mount Sinai, 70, 83
Mount Tabor, 180
mourning, 223
music, 213, 223
myrrh, 57, 197, 237

N

Naaman, 150-151
Nabal, 124-125
Naboth, 144-145
Nabu, 152
Nahor, 44
Naomi, 106-107
Naphtali, 30, 89
Nathan, 131
Nathanael, *see* Bartholomew
Nazareth, 180, 186, 198, 206
Nazirites, 100, 101
nebel, 120
Nebuchadnezzar, 152, 159, 161, 162, 163, 164
Nebo, Mount, 15
Negev Desert, 15, 42, 198
Nehemiah, 172-173
Nero, Emperor, 283, 297

New Testament, 8, 10, 180; map of, 180-181; life during, 208-209
Nicodemus, 275
Nile, River, 15, 60, 62, 66, 74
Nineveh, 15, 152, 155, 174, 175
Ninurta, 152
Noah, 24-27
Nod, 23
nomads, 33
nosering, 45

O

oak tree, 133
offerings, 22, 23
oil, 112, 117, 232; lamp, 252
Old Testament, 8, 16-17; map of, 14-15
olive oil, 112, 117, 232; tree, 266
Olives, Mount of, 183, 256, 266
Onesimus, 307
Orpah, 106
ostriches, 69
oxen, 111

P

Palestine, 14, 182
palm leaves, 257
Pamphylia, 298
papyrus, 10, 189
parables, 208; the good Samaritan, 232-233; Lazarus and the rich man, 244; the lost coin, 239; the lost sheep, 238; the Pharisee and the tax collector, 245; the prodigal son, 240-241; the sower, 224-225; of the talents, 254-255; the unmerciful servant, 242-243; the wedding feast, 251; the wise and foolish maidens, 252-253; workers in the vineyard, 250
parchment, 8
Passover, Feast of, 76, 200, 209, 262
Patriarchs, 30-31
Paul, 282, 283, 289, 290-291, 296-303, 304-305, 306-307; see also Saul
Penninah, 108
Pentateuch, 8
Pentecost, Feast of, 209, 283
Perea, 181
perfume, 168
Persia/Persians, 153, 165, 166, 168
Peter, 211, 222, 231, 234, 242, 262, 263, 265, 266, 267, 268-269, 282, 283, 285, 286, 287; and the Resurrection, 276; and the Ascension, 280-281; and Cornelius, 292-293; in prison, 294-295
pets, 131
Pharisees, 211, 217, 238, 245, 287
Pharaoh, 67, 73; and dreams, 60-61; and the children of Israel, 68-69; and Moses, 72-73; and plagues, 74-77; and crossing of Red Sea, 78-79
Philemon, 307
Philip, 211, 282, 302
Philip, son of Herod, 182
Philippi, 299
Philippians, Paul's letters to, 307
Philistines, 89; and Samson, 100-105; and Ark of the Covenant, 110-111; and Saul, 115, 118-119, 126-127
phylacteries, 182, 245
pigs, 221, 240
pipes, 213, 223
Pisgah, Mount, 91
plagues of Egypt, 74-77
plough, ploughing, 209
pods, carob, 240
Pontius Pilate, 180, 182, 270, 272-273, 275
Potiphar, 58-59; wife of, 58
potter, 158, 159
prayer, Jewish, 245
prayer shawl, 182, 245
promised land, the, 14, 88, 90-91
prophetess, 156, 195
Psalms, 17, 176; book of, 176-177
Publius, 305
Purim, 171

Q

quails, 80
Qumran, 9

R

rabbi, 8, 108
Rachel, 30, 50-53, 56
Rahab, 93, 95
ram, 43;
ram's horn, 95
Rameses, 15
Ramesses II, 93
raven, 27, 140, 141
Rebekah, 30, 44-45, 46-48
Red Sea, 15, 78
Rehoboam, 89, 140
Reuben, 30, 57, 89
Revelation, book of, 10, 308-309
Rhoda, 295
ritual washing, 272
roads, Roman, 296, 307
Romans, 182, 219, 283, 287, 303
Rome, Paul in, 296, 297, 305
roofs, 93, 217
Ruth, 106-107

S

Sabbath, 8, 81, 206
sacrifices, 16, 115
saddlebag, 42-43, 77
Sadducees, 286, 287
Salome, 226-227
salt, 39
Samaria, 15, 180
Samaritans, 233
Samson, and the lion, 100-101; and Delilah, 102-103; in the temple, 104-105
Samuel, called to serve God, 108-109; and Saul, 112-113, 115, 126-127; and David, 116-117
Sanhedrin, 183, 261, 269, 270-271, 287
Sarah/Sarai, 32-35, 36, 40
sarcophagi, 119
Satan, 20, 204-205, 221, 224
Saul, 289, 290-291; *see also* Paul
Saul, King, 89; becomes king, 112-113; and the Ammonites, 114; and the Philistines, 115, 118-119; and David, 120-123; death of, 126-127
scales, 259
scribes, 287

scriptures, 8
scroll, 8, 156; case, 171
Sea of Galilee, 206, 207, 210, 220, 230
Sea Peoples, 119
Seleucia, 298
Sennacherib, King, 152, 155
seraphs, 154
Sermon on the Mount, 214-215
serpent, 20, 21, 73
servants, 243, 254
Shadrach, 162-164
Shapham, 156
Sheba, 139; Queen of, 138-139
sheep, 23, 177, 209
Shem, 24
Sheol, 126
shepherds/shepherdesses, 23, 50, 117, 118, 209; and birth of Jesus, 192-193; tools, 192
Shiloh, 15, 108, 110
Shinar, 28
Shittom, 15
shophar, 17, 95
shrines, 300
Shumem, 15, 147, 148; woman of, 147-149
sickle, 209, 241
Sidon, 15, 140
sifting grain, 225
Silas, 297, 299, 300
silver; cups, 65, 172; thirty pieces of 261, 271; used as money, 63
Simchat Torah, 8
Simeon, 89, 195
Simeon, son of Jacob, 30, 63, 64
Simon the Cyrene, 274
Simon the Zealot, 211, 282
Simon Peter, 210, 211; *see also* Peter
Sinai Desert, 70, 80, 198
Sito, 73
slaves/slavery, 58, 67, 72, 243
sling shot, 118
Sodom, 15, 33, 37-39
Solomon, birth of, 132; wisdom of, 134-135; and Queen of Sheba, 138-139; *see also* Solomon's Temple
Solomon's Temple, 42, 128, 135, 155; building/repair of, 17, 136-137, 156; destruction of, 161
Son of God, 10, 187, 207, 234, 235, 252, 270
sower, 209, 224
spikenard plant, 260
St. Paul's Bay, Malta, 305
Stephen, 283, 288-289
stonemason, 173
Succoth, 15
Sukkoth, 208
sycamore tree, 14, 248
synagogue, 153, 182, 222
Syria, 150

T

Tabernacle, 16, 89, 129, 208
Tabor, Mount, 180
talent, 255
tambourine, 78, 98, 213
tanner, 292
tax collector, 249
Temple, *see* Herod's Temple, Jesus, Samson, Solomon's Temple
Ten Commandments, 16, 82, 83, 84, 85, 91
tents, 31, 34
Thaddaeus, 211, 282
thirty pieces of silver, 261, 271
Thomas, 211, 279, 282
threshing, 209
throne, Pharaoh's, 60
Tiberias, 180, Sea of, 207
Tiberius, 182
timbrel, 98
Timothy, 307
tomb, 276
Torah, 8, 9, 233
tower of Babel, 28-29
transfiguration, 234-235
Tree of Knowledge, 20-21
Tree of Life, 20-21
trees: almond, 158; carob, 240; cedar of Lebanon, 136; cyprus, 24, Judas tree, 271; oak, 133; olive, 266; palm, 257; sycamore, 14, 248
Troas, 301
trumpet, 95
twelve tribes of Israel, 30, 89
Tyre, 15

U

Ur, 15, 29, 30
Uriah, 130-131

V

Vashti, 168
Via Dolorosa, 274
vineyard, 144, 209, 250

W

wadi, 125
wall painting, 59, 66
water carrier/skin, 40, 44; jars, 212
weaving, 102
weddings, 52-53, 212
wells, 44
Western Wall, 17, 258, 286
whales, 174
wine, 212, 232, 264; making, 64
winnowing, 209
wise men, 196-197, 198
witch of Endor, 126-127
women, daily life, in Egypt, 58; in Galilee, 208
worship, by the Hebrews/Jews, 16, 182
writing tools, 189

X,Y, Z

Xerxes, 168-171
Yahweh, 71
Zacchaeus, 248-249
Zealots, 182
Zebedee, 210
Zebulun, 30, 89
Zechariah, 184-187
Zedekiah, 159, 160-161
Zeus, 298
ziggurats, 29, 152
Zilpah, 30
Zipporah, 70
Zoar, 38, 39
Zodiac Signs, 160

Acknowledgments

Photographic Credits
l=left, r=right, t=top, c=center, b=bottom.

Ancient Art & Architecture Collection: 60tl.
Ardea:/Wardene Weisser: 80tl.
ASAP:/Aliza Auerbach 14b, 161tr /Lev Borodulin 215br / Mike Ganon 212tl /Avi Hirshfield 269tr /Garo Nalbandian 208cl, 217tr, 230bl, 268tl, 275tr, 278tl /Israel Talby 88b.
A-Z Botanical Collection: 136tl.
Barnaby's Picture Library: 54bl.
BBC Radio Vision: 8br, 9tl.
Bijbels Museum, Amsterdam,1992: 108tl.
Bridgeman Art Library: 8tl, Royal Library Stockholm; 10c,10cr, 10bl, 10br British Library; 11t Agnew & Sons; 187tr British Library.
Trustees of the British Museum: 9c, 20bl, 32tl, 32tr, 33t, 64, 68tl, 68bl, 69tr, 73br, 87br, 103tr, 137br, 144bl, 146bl, 154br, 160cl, 166tl, 167br, 168tr, 297br, 298cl.
Peter Clayton: 65tr.
Bruce Coleman Ltd: 175br, 203br.
Professor A. Danin, Jerusalem: 80cl.
DAS/Jamie Simpson: 257br, 274tl.
E.T.Archive: 280bl; 283c Archaeological Museum of Merida.
Mary Evans Picture Library: 26tl, 260tl.
Chris Fairclough: 93cr, 286c.
Werner Forman Archive: 62tl; 265br National Library of Athens.
Giraudon: 59br; 279tr Musée Condé, Chantilly.
Sonia Halliday Photographs: 11tl, 17bc, 31b, 43tr, 78bl, 83tr, 91br, 95tr, 97tr, 102bl, 107tl, 117tr, 127tr, 135tr, 147tr, 151tr, 155tr, 156bl, 157br, 158tl, 181bl, 182tr, 186tl, 204tl, 206b, 209tl, 209br, 222cl, 233tr, 234bl, 235tr, 250cl, 256bl, 258tl, 262bl, 267tr, 288bl, 291br, 295cr, 300tl.
Hamburger Kunsthalle: 51t.
Robert Harding Picture Library: 15bl, 29tr, 50b, 53tr, 59tr, 61cr, 63cr, 72cl, 76bl, 111tr, 123cr, 148bl, 174tl, 191tr, 200tl, 215tr, 219tr, 296bl, 310cr.
Michael Holford: 58bl, 73tr, 84tl, 132bl, 152b.
Hutchison Picture Library: 9b, 33br, 34tl, 35tr, 51b, 125cr, 139br;/Sarah Errington 52bl /Bernard Régént 302cl.
Image Bank: 128tl, 189tr /Lise Dennis 275br /T.Jacobi 236tl / F.Roiter 131tr /J.L.Stage 108bl.
Israel Museum,Jerusalem: 9tr The Shrine of the Book, D.Samuel & Jeane H. Gottman Center for Biblical Manuscripts; 171tr /David Harris 271tr.
Kunsthistorisches Vienna © Mayer: 66t.
Erich Lessing Archive: 101cr, 150bl, 170bl, 172bl, 184tl, 216tl, 238bl, 243tr, 276bl.
Life File: 149tr.
Magnum:/René Burri 207c.
NHPA:/Anthony Bannister 20tl /Vincente Garçia Canseco 240bl.
Oriental Institute, Chicago:/John Hudson 159br.
Oxford Scientific Films: 45tr.
Planet Earth:/Richard Coomber 141br /Peter Stephenson 46tl.
Dino Politis: 25br, 29br, 87tr, 173tr, 207tr, 210bl.
Zev Radovan: 23tr, 24tl, 27tr, 39br, 40br, 41tr, 98tl, 119br, 130bl, 133br, 142tl, 143br, 185tr, 188bl, 195tr, 203tr, 205tr, 213tr, 232tl, 248bl, 260bl, 266bl, 272tl, 289, 292cl.
Rheinisches Landesmuseum, **Trier**: 249tr.
R.M.N: 221br Louvre.
Scala: 40tr, 197tr, 226bl; 272bl Museo Nazionale Naples; 307tr.
Harry Smith Collection: 240cl.
Spectrum Colour Library: 106bl.
Sheila Weir: 45br.
Zefa: 17br, 42tl, 42bl, 44bl, 66bc, 128bl, 183tr, 266tl, 271cr, 293tr, 305tr.

Dorling Kindersley would like to thank:
Alan Gilliam and Paul Halliday for use of artifacts from The Bible Comes to Life Exhibition; Tim Ridley, Nick Goodall, and Gary Ombler at the DK Studio; Dorian Spencer Davies; Antonio Forcione; Christopher Gillingwater; Polly Goodman; George Hart; Alan Hills; James W. Hunter; Robin Hunter; Marcus James; Anna Kunst; Michelle de Larrabeiti; Antonio Montoro; Anderley Moore; Jackie Ogburn; Derek Peach; Lenore Person; Dino Politis; Lara Tankel Holtz, and Martin Wilson for their help in producing this book.

The map of Jerusalem on page 183 is based on the illustration of Ancient Jerusalem from *The World Book Encyclopedia*. © 1993 World Book, Inc. By permission of the publisher.

Picture research: Diana Morris

Index: Lynn Bresler